After studying for an art degree at Middlesex University, Sarah Bartlett went on to become a consultant astrologer, acquiring the diploma in Psychological Astrology, an in-depth three-year professional training programme, combining astrology and mythology, and humanistic and transpersonal psychology. She is the author of sixteen psycho-spiritual books, including the bestselling *Tarot Bible* and more recently the *Mythology Bible*, and has been an astrologer for the *London Evening Standard*, as well as many women's magazines, including *Cosmopolitan, She* and *Spirit and Destiny*. Sarah currently contributes to the BBC Radio 2 show *Steve Wright in the Afternoon*. She divides her time between London and the south of France, where she teaches and practises astrology and other occult arts. Find out more about Sarah at www.sarahbartlett. com and www.theastrologyroom.com

Recent titles in the series

A Brief Guide to Secret Religions
David Barrett

A Brief History of Witchcraft
Lois Martin

A Brief History of Roman Britain
Joan P. Alcock

A Brief History of the Private Life of Elizabeth II
Michael Paterson

A Brief History of France
Cecil Jenkins

A Brief History of Slavery
Jeremy Black

A Brief History of Sherlock Holmes
Nigel Cawthorne

A Brief History of How the Industrial Revolution Changed the World
Thomas Crump

A Brief History of King Arthur
Mike Ashley

A Brief History of the Universe
J. P. McEvoy

His Finest Hour: A Brief Life of Winston Churchill
Christopher Catherwood

A BRIEF HISTORY OF

ANGELS
AND DEMONS

SARAH BARTLETT

RUNNING PRESS
PHILADELPHIA · LONDON

ROBINSON

Constable & Robinson Ltd
3 The Lanchesters
162 Fulham Palace Road
London W6 9ER
www.constablerobinson.com

First published in the UK by Robinson,
An imprint of Constable & Robinson, 2011

A copy of the British Library Cataloguing in
Publication data is available from the British Library

ISBN 978-1-84901-698-8

1 3 5 7 9 10 8 6 4 2

First published in the United States in 2010 by Running Press Book Publishers

9 8 7 6 5 4 3 2 1

Digit on the right indicates the number of this printing

US Library of Congress Control Number 2010940975

US ISBN 978-0-7624-4278-2

Running Press Book Publishers
2300 Chestnut Street
Philadelphia, PA 19103-4371
Visit us on the web!

www.runningpress.com

Printed and bound by CPI Group (UK) Ltd, Croydon, CR0 4YY

CONTENTS

Acknowledgements   *ix*
Foreword   *xi*
Introduction   *xiii*

PART 1: ORIGINS
  1 ROOTS AND ILLUSION   3
  2 EARLY MESSENGERS   13
  3 DAIMON TO DEMON   27
  4 THE DIVINE SPLIT AND ZOROASTRIANISM   43

PART 2: RELIGION AND BELIEF
  5 FROM 'MESSENGER OF THE GODS' TO
     'GOD'S MANY MESSENGERS'   63
  6 BETTER THE DEVIL YOU KNOW   77
  7 THE GOSPEL TRUTH   91
  8 ANGELS GROW WINGS   117

PART 3: CULTURE, FEAR AND SALVATION
  9 ALL AN ANGEL IS   137
 10 THE VAIN BABBLINGS OF IDLE MEN   161
 11 TRACKS OF ANGELS IN THE EARTH   185
 12 DEVIL ON HORSEBACK   203
 13 TOUCHED BY AN ANGEL   223

Last Words   245
Epilogue   247
Bibliography   249
Index   253

To Jess, and all the other angels I've ever known

ACKNOWLEDGEMENTS

I would like to thank everyone at Constable & Robinson for their efficient, calm creativity, particularly editors Leo Hollis and Jo Stansall, and copy-editor Marion Paull.

I would also like to thank my agent, Chelsey Fox, for over fifteen years of invaluable support, my children Jess and Damien for believing in what I believe to be the truth about the cosmos, and my long-suffering partner, Patrice, for his gallantry.

Thanks also to the Presbytery of L'Eglise St Jacques-le-Majeur, Bar-sur-Loup, for their kind assistance; Professor David Brakke of Indiana University for his scholarly help with the machinations of early Christianity, and writer Patrick Harpur for his always insightful daimonic advice; not forgetting the Internet Sacred Text Archive, one of the most invaluable libraries on earth.

No longer on this earth, but without whom I would not have been able to write this book, I would also like to thank my father, Plato, Plutarch, John Dee, Meister Eckhart and Trithemius for their words of wisdom, and Cornelius Agrippa, my favourite *daimon* of all, for his secret whispers.

ACKNOWLEDGMENTS

FOREWORD

Throughout history, the human quest for divine knowledge has ruffled the wings of many an angel and tested the wrath of the demons. Enigmatic angels have always been a powerful symbol of sanctity and guidance. Demons, whether fallen angels or the much debased Lilith, have had a bad press. This historical journey, whether through personal stories, literature, myth, religion or art, tells the fascinating story of how belief in angels and demons has cast a powerful spell over the popular imagination, and how the ultimate angel of darkness has proved to be man himself.

This book not only traces the history of angels and demons from their earliest mythological roots to their modern-day renaissance, but also reveals their most treasured secret.

INTRODUCTION

'So very difficult a matter is it to trace and find out the truth of anything by history.'

Plutarch (46–122 CE)

High above a rushing gorge, not far from the glitterati of the French Riviera, perches the Provençal village of Bar-sur-Loup. In the cool, dark interior of the tiny Gothic church, St Jacques-le-Majeur, hangs a fifteenth-century oil painting – not, as one might expect, a Madonna or heavenly choir of angels, but a 'Dance Macabre'. On closer inspection, this is no ordinary 'dance of death', a genre of painting popular in late medieval art, where Death leads souls on their dance towards heaven or hell. This is strikingly different. A poem, written in Provençal dialect in two columns directly beneath the crackled oil, tells the legend of the unrepentant hedonist, Count Betrand of Grasse, whose château became a centre for local *parfumiers* to test out the 'swoon-ability' rating of their new fragrances on debauched lovers.

There are two versions of the legend of the Count's Lenten Ball, infamous in the region as a yearly Bacchanalian bash. The first account simply states that several of the Count's party-goers had the misfortune to fall to their deaths through the rotten floorboards. (No doubt he was not insured and had signed a pact with the Devil). The other version tells that during the drunken antics of the night, and due to the intoxicating effects of drug-like perfumes in overheated bedchambers, several of his guests died in their sleep, one being his cousin, the beautiful Beatrice, with whom he had fallen in love that very night. Mad with remorse, the wretched Bertrand fled the château to repent in the mountain wilderness with goats and assorted self-flagellating hermits. Tortured by the memory, he eventually returned to his château, tore down the beautiful tapestries, closed up the open chimneys, refused to see his rich, fragrance-obsessed friends, and lived alone in his austere hilltop retreat for the rest of his guilt-ridden life.

In the painting, the Count plays a Provençal flute and *tamborin*, guests dance, the devil shoots arrows at the party, a tiny demon dances on the head of each of the revellers, other devils lead souls to Hell and the archangel Michael flutters benignly above it all, weighing out the sins and virtues of the dancers. This is a superb allegory for the failings of the human lot, and the price we must pay unless we have faith in God and live a vice-less life.

Yet, this painting and its haunting lines, '*Et vous danseriez en la terrible danse*', is also symbolic of an esoteric secret that lies hidden in the painting's imagery and encoded within this book – the secret of our own eternal dance with angels and demons.

PART I:

ORIGINS

I

ROOTS AND ILLUSION

'Who, if I cried out, would hear me among the angels'
hierarchies? and even if one of them suddenly
pressed me against his heart, I would perish
in the embrace of his stronger existence.
For beauty is nothing but the beginning of terror
which we are barely able to endure and are awed
because it serenely disdains to annihilate us.
Each single angel is terrifying.'
Rainer Maria Rilke (1875–1926) *Duino Elegies*

For around two thousand years, our Western concept of angels
and demons has hinged on a simple but artful Judaeo-Christian
marketing device: angels are God's messengers, and demons the
devil's consorts.

But where did these go-betweens of the divine and earthly
worlds originate? Are they merely orthodox religious devices,
or do they have their roots embedded way back in the mists of
time? Do angels have truly pagan or heretical roots, which by a

clever twist in the serpent's tail, the Judaeo-Christian fathers had no choice but to assimilate into their own system?

Religion isn't just confined to the 'big ones' as we know them today. Worldwide, there are probably more underground religious beliefs than there are overtly orthodox ones. Due to length restrictions, this book focuses mainly on European tradition and its esoteric or occult offshoots, where we find paradox and religious '*parfumiers*' – the manipulators of the divine essence itself – aplenty.

WHAT IS RELIGION?

The etymology of the word 'religion' falls into two camps. *Klein's Etymological Dictionary*, the main etymological source throughout this book, refers us to Cicero's definition of the Latin word *relegere*, which originally meant 'to go through again, in reading or in thought'. The term suits the orderly, authoritarian Roman system, which assimilated all the Greek gods and goddesses, spirits and other assorted messengers into their own pantheon. It wasn't an experiential, orgiastic engagement with the gods, like the cathartic practices of the ancient Greeks, Minoans or Sumerians, although the Romans did have the perverse self-castrating cult worship of Cybele and Attis.

The word 'religion' is also rooted in the Indo-European word *leig-*, meaning 'to bind' or 'to gather together'. Depending on our personal perception of religion, we will side with one camp or the other. Let's say, in this book, we're taken by the *leig-* camp.

Here, religion gathers and binds people to the source, the invisible, the universe, the place you were before you were conceived, the numinous. Religion also binds us to each other, not only for a mass purge – like any football crowd of today – but also to remind us of our sense of oneness with the rest of humanity. Our loneliness is the universal human bond.

And religion offers us a way to sublimate our innate spiritual or divine longings. To find a way back to the source is, according to psychologist Carl Jung, a perennial human need.

Jung believed we were deeply connected to the ancient past through what he called 'the collective unconscious'. Briefly, the farther back in time we go, Neolithic and beyond, the more likely we are to meet the most instinctive energies that are swimming around in our own unconscious. If we go back to before anything that was ever known, we arrive at the place when all was One, and somehow through the dizzy distant past, we are intrinsically connected to these basic primitive instincts and energies of millions of years ago.

Gods and goddesses, angels and demons are, on one level, metaphors for these basic primitive forces. They represent the connection to the divine within us that has got lost on the way. Whether a god is personified as the great Zeus, or merely an abstract spiritual force, such as *ate* (delusion), Jung's philosophy rings true. Yet do the angel and demon, apart from being metaphors for our inner qualities, exist in some invisible realm? Or are they both, simultaneously, within us and without us?

The emergence, development and evolution of both angel and demon in history holds up a mirror to the collective psyche or soul of the time. It reveals how we have polarized the cosmos into black and white, good and evil, and now long for anything other than that polarity, ironically enough, by a revival of the angel without the demon.

If we follow Jung's belief that we all carry the pool of humanity's archetypes, which have been around for some two million years, then we have a hell of a lot of stuff to process. Our collective religious instinct encompasses the archetype of angels and demons and what they represented before they became angel equals 'good' and demon equals 'bad'. It goes back to a time when they were one; but maybe they have always been out there, too.

FIRST ROOTS

The roots of a word tell us the secret of the word, and the etymology of 'angel' and 'demon' reveals that the two are not mutually exclusive, but intrinsically linked.

The root of angel derives from the Latin *angelus*, which is from the Greek *angelos*, meaning 'messenger', thought to be a loan word from *angaros*, 'mounted courier', from an unknown Oriental source, related to the Sanskrit *ajira*, 'swift'. The word *angelos* was used in the first Greek translation of the Bible, for the Hebrew word *mal'akh* (*yehowah*), 'messenger (of Jehovah)', from the Hebrew base *l-'-k*, 'to send'.

With so much confusion over the words demon, daemon and daimon, we need to get this absolutely clear in our minds. It was the impartial yet ambivalent Greek daimon who became Christianity's enemy number one, the demon.

Demon comes from the Latin *daemon*, which is a transliteration from the Greek word *daimon*. The Greek *daimon* derives from the Indo-European word *daiô*, or *dai*, meaning 'distributor of destinies', also considered to be 'individual destiny', and from an even earlier Proto-Indo-European word *dei*, which means 'god', 'divine', 'divide', 'cut off', 'separate', 'distribute'. The general agreement is that *daimon* means 'distributor of destinies'.

Whether sending messages or distributing destinies, on horseback or by mouth, once upon a time, daimons or mal'akhs were neither good nor bad, until the sender of the message and the recipient of the message began to have very different perceptions of the message itself. The neutral messenger was to be cast in either a positive or negative light.

HISTORICAL BACKGROUND

'It is not that the divine is everywhere: it is that the divine is everything.'
Joseph Campbell (1904–87), mythologist and historian.

Where did the messenger archetype originate from? How did we get to Hermes and his winged sandals, let alone winged angels? It is in the mythology of the earliest civilizations where we find angels first spread their wings.

Until about 3500 BCE, matriarchal goddess cultures were still widespread from the Indus valley in India to old Europe. Joseph Campbell observed that similar symbolic images were prevalent from the Aegean Sea to the Indian Ocean. Whether the Great Goddess was worshipped as cow, bird, lion, bull, rain, moon or stars, all was sacred. Shared worldwide themes in mythology, such as the hero, the trickster, or messenger, reveal how these universal archetypes captured the collective imagination.

In ancient Sumerian mythology, wind, fire, water, air and earth were personified, while nature spirits became go-betweens of the visible and invisible realms. Sumerian tablets discovered in early twentieth-century excavations at Nippur, Iraq, reveal spirit messengers dating back to the third millenium BCE. The universe, to the Sumerians, consisted of heaven and earth, between which was a breath-like vapour or airiness called 'Lil', described as 'air', 'wind' or 'spirit'. The moon, planets and sun were made from this spirit, yet endowed with luminosity.

Enlil, the air god, established the world; the water-god, Enki, got it all working. The in-between world of Lil, between the gods and man, filled itself with innumerable spirits, known as Utukku. Some were benevolent, others were not, such as those called the Edimmu. The Utukku were found in every rock, bird, fish or hollow. Everything on the earth and in the sky was imbued with this 'spirit'. In Sumerian cuneiform texts in the British Museum, the Utukku are described as 'winds ever sweeping along'.

In ancient Greek religion, daimones were assorted guardian spirits and messengers, but of lesser power than the gods. They were neither good nor bad, and sometimes both. Whether consciously or not, it was through translation, modification, redaction and the diverse viewpoints of scholars, Church patriarchs and translators, that all pagan gods and lesser spirits eventually fell under the umbrella term 'daimon', to become associated with 'Evil'. The devilish brat pack, in Christian eyes, was an ingenious marketing device, as we shall see later. Yet, long before Christianity came into being, there were other darker, insidious goings on. The Devil had been on horseback for quite some time, not underground ruling some hellish inferno, but attempting to ride his own chariot across the skies alongside the gods – man himself.

THE BRONZE AGE

With the coming of the Bronze Age, the old universal oneness was gradually being replaced by patriarchal power games. The cyclic nature of the universe was slowly creaking forward another notch, but for what? What message was being relayed, if any?

The era from around 3500–1250 BCE brought not only the discovery of bronze and how to make useful tools, weapons, ornament and idols, but the discovery of writing. Man began to communicate by means other than just sign language, speech or marking images on cave walls. Throughout ancient Mesopotamia and ancient Egypt, stories that had once been orally transmitted were written down. Tales such as those of Neith, the Egyptian goddess of magic and weaving, and the 'Epic of Gilgamesh' in Sumeria, were recorded on clay tablets or strips of papyrus. These myths revealed the divine imagination of the ancestors both as a testament to their beliefs and to ensure the stories were passed down to future generations. The primordial Great Goddess of the Paleolithic and Neolithic eras was gradually absorbed into the pantheons of gods and goddesses, spirits and a range of deities who personified everything that was once part of nature.

The ancient pastoral and apparently peace-loving Great Goddess culture was gradually being usurped by her own offspring – civilization. In ancient Sumeria, the goddess Inanna, also identified as Isis of Egypt, and Cybele in Anatolia, was another aspect of the Great Mother, representing both life and death. Her dark and light power is reflected in the story of her dying and resurrected son-lover, Dumuzi, who was cursed to spend winter in the underworld and rose every spring to be born again. Inanna also guarded the *Me*, the Tablets of Destiny, and the key to universal knowledge. If the Goddess hid her knowledge, then perhaps she has returned to offer the messages to us again, in her role as new age angel?

In ancient Egyptian mythology, *c.* 3100–2890 BCE, the seamstress of the universe, Neith, was one aspect of the Great Goddess of the Nile Delta region. She arose spontaneously from the primeval nothingness, gave birth to the Great God, Ra, and created the universe by stringing the sky across her loom. Similarly, new myths developed and became woven into the tapestry of life, just as Neith weaved the universe and all that is in it. Egyptian civilization, as insular as Mesopotamian was expansive, eventually included a deity or spirit for every thing in nature. Ra single-handedly (literally, some cults believed he masturbated himself into being) created Atum, an aspect of himself. Finally, the pantheon expanded to include the eternally warring gods Set and Horus in their battle for power.

From early Mesopotamian mythology and the first Babylonian dynasty of 2057–1758 BCE comes the tale of the battle between Marduk and Tiamat, perhaps one of the oldest surviving examples of good versus evil. The cycles of creation and destruction were echoed in the early Vedic myths, where Indra, originally the Aryan's chief deity, is the most talked about god. With a thousand testicles and the lust to go with it, Indra formed a duality with Varuna, god of the sky, the pair embodying morality and amorality.

MOVEMENT AND CHANGE

The cultural revolution on the ground was massive. Indigenous peoples moved from village or nomadic caravans to city life. Civilization came with its own big bang, and marked the final split of human psyche from nature. Humanity taught itself to fear nature's cycle of growth and decay, of life and death, rather than merge with it.

Hierarchies developed, women were treated differently, men had to defend themselves from alien peoples. Tilling the land and being at one with it, whether giving sacrifice or communing with nature, was no longer in vogue; fortresses were. Patriarchal sky gods were given star quality and the Great Mother Goddess lost her power. Both early Sumerian and Egyptian cosmology reveal this first real split between Heaven and Earth, and the two civilizations and their open roads led easily towards the new cosmology and monotheistic beliefs of the future Iron Age. These diverging roads were the main channels through which the ancient archetype of the spirit messenger travelled to become 'angel' and 'demon'.

Men got braver and more like gods. The hero archetype ruled, too. The hero, who was born to a mortal and a god, a demi-god, became particularly important for the emerging patriarchal consciousness, like the later well-known Greek heroes, Achilles, Perseus and Theseus. The myth of the hero endorsed the hostile, conquering, competitive qualities of patriarchal society. Tribal peoples moved, migrated, encountered strangers, wanted what those people had and got what they wanted by force.

The Warrior

Along with the Semetic and Aryan warring peoples came big trouble. As Campbell points out:

> mythologies of the goddess mother were radically trans-
> formed, reinterpreted and in a large measure even

suppressed by those suddenly intrusive patriarchal warrior tribesmen whose traditions have come down to us chiefly in the Old and New Testaments and in the myths of Greece.

Like the earlier Kurgan migrants of around 3000–2500 BCE, the Ayrans were essentially warriors. They swept down from the northern plains, bringing with them their own sky-gods, while the Semetic peoples from the desert lands between northern Syria and the tip of Arabia brought 'spirits'.

Included in these invasive groups were the earliest Akaddians, Amoritic Babylonians and the Canaanites, who were later conquered by the Hebrews, who were later conquered by the Assyrians. Northern old Europe still had traces of goddess worship, which had been hidden underground with the onslaught of the warring conquistadors known as the Celts. The pagan religions of Europe were a melange of individual tribal religious cults, peppered with deities such as the horned god, who appeared in many different guises, for example Cernunnos in Celtic myth, one of the many wonderful role models for the Christian devil. All these invaders imposed their dualistic belief of light versus dark, or good versus evil, wiping out the earlier unity of light and dark as one. Nature was no longer sacred. Human life was worthless. Attitudes changed – life was no longer a cyclic process, and death was now to be feared.

The ethos of conquest was the means of survival for these peoples. For example, the Ammorite King Hammarabi, who conquered Sumer in 1763 BCE, was responsible for one of the first codes of laws and the well-known adage 'an eye for an eye'. Great civilizations rose and fell. The Vedic period unfolded in India between 1600 and 1000 BCE, and then came Zoroaster, the Persian prophet, as much responsible for the split of 'good god' and 'evil god' as anyone. Around 1250–1200 BCE, the Hebrew people returned to Canaan from Egypt, to begin their own power struggles.

BABYLON

Women's status changed dramatically, and death was an absolute, an end and to be feared. Then, with the astronomical observations of the Babylonians, came measurement, calculation, fixed stars and patterns emerging in the sky. This knowledge provoked a new vision of that which is above – the heavens – and that which is below, no longer separate, perhaps united. Astrology, a new astral religion, was developed as the stars became identified with the gods; and with use of magic, or divination, man's soul could transcend the absolute of death and return to the heavens.

In 539 BCE, the Babylonians were conquered by King Cyrus of Persia, and their magical beliefs spread out into the far reaches of Persia and southwards to Egypt. The fusion of ideas, the cross-cultural changes across the whole of the Mediterranean excited the Greeks, forever a race of people who wanted to know answers, and they began to ask even more questions.

Pagan religions and cults continued to flourish. The gods were our ancient messengers, bringing ideas, personifying archetypes, bringing man closer to the divine. Thousands of unnamed deities and lesser spirits waited in the wings to imbue every new offspring with its accompanying guardian spirit. But the profound message being transmitted was that humanity was on its way not only to splitting the atom, but to polarizing the divine messengers into good and bad for ever.

2

EARLY MESSENGERS

'Truth is one, the sages speak of it by many names.'
The Rig Veda, Hindu text

An old Chinese myth about a jilted warrior-lover tells how he rode his stallion along a road to nowhere, a land beyond a snow-capped mountain. On the other side of the mountain he came across a wishing stone, imbued with angelic spirits and dancing gods. He stopped to pay homage to the deities, and was immediately enlightened. Hadn't the mountain he'd already passed before the wishing stone been infused with kindly gods, too? Hadn't he himself been filled with 'angels and gods' long ago, in some other life, before he ever reached the road, the mountain or the wishing stone? If he had been with the gods before, love had been known before and love would be known again, because it had never gone away. The jilted lover became the lover of the angelic spirits, and the warrior became a monk, knowing these divine beings would never leave him, and never had.

The symbolic inference of this ancient story is that if we dig even further back into the past, hidden among the tombs, temples and caves of ancient peoples we can discover remnants of the winged messenger when he or she first flitted into human consciousness. But where did the motif originate? Was it from some hazy recollection of the bird from which we possibly evolved, or just our human longing to fly home, to be reunited with the Source?

Symbolic imagery of birds appear in most ancient civilizations. Archaeologists have unearthed Neolithic bird goddess figurines from Mesopotamia, and discovered flying-bird symbols in a burial chamber in Mal'ta, Siberia, dating back to about 16,000–13,000 BCE. A bird, shaman and bison picture was discovered in a secret well in the Lascaux cave, c. 15,000–12,000 BCE. Drawings of shamanic vulture goddesses, c. 6100 BCE, were found at the Catal Hayuk shrine in Turkey. Enough evidence exists to reveal a magical world of shaman, goddess and bird prospering long before the angel was even conceived.

But are we, in the twenty-first century, merely projecting our obsessive need to discover profound truths in ancient imagery, or were they as meaningful at the time as we believe or hope?

The bird goddess, originally a beaked, winged female form, appears in Minoan mythology with human face and epiphanous raised arms. In indigenous societies in North America, shamans took on the spirit of a bird to travel to spiritual or supernatural realms, and in some mythologies, shamans were mothered by birds. For example, in the Yakut mythology of Central Asia, each shaman has a mother bird, who appears just twice in the shaman's life – at his spiritual birth, and at his death, when the mother bird takes back the shaman's soul. In other Yakut myths, the mother bird nests in a tree where she lays eggs containing the shaman's soul. Great shamans are born at the top of the tree, lesser ones at the base.

A story is being told in the shaman drawing in Lascaux, but which story? A bird-man lies prostrate on the ground with erect phallus, one claw-hand pointing to the bison, the other to a bird sitting on the end of a wand or stick. Is the shaman-bird attempting to contact the soul of the dead bison, to learn the mysteries of death? Was this a shamanic ritual, as many suggest, or simply a tribal statement of a kill?

The Romanian religious historian Mircea Eliade (1907–86) points out in his book *Shamanism* that all indigenous shamans 'fly', and adds, 'the bird perched on a stick is a frequent symbol in shamanic circles', as are birds who guide souls to the realms of the dead in Greek mythology. Shaman bird-men are found in other archaeological sites, too. In the 1950s, archaeologists Rose and Ralph Solecki excavated a site in Kurdistan, a burial site for the Zawi Chami peoples of around 8800 BCE. Skeletons of massive vulture wings are probably a sign that the wings had been worn or used in some kind of shamanic ritual or ceremony, similar to the Catal Huyuk shrine in Turkey.

Angel-cult worshippers, known as the Yezidis, of Iraqi Kurdistan believe that God placed the world under the care of seven angels; Melek Taus is the supreme being, known as the 'peacock angel'. Their ancient bird statues, according to Kurdish scholar Mehrdad Izardy (b.1963), resemble not so much a peacock, but a predatory bird called the 'sanjaq', which is not unlike the hooked-beak genus of vultures venerated by the Zawi Chami peoples. Could angels originally have been birds?

THE NAVIGATION OF THE MESSENGER

One of the most esoteric and yet well-known secret codes recorded is the Emerald Tablet of the magician god, Hermes, which reads: 'As above, so below'. The 'above' of heaven, constellations, and planetary cycles reflects the 'below' of the world. Winged messengers are the mediators between the above and the below. Wings go with all things heavenly. They free us from our earthly chains, and anything that forms a bridge between the two, such as the bird or shaman, becomes a sort of divine catalytic convertor.

From its earliest roots, the messenger archetype in European history evolved through two divergent streams of civilization. Rowing its boat gently down one stream, the messenger navigated the waters of pre-dynastic Egypt, on into Hellenistic Greece to trickle into the neatly laid-out sewers of the Holy Roman Empire and the growing conversion of all things pagan to Christianity. The other stream was trickier. The messenger had to navigate torrents, white water, waterfalls and the raging currents of the earliest Sumerian mythology, the Aryan and Semitic invaders and the subsequent influence of Zoroaster, until reaching the crystal waters of Jewish monotheism. Our messenger was gradually reshaped, re-visioned and sculpted into what each era's or civilization's belief system needed the messenger for. Then they converged.

ANCIENT EGYPT

The first records of the existence of peoples in pre-dynastic Egypt were discovered in the Naqada region on the east bank of the Nile in Upper Egypt, dating from between 5000 and c. 3000 BCE. Finds included pottery figures of a dancing goddess with arms or wings raised above her head. The Naqadas were agriculturists, but they also traded far and as wide as the eastern desert of Arabia. Similar iconography has been discovered on pottery found on trading routes between the Red Sea and Naqada. It is believed an exchange of ideas and beliefs between Sumeria and Egypt must have occurred at some point in history, but no one really knows if it was the Egyptians who influenced the Sumerian culture or the Sumerians who influenced the Egyptians, or if both flourished simultaneously, as do flowers on the same stalk.

Hathor

Hathor, sometimes considered to be a later aspect of Neith, was one of the earliest messenger goddesses to be worshipped in Egyptian mythology. She has been described as 'the great mother of the world'. The cosmic Hathor was the personification of the great power of nature, which was perpetually conceiving, creating, bringing forth, rearing and maintaining all things, great and small. It was said that when a child was born, seven Hathors – aspects of Hathor, guardian spirits, or what we would now call guardian angels – were present at the birth to announce the child's fate. The Hathors would exchange a prince born to bad fortune with a more fortunate child, therefore protecting the dynasty and the nation. During Ptolemaic times – when the Greeks ruled over Egypt – the seven Hathors were identified with the constellation, the Plaeides.

The Hathors were, in a sense, our first fleeting acquaintance with guardian angels, although some kind of guiding spirit has appeared in most worldwide mythologies. On the northwest coast of America, for instance, totem spirits included a bear protector, and Melanesia had bird and fish protective spirits. The guardian spirit is as much part of our million or so years of psychic inheritance as is the trickster, the hero, the magician.

Isis

More human than goddess, Isis represents a go-between, a messenger, the first real 'angel' between man and the divine, who also offered divine protection. She was both a guardian angel of everything, but also the epiphanous angel, the first goddess-angel of good tidings.

The Greeks called her Isis, the Egyptians called her 'Au'Set', or 'Ashesh', meaning 'pouring out' or 'supporting', and the Hebrews called her Asherah. Hathor is probably an even older version of the winged goddess, Isis, revered for over three thousand years until the rise of Christianity. From around 2500 BCE, the iconography of the winged goddesses Isis and her sister Nephyths dominated Egyptian culture. Isis was the dawn, Nephyths the twilight, Isis the morning star, Nephyths the evening star. As first/second-century Greek historian and biographer Plutarch noted, 'Isis is the visible world, Nephyths the invisible.'

At one end of the tomb of Rameses III (1194–1163 BCE) kneels a winged Isis, supporting the throne on her head, and at the other end, guarding the pharaoh, kneels a winged Nephthys. Isis was also depicted as the pharaohs' throne itself. Each pharaoh would 'sit' on Isis's lap to be enveloped by her gigantic, comforting wings. On Tutankhamun's tomb (c. 1325 BCE) the sisters face one another, their wings raised yet outstretched, protecting Tutankhamun's mummy, but welcoming his resurrection so that he can join Ra's boat on its journey across the heavens every day.

A later Greco-Roman cult developed out of the story of Isis's power to bring to life Osiris, so she could give birth to a saviour son. In the story of the resurrection of Osiris, she takes the form of the kite bird, and with the beating of her wings, generates enough wind to breathe life into Osiris, enough to enable him to impregnate her and subsequently she gives birth to Horus, her much-loved child.

Plutarch portrayed Isis as the universal principle:

Isis is, in fact, the female principle of Nature, and is receptive to every form of generation, in accord with which she is called by Plato the gentle nurse and the all-receptive and by most people has been called countless names ... She has an innate love for the first and most dominant of all things, which is identical with the good, and this she yearns for and pursues; but the portion which comes from evil she tries to avoid and reject.

Sounds like an angel.

Isis continued to wing her way as symbolic life-bringer until the fourth century, bearing the message of eternal life and the soul's merger with the divine. Isis, rather like the Mesopotamian Inanna, imparts human vulnerability to the usually untouchable character of a goddess. We sympathize with her for her loss and grief; we have compassion for her child saviour, Horus. This familiar scenario is reinterpreted later in the story of Mary and Jesus.

After Alexander the Great conquered Egypt in 322 BCE, the insular mythology and religion of Egypt merged with that of Greece. Isis worship continued to be encouraged by the Ptolemaic kings, and Isis's cult was brought to Athens by traders. On Delos, a temple to Isis stood alongside temples to all the Greek deities, and the Isis Mysteries flourished until about the fourth century.

Apuleius, the second-century Latin writer, an initiate of the Mysteries of Isis, described her as 'the universal mother . . . known by countless names'. His hero, Lucius, in the book *The Golden Ass*, recounts how she appeared to him in his own initiation, and 'On her feet were slippers of palm leaves, the emblem of victory'. Curiously, Isis here sounds more like Nike, the Greek winged goddess of success. Perhaps Apuleius's brain was slightly addled by his initiation rites and confused the two goddesses; or perhaps they had already been one, a long time before? Did a lingering symbol of the protective wings of the Mother Goddess emanate through such symbols as palm leaves, birds, wings and the air?

Ka and Ba

A confusion of soul, spirit and wings of a different kind lurked in ancient Egypt, namely, the Ka and Ba.

Ka was essentially the 'life-force', or spirit, that transcended the death of the physical body. An energy, force or spirit, like the Polynesian mana, or the Taoist chi, the Ka was inherent in all things. The hieroglyph for Ka shows two arms raised high, not unlike the figurines of bird goddesses and dancing angels.

Khnum the potter god fashioned the individual Ka for the gods, enabling them to manifest in myriad aspects, imbuing statues, magical totems or symbols with the Ka essence of that particular god.

The Ka can be likened to something given to the individual from outside of oneself. It represented the pool of psychic energy of the ancestors, of which the individual was merely a part. The Ba, on the other hand, was more like the personal identity or 'soul character' of an individual.

The Ba was depicted with the head of a human and body of a bird, usually a falcon, who hovered over the deceased like Isis hovering over Osiris. The Ba waited to unify with the Ka and thus animate the Akh, the 'effective one' or the soul itself, for its continued journey into the afterlife.

For royalty and the elite, the Ka was a personal guide, often depicted as a shadow walking behind the pharaoh. Pepi II, who reigned c. 2278–2184 BCE in the Old Kingdom Dynasty, and whose throne was named Neferkare – Nefer-ka-Re, 'Beautiful is the Ka of Re' – commented:

It goes well with me and my name;
I live with my ka.
It expels the evil that is before me.
It removes the evil that is behind me.

The Akh's confusing amalgamation of Ba and Ka lived on after death and, it was believed, would manifest as a star in the night sky. This resonates well with the Orphic-cult belief that purified souls became stars, and the later Platonic philosophical concept that the Sirens and daimons had some kind of cosmic function, singing the very music of the spheres to keep the universe spinning.

Other contenders for early guardian-angel status included the Hunmanit, a group of spirits portrayed as rays of the sun, similar to the Christian representation of the angel choirs, the Seraphim. The Hunmanit had a responsibility to look after the sun, and in doing so, protected humanity at the same time.

GREEK MESSENGERS

In the colourful world of ancient Greek mythology, messenger gods, such as Iris and Hermes, were also at the root of the Western Christianized angel. Greek mythology is vivid. It resonates in our modern-day psyche because dynasties rose and fell, gods and goddesses interacted with mortals, heroes and heroines bothered great kings and immortals, and life was a pig.

Iris

Iris was an envoy of the Olympian gods, usually described as a virgin goddess, but married to Zephyrus, the god of the west wind. Daughter of Thaumus (wondrous one) and Electra, she was considered to be a daimon and sister to the Harpies.

Iris's name contains a double meaning – 'rainbow' and *eirein*, or 'messenger'. On golden wings and carrying a pitcher of nectar, Iris ran errands for the other gods, but also between gods and mortals. Her name is derived from *erô*, or *eirô*, 'speaker' or 'messenger', and means 'I join'.

In Plato's *Cratylus*, Socrates constructs some boring philosophical reasons for the roots of the names of the gods:

Let us inquire what thought men had in giving them [the gods] their names . . . The first men who gave names [to the gods] were no ordinary persons, but high thinkers and great talkers . . . Iris [like Hermes] also seems to have got her name from *eirein*, because she is a messenger.

Iris bridges not only the world of gods and mortals, but as personification of the rainbow, she spans the heavens to form an arch or bridge down to earth. Servius, a renowned fourth-century Roman grammarian and commentator, believed the rainbow was merely the road on which Iris travels, appearing when she wants to visit earth, disappearing when she has completed her mission.

Iris appears frequently as a messenger in Greek mythology – in the Trojan war, on the voyage of the Argonauts, the labour of Leto, the journey of Aeneas and as a go-between for Hera and Hypnos, the god of sleep. A Homeric hymn to Demeter, *c.* seventh century BCE, recites, 'First he [Zeus] sent golden-winged Iris to call rich-haired Demeter' to implore her return from her self-imposed exile after her daughter Persephone was abducted to the underworld by Hades.

She also appears in Homer's *Iliad*:

Now to the Trojans came as messenger wind-footed Iris,
in her speed, with the dark message from Zeus of the *aigis*.

But Iris, like many of her feminine contemporaries, became less important as a goddess due to the misogynistic intellect rife in antiquity. Cicero, the first-century BCE Roman rhetorician, in *De Natura Deorum* comments glibly:

Why should not the glorious Rainbow be included among the gods? It is beautiful enough, and its marvellous love-liness has given rise to the legend that Iris is the daughter of Thaumus (Wonder). And if the Arcus (Rainbow) is a divinity, what will you do about the Nubes (Clouds)? The rainbow itself is caused by some coloration of the clouds.

Iris's epithets had once included *Khrysopteron*, 'golden-winged'; *Aellôpsos*, 'storm-footed'; and *Thaumantos*, possibly the one epithet Cicero would have liked for himself, 'wondrous one'. With Iris's close identification to Isis and her golden-winged cult, it was timely to reinvent Iris as nothing more than 'some coloration of the clouds'. There was a lot more to Iris, dare I say it, than meets the eye.

Nike

According to Hesiod (c. eighth/seventh century BCE), Nike (originally Nice) was the daughter of the river Styx and the giant, Pallas. She was sent to fight on the side of Zeus in the war against the Titans, and although she had no specific cult, she was extensively worshipped as goddess of victory and success. In Greek art, she is usually winged, carrying an olive branch or Hermes' caduceus – the symbols of mediation between divine and mortal. 'Trim-ankled' Nike represented the soaring flight of victory in later Greek culture as an aspect of Athena. She also became a favourite goddess in Roman mythology in her emanation as Victoria.

Hermes

Hermes was the street-trader of the Olympian pantheon, the go-between of all worlds, including the underworld, the god of thresholds and transitions. Hermes was a psychopomp – an escort and guide through transitional changes, and to the afterlife – like Iris and the Harpies, but also the ubiquitous god of trade, cunning, thieves, boundaries, writing, travellers and commerce. A precocious, wily and promiscuous god, he had many lovers, such as Dryope, Aphrodite, Penelope and Crocus.

In the Homeric Hymn to Hermes, which describes the psychopomp's birth and his adventures, Hermes is

> One of many shifts (*polytropos*), blandly cunning, a robber, a cattle driver, a bringer of dreams, a watcher by night, a thief at the gates, one who was soon to show forth wonderful deeds among the deathless gods.

He was the god of the shape-shifting messengers and shamans themselves. In Hellenistic Egypt, Hermes became identified with the Egyptian god of magic and writing, Thoth. The Egyptians were religiously insular, but had politically subjected themselves to Alexander's conquest of the Nile Valley. Despite remaining fiercely protective of their own esoteric mysteries, rituals and cults, the syncretism of Hermes with Thoth became the catalyst for the infamous corpus of secret wisdom, the Hermetica, and its affect on Renaissance thought.

Plato's *Cratylus* adds some pedantic nit-picks to Hermes' name:

> This name 'Hermes' seems to me to have to do with speech; he is an interpreter (*hêrmêneus*) and a messenger, is wily and deceptive in speech, and is oratorical. All this activity is concerned with the power of speech. Now, as I said before, *eirein* denotes the use of speech; moreover, Homer often uses the word *emêsato*, which means 'contrive'. From these two words, then, the lawgiver imposes upon us the name of this god who contrived speech and the use of speech – *eirein* means 'speak' – and tells us: 'Ye human beings, he who contrived speech (*eirein emêsato*) ought to be called Eiremes by you.' We, however, have beautified the name, as we imagine, and call him Hermes.

Hermes was also the god of the birds of omen, which were despatched from heaven under the divine inspiration of the prophetic Apollon. Only clairvoyants, under the god's patronage, could distinguish birds of omen from those 'idly chattering', and only oracles and seers were allowed to interpret their divine messages.

Our Greek messenger deities became heretical fodder for orthodox religion, but secret ambassadors for later occult beliefs. Hermes became safely assimilated in the Roman pantheon as Mercury. He'd already fused with Thoth in some divine pomander, to steer the souls of secret mystery cults, such as the Hermeticists, on their own journey to the deepest mystery of all. Iris became the rainbow and Nike the symbol of victory, but what of the other winged spirits in Greek mythology, the daimones and the keres? Here was a bigger challenge for the patriarchal intellect, especially now that evil was less associated with man's fate and more with man's choices.

3

DAIMON TO DEMON

'Two strands then clearly emerge, daimones as independent spirits, and as the souls of the departed, and it is fair to say that the strands could never be completely unraveled once they had become tangled.'

Frederick E. Brenk, *In the Light of the Moon: Demonology in the Early Imperial Period.*

As already mentioned in the first chapter, *daimon* is generally agreed to mean 'distributor of destinies'. This distributor is like a cash machine. The cash machine doesn't decide how much it will give you – although if you ask for too much, you won't get it. It's you who decides; you have your own personal code and an amount you have in mind, or a desire, to retrieve. The daimon gives you what you ask for, or what you already know you can account for. The daimon isn't a 'fated' given, as we shall see, it is the guardian angel or spirit guide who helps you become who you already are. According to Platonic thought, the daimon is both an aspect of your individual soul and the spirit that guides that soul – the cash-distributing guardian angel.

DAIMONES IN ANCIENT GREEK RELIGION

Depictions of daimones occur as early as *c.* 3000–1100 BCE, on Minoan vases. The Minoans considered the daimon to be a servant or emanation of their vast array of gods, a lesser spirit among many. This is similar to the beliefs of many indigenous peoples, from the white-winged Doji spirits of Japan, and the Vodianoi of Slavic mythology, to the Tuatha-de-Danaan of Celtic Ireland.

Spirits are the interlopers between the invisible and visible worlds. They come as shape-shifters and tricksters, merging, appearing, disappearing. Later, some are known as imps and fairies; others surface as ghostly spirits or in animal guise. They can be good or bad, or both.

In ancient Greece, there were hosts of daimones, from air, earth, sea and the underworld. There were nature spirits, nymphs, fauns and satyrs, as well as abstract personifications, such as Achos (pain of body or mind), Anance (necessity, compulsion), Himerus (sexual desire), Lethe (forgetfulness), Hybris (excessive pride), Ate (delusion) and Zelus (jealousy). Some daimones who achieved a higher status were often personified in Greek art, including Nemesis, Sophia, Eris, Harmonia and Nike.

Daimones Proseoous (eastern spirits) haunted the dark caverns around the island of Rhodes, but good daimones bestowed luck and blessing. A popular good spirit in Greek folk religion was Agathos Daimon, who presided over vineyards and grain fields. Considered to ensure happiness and a successful harvest to those who were good and true, Agathos was precursor of the 'genius' of Roman mythology.

THE KERES

Hesiod, Homer and Virgil refer to the Keres as evil. Originally winged spirits that flitted across many a funeral vase or fifth-century

BCE Greek jar, they evolved into the Erinyes, the Harpyiai and the much-maligned Sirens. All were personified as females with wings.

Ker, according to classical scholar Jane Harrison (1850–1928), in her book *Prologomena to the Study of Greek Religion*, is one of the most difficult of ancient Greek words to translate. In her academic, but accessible, work of 1904, Harrison admitted she was not a great philologist and most of her evidence for her book came through archaeological depictions. However, she did draw on the etymology of an obscure but richly revealing Greek lexicon, the *Hesychiii Alexandrii*, said to have been compiled by Monsieur Hesychius of Alexandria himself, in the fifth century. Filled with lost words from local dialects and names of places where words were in common usage, the book has over fifty thousand mouthwatering entries. However, the only surviving complete manuscript is the corrupt fifteenth-century version, which was heavily interpolated by later writers and is currently in the library of San Marco in Venice. Yet its wealth of information is still mind-blowing.

Hesychius's entry for *ker* is defined not only as 'goddess' or 'angel of death', but has a racing stable full of wonderful connections, such as 'soul', 'messenger', 'a priestly race descended from Hermes', 'life bringers' and 'death bringers'. On further investigation, *ker* also corresponds to another root – 'herald or messenger's wand'. We also find in Hesychius's lexicon, an interesting reference to Artemis identified as *angelos*. In fact, 'Angel' was the goddess's title at her shrine in Syracuse. Along with Hecate, who was considered to be ruler of the daimones, Artemis was identified with the planet Venus as Morning Star, and later personified as Phosphorus, the bearer of light, known later by the Romans as our friend Lucifer. Could the lovely Artemis, curiously enough, have been the goddess who embodied both angel and demon?

The Keres were also associated with disease and bad spirits, and with the rise of patriarchal civilization, they soon became associated solely with evil. Homer, perhaps more than any other writer, saw the Ker as the angel of death, doom and fate itself, and later as a personified she-devil of destruction. In the *Iliad*, a Ker appears to Achilles on the battlefield:

> And in the thick of battle, there was Strife,
> And clamour, and there too the baleful Ker.
> She grasped one man alive, with bleeding wound.
> Another still unwounded, and one dead
> She by his feet dragged through the throng.
> And red her raiment on her shoulders with man's blood.

The Harpies and the Erinyes, later versions of the Keres, were both as unwelcome. Virgil, in the first century BCE, describes the Erinyes in the *Aeneid*:

> Two demon friends there are, called by the name of the Furiae [Erinyes] whom darkest Nox brought forth at one and the same birth with hellish Megaera, breeding all three alike with the twining coils of serpents and giving them wings like the wind.

The Harpyiai, or Harpies, 'swift robbers', were the spirits of sudden gusts of stormy wind. Depicted as winged women, sometimes with bird bodies, they were sent by the gods to punish the blind King Phineus of Thrace for his theft of the secret of immortality. Swooping down every time food was laid in front of the king, they'd snatch it away. However, Hesiod, the ninth-century BCE Greek misogynist, in his poem 'Theogony', spoke quite fondly of them:

> The Harpyiai of the lovely hair, Okypete and Aello, and these two in the speed of their wings keep pace with the blowing winds, or birds in flight, as they soar and and swoop, high aloft.

'Theogony' was Hesiod's marvellous soap-operatic creation myth to rival all others, before and after. Virgil, several hundred years later, spoke less favourably:

> Bird-bodied, girl-faced things they are; abominable their droppings, their hands are talons, their faces haggard with hunger insatiable.

Say no more. In his poem 'Works and Days', Hesiod writes:

> Then, when the dog-star (Sirius) comes and shines by day
> For a brief space over the heads of men Ker-nourished.

Here the nourishing Ker resembles some kind of guardian daimon, a spirit who would guide man's fate rather than seal it in some hellish tomb. Perhaps the Ker does both. The Ker daimon was both guardian angel of the soul, yet the enemy of the body, both evil and good, the distributor of individual destiny and yet still 'to mortals at their birth' the Ker gave 'good and evil both'.

The Kakodaimones, mothered by the daimon Eris (strife), were the evil abstractions sent to plague mankind, and included the Algea (pains), the Neikea (quarrels), the Phonoi (Murders) and the Makhai (battles).

The Keres were eventually known as the female daimones present at violent and cruel death. They were agents of the Moirai (the Fates), the three goddesses who measured out man's life at the time of birth. Hungry for blood, the Keres feasted on corpses after ripping out the soul and sending it on its way to Hades. Usually depicted as winged, fanged and taloned women, the Keres appeared on battlefields. Their presence meant you were likely to drop dead at any moment. In Homer's *Iliad*, Zeus says to an impatient Hera, hoping for Paris's death, 'Aphrodite forever stands by her man [Paris] and drives the Keres away from him.'

GUARDIAN SPIRITS

Hesiod, in his poem 'Work and Days', describes how Zeus transforms the men of the Golden Age, living in the time of Kronos, into the kindly guardians of mortals. These daimones, known as the Daimones Khryseoi, the 'golden spirits', were 'air-dwelling, thirty thousand in number' and 'the watchers' who observed the deeds of mankind and rewarded them with a bountiful harvest if they were just and true. This is one of the earliest associations of 'daimons' or 'guardian angels' with the 'watchers' later to be associated with the fallen angels in the apocryphal Book of Enoch 1.

Hesiod, however, says:

> They were kindly, delivering from harm, and guardians of mortal men, for they roam everywhere over the earth, mist-apparelled and keep watch on judgements and cruel deeds.

In Hellenistic Greece, the spirits were divided into the Eudaemons and the Kakodaemons, good and bad respectively. Eudaemons were guardian spirits, and the word *eudaemonia* came to mean 'wellbeing' or 'happiness'. Hesiod also described a race of silver spirits, Daimones Argentus, who burnt themselves out by 'foolishly sinning and wronging one another, until Zeus made them blessed spirits under the earth, a second order, worthy of honour'. It would be easy here to polarize the daimon into heavenly good and hellishly bad from Hesiod's golden and silver groupings. Hesiod, however, had honoured them both.

Plato, several centuries later in his *Laws*, used the myth of Kronos in his description of an ideal state ruled by a philosopher elite:

> He [Kronos] then appointed as kings and rulers for our cities, not men, but beings of a race that was nobler and more divine, namely *Daimones*.

Diotima, the priestess of Plato's *Symposium,* taught Socrates that love is a 'great *daimon*', and then describes the daimon as:

> Interpreting and transporting human things to the gods and the divine things to men: entreaties and sacrifices from below, and ordinances and requitals from above . . . [She tells Socrates] everything daimonic is between divine and mortal [and] only through the daimonic is there intercourse and conversation between men and gods, whether in the waking state or during sleep. And the man who is an expert in such intercourse is a daimonic man . . .

In Homer's *Odyssey*, the daimon is an ambivalent lone ranger. He/it/she is a supernatural intermediary, who appears through the experience of some crisis within the individual, or outer event.

Earlier, in *Timaeus 3*, Plato had associated the daimon with oracles and divinations:

> Through [the daimon] are conveyed all divination and priestcraft concerning sacrifice and ritual and incantations, and all soothsaying and sorcery.

According to Hans Betz's work, *Greek Magical Papyri in Translation*, magicians called upon daimons both malevolent and beneficial in their spells and incantations, commanding, 'send me the daimon who will give responses to me about everything which I order him to speak about'. This early association of the daimon with magic or divination was not a particularly helpful marketing job for its later evolution.

Sirens

Winged enchantresses, depicted in early Greek art as part bird, part woman, the Sirens resemble our goddess friends Inanna, Isis and the ancient Neolithic bird goddess. The sirens first appear in Homer's *Odyssey* to lure Odysseus and his men to the island.

They lull him with murmur of sweet sound crouching
within the meadow; about them is a mound of men that rot
in death, their skin wasting the bones around.

Rather like the mysterious Sphinx, the Sirens can see past and
future. They live on an island, not in the sea, they are birds,
often represented as the singing souls of the dead, similar to the
Ba of Egyptian mythology.

At the end of the *Republic,* Plato, summing up his cosmology,
writes:

The spindle turns on the knee of Ananke, and on the upper
surface of each sphere is perched a Siren, who goes round
with them hymning a single tone. The eight together form
one Harmony.

First century writer Plutarch had a hard time accepting the idea
that the Sirens, by then assumed to be evil, could be at the root
of the music of the heavenly spheres. But he eventually justified
this, through the opinion of one of his guests in the *Symposiacs,*
who offers a mystical significance to Homer's description in the
Odyssey:

Even Homer means by their music not a power dangerous
and destructive to man, but rather a power that inspires in
the souls that go from Hence Thither and wander about
after death, a love for things heavenly and divine and a
forgetfulness of things mortal, and thereby holds them
enchanted by singing.

And as we know, angels do like singing.

THE DAIMON AS GUIDING SPIRIT AND SOUL

*'Zeus has placed by every man a guardian, every man a
daemon, to whom he has committed the care of the man;
a guardian who never sleeps, is never deceived.'*

Epictetus (55–135 CE), Greek Stoic philosopher,
Dissertation 1, Chapter 14, 12

The mystical philosopher Pythagoras (sixth/fifth century BCE)
was probably the first Greek to develop the notion of the relationship between the 'soul' and the daimon. It may be that he
drew on initiations he underwent in Egypt, where he learnt about
mysticism and the soul's journey. A line from the Pythagorean
'Golden Verse', a collection of moral lines and fragments, said to
be based on original sayings either by Pythagoras or his pupils,
dating back to the third century BCE, reads:

Father Zeus, O free them all from suffering so great or
show unto each the *daimon*, who is their guide.

The Pythagorean school of thought believed that a part of man,
called the Higher Self or Divine Spark, could be purified in life,
and thus transcend the body's death to become a higher being.
And then, of course, there was the first declared extraordinary
daimonic man himself, Empedocles.

'A twofold tale I shall tell'

The pre-Socratic wanderer, healer, philosopher and poet,
Empedocles (490–430 BCE) believed he was a daimon, or that he
lived a 'daimonic life'. According to Diogenes Laertius in *Lives of
the Eminent Philosophers*, Empedocles was a charismatic philosopher, claiming among other things, divine or magical powers. He
wandered about wearing purple robes and bronze sandals, not
forgetting a magnificent golden belt. Various apocryphal stories
emerged about him in late antiquity, concerning his means of

death. One story recounts how he leapt into Mount Etna's crater so no one could refute his ascension to divine status. Unfortunately, one of his bronze sandals was later thrown up by a new eruption, thus proving to onlookers that he had died as any mortal would if they fell into a volcano.

Empedocles studied with Parmenides, Pythagoras and Anaximander. Flamboyant and attractive, he was also a bit of a politician. In his personal work he considered himself to be a wandering healer, 'distributing prophecies' and working miracles, such as reviving the dead and controlling the wind or rain. He was the 'distributor of destinies', the *dâio* man himself. A mystic, philosopher, politician, and poet, Empedocles's teachings were concerned with the soul's journey to achieve harmony and perfect Love. His world-view was that of a constant cycle of eternal growth and decay, where Love and Strife personified the eternal 'exchange of position'. He imagined the Golden Age of the past, when universal harmony existed, and no doubt he had been inspired by Pythagoras as well as the ancient mythology of the Great Goddess – 'They did not have Ares as god or Kydoimos, nor King Zeus, nor Kronos, nor Poseidon but queen Kypris [Love].'

In his poem 'On Nature', he also comments, 'there is an oracle of necessity, an ancient decree of the gods, eternal, sealed with broad oaths', and it was this message he was intent on delivering himself.

The discovery of ancient fragments of his work by Strasbourg University in the 1990s gave scholars more to scratch their heads about. In one fragment, he describes his daimonic incarnation. In his previous manifestation, he had been banished from the company of the gods for eating meat and shedding blood (like Pythagoras, he was a dedicated vegetarian) and now must face thirty thousand years, or 'three-times countless years', of the transmigration of the soul back to its divine state. However long his banishment, he must pay for his sins by being reincarnated into every living form of Nature, and confessed to his present state as daimon:

I too am now one of these, an exile from the gods and a wanderer, trusting in mad strife.

The purification process worked at all levels of the cosmos. It meant he would eventually be reborn immortal. In his current, higher than human, shamanic, in-between, magical state, he commented that there are other 'daimons' who 'come among men on earth as prophets, minstrels, physicians and leaders, and from these they arise as gods, highest in honour'. We shall meet more of these later.

If the daimon and the shaman are intermediaries between the human and divine worlds – the daimon working on behalf of the gods, and the shaman, a man who can engage with the spirit world – according to Empedocles, he was both.

Heraclitis

Another fifth-century BCE philosopher, Heraclitis, became famed for his well-known *Ethos anthropos daimon* catchphrase, which became an important doctrine of Platonic followers. Usually translated as 'character is fate', what did Heraclitus mean? From Hegel to Heidegger, many have wrestled with the true meaning behind this profound riddle. Poet and writer W. B. Yeats noted in his book *Mythologies*:

> It was Heraclitus who said, the Daimon is our destiny . . . I understand why there is a deep enmity between a man and his destiny, and why a man loves nothing but his destiny . . . I am persuaded that the Daimon delivers and deceives us, and that he wove the netting from the stars and threw the net from his shoulder . . .

Perhaps the translation is better reworded, as simply 'your character *is* your daimon'.

Plato (427–347 BCE)

Like Pythagoras, Plato believed that a spirit, separate from us, accompanied us at birth into life, and guided us through life and after death, namely our personal daimon. He calls it 'the daimon which has received us as its portionment'. Whereas Hesiod's golden daimones, and good spirits such as the Agathos Daimon, were protectors of all mankind to be propitiated to ensure goodness and wellbeing for everyone, Plato believed that the personal daimon was exactly that – a lifelong, and deathlong, guardian angel or divine companion.

Socrates (c. 469–399 BCE) apparently knew his daimon, although he never called it by that name, describing it as 'a sign' or 'a something', and 'a marvellous gift which has never left me since childhood. It is a voice which, when it makes itself heard, deters me from what I am about to do and never urges me on.'

Sumerian cosmology and its fleet of messenger spirits was probably at the root of Hebrew myth and its more officious, role-bearing messengers, who were described as such because of what they do, not who they are. Residing in the invisible world, they fleetingly appear, more often in dreaded form than desirable one. They play a role for God, they are emanations of God, but they are not the guardian daimon/angel of Pythagoras, Empedocles or Plato, which has character traits as any mortal or god.

In *Phaedo*, Plato discusses the true nature of the daimon:

It is said that after death, the tutelary genius (*daimon*) of each person, to whom he had been allotted in life, leads him to a place where the dead are gathered together; then they are judged and depart to the other world with the guide whose task it is to conduct thither those who come from this world; and when they have there received their due and remained through the time appointed, another guide brings them back after many long periods of time.

And the journey is not as Telephos says in the play of Aiskhylos; for he says a simple path leads to Haides, but I think the path is neither simple nor single, for if it were, there would be no need of guides, since no one could miss the way to any place if there were only one road. But really there seem to be many forks of the road and many windings; this I infer from the rites and ceremonies practised here on earth. Now the orderly and wise soul follows its guide and understands its circumstances; but the soul that is desirous of the body, as I said before, flits about it, and in the visible world for a long time, and after much resistance and many sufferings is led away with violence and with difficulty by its appointed *daimon*.

But it was Plato's pupil Xenocrates who may, intentionally or not, have led the way to the ambiguous nature of daimons. Plato's notion that the heavenly bodies are moved by divine souls, or in Aristotle's theory 'intelligences', gave rise to the idea that there must be a hierarchy of all things supernatural and natural, somewhere between the Soul of the World and the Earth. The author of the pseudo-Platonic *Epinomis* (*c*. 347 BCE), probably Philip of Opus, another of Plato's pupils, puts forward the elaborate theory that daimons inhabit the three middle elements between the stars, which are fire, and men. These are the daimons of aether (an added element), air and water. Xenocrates made this even more complex by introducing a triangular analogy to show how daimons related to man and the divine. Plutarch describes this obscure geometry in his *Theosophical Essays*:

Xenocrates, the friend of Plato, has taken the different kinds of triangles, comparing the equilateral to the divine, the scalene to the mortal, the isosoles to the nature of daemons [daimones]. For the first is equal in every way, the second unequal in every way, the third equal in one way, unequal in another, just as the being of daemons which has in it mortal passions and divine power.

Plutarch again comments in his essay on Osiris and Isis that:

Combined with the nature of the soul and the senses of the body, susceptible of pleasure and pain, and all other emotions the result of these, that by their vicissitudes disturb, some in a greater, others in a less degree; for, in that case, as amongst men, so amongst dæmons, exist degrees of virtue and of vice.

In other words, daimons were capable of both positive and negative human characteristics. Imbued with human traits, evil had been let loose.

THE GENIUS
If, as the ancients believed, divine power emanates through everything, whether animal, rock, person or place, the Roman idea, rooted in pagan polytheistic worship, was that every mythological god or creature was itself a genius, but also every individual place, person or thing had its own personal genius, too. This latter idea developed out of the traditional belief that the 'genius' of the home – what a scientist might now call the genes of the ancestors – was the guiding power on the male side of the family.

Genius is rooted in the Indo-European word 'gen' meaning to 'beget, produce'. Thus the genius was, literally, the 'generative power' of the family. The concept developed to include the genius of virtually everything, from the festival, vineyard, the Roman army, to places, such as streets, gates, doorways and temples. There were genii for each family member. For example, the genius Juno represented female reproductive power, while Jupiter the male equivalent.

Discovered among the ruins of Pompeii and its outlying villages were hundreds of shrines, or *lararia*, embellished with frescoes of pairs of genii, ubiquitous token serpents, the Juno and Jupiter family members, and a central genius – the family genius itself.

A beautiful, beguiling, yet frightening fragment of a fresco found in the remains of a villa in Boscoreale, near Pompeii, belonged to a Roman with an equally intriguing name, P. Fannius Synistor. It shows a winged genius, hair swept back off his face to resemble a halo, his eyes not quite human, but still dazzling and inviting. Almost ghostly, almost man, almost divine, this fresco is on show in the Louvre, but be prepared for the compelling gaze of Mr Synistor's sinister genius. Gaze at your peril.

WHERE TO GO?

To the early Greeks, the daimon was both man's guardian angel and a messenger/go-between of the spiritual and material world. The medieval alchemists and Renaissance Neo-Platonists, and more recently transpersonal psychologists, such as James Hillman, have all expanded this concept of the daimon as guardian of the soul. In the *Corpus Hermeticum* – the bible of the Hermetic followers, which was probably written in Egypt, by authors unknown, sometime before the end of the third century – daimons function as gatekeepers of the spheres through which souls pass to the highest heaven:

O son, how many bodies we have to pass through, how many bands of daimons, through how many series of repetitions and cycles of the stars, before we hasten to the One alone?

Third-century Neo-Platonist philosopher Porphyry made a distinction between good daimons, who controlled their emotions and desires, and bad daimons who were controlled by them. Archetypal psychologist James Hillman, in his book *The Soul's Code*, brings the daimon into sharp focus:

therefore you find your genius [daimon] by looking in the mirror of your life. Your visible image shows your inner truth, so when you're estimating others, what you see is what you get. It therefore becomes critically important to see generously . . . and to see deeply into dark shadows, or else you will be deceived.

So how did the guardian spirit, the daimon, the 'distributor of destinies' end up as the devil's accomplice in Christian eyes, and where did our shape-shifter find a safe place to hide? First, we have to see how the 'messenger' navigated through the waters of Sumerian mythology and floated on the raft of Zoroaster's monotheism to become known as one of God's heavenly angels.

4

THE DIVINE SPLIT AND
ZOROASTRIANISM

'In heaven, all the interesting people are missing.'
Friedrich Nietzsche (1844–1900)

If you have the time, or the inclination, to wander down the corridors of the British Museum in London, you eventually come to Room 56, a large, austere gallery of good proportions, displaying an incredible collection of early Mesopotamian objects. Not far from the wood, gold and lapis 'Ram in a Thicket' sculpture, excavated by Leonard Woolley in the late 1920s from the Great Death Pit at Ur, in southern Iraq, and dating back to about 2600–2400 BCE, is a more mysterious and spectacular plaque. Known originally as the 'Burney Relief' and now called the 'Queen of the Night' relief, this Sumerian terracotta plaque has been dated at anywhere between 2300 and 1750 BCE. The debate about who it represents, and its real significance, is ongoing.

This striking, magnificent winged goddess with taloned feet, accompanied by lions and two owls, is thought to be either Lilith, the demonic first wife of Adam, debased in Hebrew mythology (see Chapter 12), or Inanna, the earlier version of Ishtar. Inanna and Ishtar were both aspects of the Great Goddess. The Sumerian Inanna was the first to be worshipped at Uruk in 4000 BCE, Ishtar being her later Assyrian counterpart. Interestingly, Lilith was also known to be Inanna's hand-maiden, or possibly an aspect of Inanna.

Various metaphors in the imagery of the carving link the owl, lions and talons with the worship of Inanna, and a similar motif appears on what is known as the 'Ishtar Vase' in the Louvre. The winged goddess was no longer a goody-goody earth mother, but an awesome night-time bad girl. Angelic wings were tainted with ambivalence or eroticism, or both. Cruel and fickle, loving yet terrifying, she corresponds to other goddesses, such as the Hindu Kali, and the Greek Aphrodite.

In Sumerian mythology, Inanna stole the Tablets of Destiny, the *Me* (pronounced 'mai'), from Enki, the earth god, and then hid these fundamental secrets of the universe. Flushed out of sight in the murky waters of patriarchal civilization, there is an apocryphal story that the Ten Commandments were a handful of the *Me*, found by Moses on the top of Mount Sinai. From the early Uruk culture of around 3450 BCE, to the arrival of the first Semetic peoples near Byblos in the Lebanon, in 3200 BCE, the goddess began to lose not only her secret message, but also her power.

DARK SIDE OF LIFE

Witchcraft, magic and evil spirits had been around from the earliest days of the shaman. The complex religions of the Sumerians were renowned for their exorcisms, magic spells and countless spirits, such as the Gigim Xul, the evil spirit himself, the Telal, or wicked one, and Gelal, the incubus.

The Abgal in Sumerian mythology – Apkallu in the old Akkadian language – were seven mediating spirits depicted as humans with griffin heads and wings. These demi-gods were sent by Enki to teach wisdom to humans and civilize humanity. The Apkallu were the main influence on both Zoroastrian and Hebrew angels. Thorkild Jacobsen (1904–93), a renowned historian of Sumerian mythology, translated many ancient texts, including a few lines on evil spirits as:

Bitter venom of the gods, they are the storms let loose from heaven, Spawn spawned by the god of heaven.

The Sumerians embraced a belief in messenger spirits between gods and humans. They also believed that each person had a 'ghost' who remained a constant companion throughout life. Altars dedicated to guardian spirits have been found in the excavations of ancient Sumerian homes, along with stone engravings and temple wall paintings of human figures with wings.

After the polytheistic Semitic tribes had conquered the Sumerians around 1900 BCE, they developed the idea of groups of spirits answerable to each of the many Semitic gods. They organized these groups into 'ranked' hierarchies, a notion that persisted into Zoroastrianism and was taken up in monotheistic Judaism.

The Sumerian peoples were subsequently conquered by the Amorites, who introduced their own Semitic language but preserved much of the Sumerian culture. At this point, Inanna still lived on in their mythology. Around 1900–1500 BCE, nomads and ancestors of the Hebrew peoples migrated from Sumer to Canaan, and on into Egypt, led by patriarch Abraham. Gradually, Sumerian Inanna, along with the hoards of divine beings from earlier mythology, began to be assimilated into the fragmented patriarchal stories of the Hebrew peoples.

These oldest tales of Yahweh were probably based on the Ugarit mythology of El and Asherah. By the eighth to sixth century BCE, El had become identified as Elioh-Yahweh, and the other gods and spirits were mere emanations of Yahweh's power.

Between 1450 and 1200 BCE, the cosmopolitan city of Ugarit was a thriving port linked by trade to both Egypt and Cyprus. Archaeologist Claude Schaeffer discovered temples dedicated to 'Baal' the son of 'El', a palace library, a temple library and two private libraries made up of cuneiform clay tables. In Sumerian, Hurrian, Akkadian and Ugartic mythology, the Baal cycle was the basis for the religion of the Canaanite Baal, and subsequently the Old Testament.

Baal's destruction of the sea monster Yam bears a striking resemblance to the sea dragon Tiamat's destruction by Marduk, and to other myths where gods rise up against nature (the Great Goddess) and a pantheon of warrior gods and heroes arrive to restore order.

If Inanna's message of 'all is one' had been lost with the arrival of patriarchal civilization, if the Tablets of Destiny had been hidden from the gods, at least her messengers and wings lived on. The goddess wasn't quite as daft as she looked. To the patriarchal civilizations, the problem was not so much that there was a key to all knowledge, but that it was a goddess who had hidden the secret.

THE DIVINE SPLIT

As the rising sun cast an ochre glow across every sand hollow and rock outcrop, a horse and rider galloped across the desert, their mission almost complete. The dust swirled into elliptical clouds, the snorting stallion stamped its hooves before the towering Ziggarat, and the mounted courier wiped his blistered hands on his flaxen shirt.

Breathless, he handed the rolled papyrus to the king's servant: 'Say this is for Marduk, say this is the gods' reply. Say that he must slay the dragoness, Tiamat and her consort, the evil Kingu. Say that he must ride on a hurricane, take the net, the bow, the four winds, the arrow of lightning and steal the Tablets of

Destiny. With this knowledge he will be proclaimed the one and only supreme god.'

As the servant ran back to the walls of the great citadel, the courier clicked his tongue, dug his heels into the stallion's side and galloped back across the dusty trail he had already traced in the sand, the blistered hands now bleeding, the words now spoken.

Our mounted courier, *angaros* or *angelos*, had arrived not only at sunrise, but at the dawn of patriarchal civilization. The sky gods still feared the Great Goddess and all that she represented. Nammu, the creator goddess, had finally become associated with evil. But the gods, hungry for power, wanted the Tablets of Destiny stolen by Inanna. In other words, it was time for a patriarchal take-over bid.

The myth of Marduk and Tiamat – known as the *Enuma Elish* and a Babylonian rewrite of an earlier Sumerian story – became the metaphor for the end of the matriarchal religions and the old mythology of the Goddess. As the warring Aryan and Semitic patriarchs battled for power, Marduk became the hero of the people, the first god to destroy the Mother Goddess and set a precedent for most mythology that was to follow. This version dates back to around 1750 BCE, at the time when many ruling warriors, such as the Amorite king, Hammurabi, quickly identified themselves with the new solar principle, and associated imagery.

By 1000 BCE, Marduk has became identified as the sole creator god himself, and the entire pantheon of Mesopotamian gods was virtually wiped out, or introduced as aspects of Marduk. Marduk's worship was monotheistic, his myths, the propaganda of the ruling kings, and as late as the sixth century BCE, Marduk was still being worshipped as the 'tutu' or 'creator'.

If the old goddess dragon had wings, then the conquering gods were portrayed as lions. If the old goddess was originally the primeval Water, then the hero and the conquerer were Fire. Solar consciousness equalled strength, lions, the sun, power, victory, conquest, light, order, the rational and the 'good'. The winged dragon-goddess, and all that was associated with the feminine or lunar pinciple, became identified with nature, darkness, the mortality of the body, and evil. And so it was that spirit opposed soul, mind opposed body, the divine opposed evil, and the risen opposed the fallen. But where did the old matriarchal beliefs and paleolithic values go? As Jung points out, 'nothing in the psyche is ever lost.' In fact, the old beliefs went underground for a while, surfacing later, in ways known only to the few.

The *Enuma Elish* story was top of the hit parade through much of the Babylonian, Assyrian and Hittite civilizations. The epic myth continued to be recited for over a thousand years at the spring equinox, and had a strong influence on the early Hebrew myth of creation. With the dragon-serpent goddess conquered, the priestly myth-makers had cleverly reworked the earlier stories of the cyclical nature of life as something to be feared.

Joseph Campbell said that the *Enuma Elish* heralded:

A new psychology . . . a new structure of human thought and feeling . . . We have now entered a new theatre of myth that the rational, non-mystic mind can comprehend without aid, where the art of politics, the art of gaining power over men, received for all time its celestial model.

Ahuras and Daevas

A linguistic diversion had also occurred in the Proto-Indian-European (PIE) language of the Ayrans, the people who migrated west on to the Iranian plateau, and east into India, probably from the Ukranian Steppes, around 3000 BCE 'Aryan' is where Iran derived its name. Both groups maintained their original array of gods, but some strange linguistic changes occurred. The Vedic word *asura*, 'lord', was used for all high-powered deities, specifically Varuna, who was the equivalent of Ahura Mazda in Iran. Originally, there were three words for a divine being – *asura*, *yagata*, 'the one who is worthy of sacrifice', and *daêva*, 'the shining one'. In Iran, *asura* took precedence as the supreme god, transliterated as *ahura*, and *yagata* became a useful word to describe all the other aspects of the god and his spiritual deities. In earliest Persian mythology, *ahura* came to mean 'god' and *daeva* came to mean 'demon'.

In the Zoroastrian Gathas – hymns said to have been composed by the prophet Zoroaster himself – the *daevas* were 'false gods' or 'gods that are [to be] rejected', while *ahura* meant a good spirit. However, in early Vedic mythology, the *daevas* are all gods and goddesses, while *asuras* are power-seeking deities, who were often described as evil. In later Hindu mythology, *asuras* become evil spirits who war against the *daevas* (gods), *daeva* maintaining its root meaning of 'shining one'. This head-spinning confusion didn't exactly help anyone.

With the subsequent evolution of the sacred writings of the Rig Veda and its later development in Hindu mythology, the materialistic *asura* deities had the negative projection of evil dumped upon them. Subsequently, the word *asura* came to represent demonic forces in Hindu religion, completely the reverse of Iranian mythology.

IRANIAN MYTHOLOGY

The pastoral indigenous peoples of Iran, some the descendants of the Aryans, worshipped a pantheon of gods and spirits, including a triad of gods who protected the cosmos, consisting of Ahura Mazda, Mithras and Apam Napat. In the Indian Rig Veda, they were called Varuna, Mitra and Indra respectively. The popular triad regenerated in different guises over the next millenium, and cults developed, such as that of Mithras, who remained popular throughout the Mediterranean world and managed to re-emerge as a cult in late Antiquity.

Due to the reformation of Iranian religion after the rise of Zoroaster, its ancient mythology was lost or destroyed. Evidence of pre-Zoroaster Iranian mythology is scarce, but is likely rooted in the tales of the Aryans' Golden Age and their native homeland. One story tells how all was eternal harmony, ruled over by King Yima, known to the Persians as Jamshid. Yima/Jamshid somehow managed to sin, lost his immortality and died, thus ending the Golden Age and bringing on the darker one. His doppelganger, Yama in Vedic mythology, was a more benevolent deity who became a neutral god of the underworld.

Another crucial pre-Zoroaster Iranian myth concerns a primordial being who existed before creation, Zurvan Akarana, the god of time. By inseminating itself, the god created twins in its womb. One was the personification of light, Ahura Mazda, the other, Angra Mainyu, the personification of darkness. This story was to become key to the evolution of Zoroastrianism, but it was not until Zoroaster opposed polytheism with his one uncreated God of Goodness that the real problem began.

ZOROASTER

No one is absolutely certain of Zoroaster's dates, but according to most scholars and based on his sacred texts, he lived around 1100–1000 BCE. However, some schools of thought put him at 6000 BCE, and others place him around the seventh century BCE. Whatever the case, his real name, Zarathustra, meant anything from 'having many camels' to 'star in the sky', and became the stuff of which dreams are made in the Greek Hellenistic world.

From around the fourth century BCE, he was known to the Greeks as Zoroaster, and was considered to be the founder of the Magi, the original astrologers and alchemists. The word 'magus' has some complex roots, but in the original Persian simply meant someone who was 'esoterically in the know'. According to Herodotus, writing in the fifth century BCE, the magi were simply the people of the Medes. In western civilization, the word eventually became a derogatory term for a charlatan or conjurer, the plural evolving into magician.

To the Greeks, Zoroaster was a Babylonian who could read the stars and predict the future – a true prophet and wise man. Libraries-worth of literature circulated the Greco-Roman Mediterranean world concerning his exotic and mysterious wisdom. Many believed Pythagorus had travelled to Babylon to study with the prophet at first hand, and hundreds of works circulated under his name, including an astrological handbook, made up of five volumes in papyrus rolls, entitled *Asteroskopita*.

Zoroaster's philosophy

Zoroaster's simple philosophy was one the Greeks took on board with little problem. Here was something that cut through the fated icing on man's cupcake of life, and gave the wise intelligentsia much to think about. There were three principle ideas.

Firstly, one uncreated God had created all in the world as good. Secondly, man had free will to make choices between his good and bad thoughts. Thirdly, man had a soul, which existed before birth, and would transcend the death of the body. Depending on how good the individual had been in life, the soul would be elevated to a divine status. Finally, when all bad thoughts were eliminated from the world, the righteous dead would be resurrected to live in eternal harmony.

From what we know of early Greek religion and mythology, mainly thanks to Hesiod and Homer, the Greeks still relied on the premise that while the ambivalent gods continued to play eternally irresponsible games on Mount Olympus, human fate was terminal. After death, all you had to look forward to was the descent to Hades, and, hopefully, the Pool of Forgetfulness. Similarly, Babylonian and Jewish beliefs had not much better to offer. Only mystery cults led the radical individual away from this rather bleak and despairing notion of a dismal terminus.

Zoroaster's encouraging philosophy that the soul lived on was one of the major influences on the Greek Hellenistic period, at last providing a light at the end of the Hades tunnel.

Babylon

The Babylonians, whether under Chaldean, Assyrian or Hittite rule, up to their conquest by the Persian Empire, had a similar cosmology to the Mesopotamians and Sumerians. There were as many spirits as there were abstract ideas or elements in nature. Evil spirits plagued humanity, causing anything from a toothache to a nightmare, and good ones were called upon whenever divine help was deemed necessary, from blessing a birth to bringing rain. Sin if you dare, and the gods will punish you by sending evil spirits to make your life unlivable. Exorcism, protective amulets, spells and enchantments were as common as, well, consulting the internet.

After a succession of take-over bids and battles, Nebuchad-nezzar II, the Babylonian king, went on to conquer Jerusalem in 597 BCE, only to destroy it in 586 BCE. The Jews, exiled to Babylon, thus encountered the remnants of the old Assyrian mythology. Forty years or so later, in 539 BCE, Cyrus the Great, Emperor of Persia, conquered Babylon and freed the Jews again.

Cyrus was a practising Zoroastrian, and his slightly benev-olent rule quickly assimilated the old Babylonian polytheistic beliefs into the new Zoroastrian religion, influencing the exiled Jewish one. But Zoraster's philosophy, simple as it was, had already been reworked to suit the powers that be.

We know little of Zoroaster himself, except he was a benevolent spiritual philosopher, although there are docu-mented facts of family history, rather dull and not very legendary, in the Gathas. The Gathas are the only texts among the Zoroastrian archives that are certain to be old enough to have been written by Zoroaster. The main body of the archives, the Avesta, is made up of a collection of texts, including the Gathas, known as the Yasna. The Avesta contains a whole library of hymns and scriptures compiled by post-Zoroaster scribes and priests, who reveal the kind of man the patriarchal rulers might have fabricated, someone who wrestled with the demons himself.

The most crucial tenet of Zoroaster's philosophy, like Buddhism, was that man has free will to make choices, and it is not all in the hands of Fate. The conflict between our good thoughts and our bad thoughts, and the suppression of our bad thoughts, is the key to completeness; from that comes the well-known Zoroastrian catchphrase: 'good thoughts, good words, good deeds'. According to the Gathas:

Everything that is created was first a Thought.
So let your Thoughts be Good
Good Thoughts are those that are in Harmony
with the Wisdom in Creation
Let your Good Thoughts be known through Good Words
For that's when Creation first comes into Being.

Strangely, good and bad thoughts ended up linked with the twin warring gods from the older mythology. One sacred text in the Yasna proclaims:

Truly, there are two primeval spirits, twins renowned to be in conflict. In thought and word, in act they are two: the better and the bad.

When Zoroastrianism became the official religion of the Persian Achaemenid State between 549 and 330 BCE, the above line was interpreted as an eternal cosmic conflict of good versus evil. From many of the later writings *attributed* to Zoroaster, the Zurvan Akarana (god of time) myth may well be at the root of 'the twins' philosophy.

Zoroaster's legacy

Zoroaster's followers personified 'the bad thought' as Angra Mainyu. After all, it was easier to represent 'evil' by a god rather than an abstract concept. The ordinary man in the desert had evolved with superstition, spirits and gods for thousands of years, and the later writings of the Avesta, such as the Vendidad, sought to promote this dualistic concept. The original idea that through man's 'goodness' his soul would receive eternal harmony, now developed into a last judgement scene, where on the precarious bridge of Chinovat, the soul would be judged by three heavenly beings. These early angels – Mithra, Rashnu and Sraosha – determined the soul's fate, whether it should go to heaven or to hell.

What was remarkable about the Zoroastrian interpreters was their ability to twist a simple philosophy to justify the power of the ruling kings and priests over the people. If the earlier polytheistic gods had their own messenger gods, such as Nabu, the son of Marduk, then who was to transmit those messages now? If there was only one God, inaccessible, remote, far away in heaven, and the only way to reach him was through a lifetime of good behaviour, how was the message going to be put to the common or garden Joe? There was now an isolated creator God who didn't want to communicate. There was a gap and something had to fill it. Politically motivated religion was gaining power, but it needed a spiritual ally, and since a spiritual hierarchy seemed the only way forward in the eyes of the power-hungry priests, the angelic world came alive. The Amesha Spentas were defined as 'higher spiritual beings', the Yazatas as 'worthy of worship' and the Fravashis as 'heavenly doubles'. The soul, or Urvan, was given an added sprinkle of 'angelic' charm, and the hierarchy was complete.

Amesha Spentas

The name derived from a word meaning 'bounteous, holy'. The Amesha Spentas were originally aspects of Ahura Mazda, or his 'divine sparks'. These are the moral qualities that man must develop in himself to align with the good thought, good deed, good action ethics of Zoroaster's original teachings. They are known as:

Vohu Manah – Good Purpose
Asha Vahishta – Righteousness, Truth
Kshathra Vairya – Desirable Dominion
Spenta Armaiti – Holy Devotion
Haurvatat – Wholeness
Ameretat – Immortality

Their later correspondences were associated with cattle, fire, metal, earth, water plants and humanity, and were transformed into supernatural beings in their own right, on a par with the later archangels of Christianity.

Yazatas

Yazatas are useful, kindly spiritual beings. In the Gathas, the Yazatas are worshipped collectively, and whether they were considered abstract concepts or manifest as beings is not verifiable. In the texts known as the Younger Avesta, written around the fifth century BCE, they become divine beings, personified as both male and female, with specific duties to perform, associated with specific days of the month or protecting man from evil spirits. They are too numerous to mention them all, but they include Ushah, female spirit of the dawn, and Sraosha, a male spirit who guards the soul for three days after death. Along with Mithra and Rashnu, Sraosha guards the bridge where the souls are judged. Others are Raman, spirit of joy; Erethe, female spirit of truth; Drvaspa, female spirit personifying cattle; and Chisti, another female spirit personifying wisdom. These are all re-visioned gods from earlier mythology. The Yazatas, meaning 'adorable ones', are nowadays likened to the Christian angels.

Fravashis

The Fravashis are similar to the Egpytian Ba, the genius of Roman mythology and the Greek daimon. The Fravashis aren't mentioned in the Gathas. The earliest mention is in the Yashts – songs of praise of widely divergent context and date, separate from the Avesta – where a hymn is addressed to thousands of 'heavenly doubles', who inhabit the stratosphere and help mankind fight evil. The date is dubious but certainly the first few centuries of the Christian Era. In the Avestan language, Fravashis are female.

According to the Yasht, each person is accompanied by a guiding spirit throughout life, personified as winged female, who equates with the soul of righteous people. As Zoroastrian scholar Mary Boyce points out, the Fravashis could well have been a later addition to ensure the religion was more acceptable to the old tradition of ancestor spirit worship.

The old Iranian hero cult worship, of around 1500 BCE, still held sway in some places, and the deavas, or evil spirits, that Zoroaster wanted to stamp out were simply the old pagan gods and hero spirits still hovering in the stratosphere. These hero spirits were venerated along with the ancestors, and thought to be assigned as spiritual protectors, warlike more than angelic. The ingenious inclusion of the Fravashis may well have been the saving grace for the zealous Zoroastrian priests. They became an acceptable symbol for the mainstream worshipper, whose collective and individual psyche still thrived on traditional polytheism.

Fravashis could be warrior-like, too, but were usually pictured as winged females that lived in the air, then on earth, answering and delivering prayers and responding to calls for help. The thirteenth Yasht describes a Fravashi as flying like a winged bird, and the winged figure of Ahura Mazda shown on Persian sculptures was thought to be the Fravashi of God. Even Ahura Mazda had a heavenly double and his own bird.

Daevas again

An epithet for those who worshipped 'other gods' was *daeva-yasna*, 'one who sacrifices to the daevas'. In the Gathas, Zoroaster 'rejects the daevas'. The pagan gods were not in themselves 'evil' but as Zoroaster was clear to point out, they didn't know the truth from a lie, and therefore were unreliable and erroneous. The ambiguity of the Gathas led to the later Avestan text writers building on the original hymns to associate daevas with 'evil', and later identifying them 'as evil' beings.

In one text from the Yasna, they deceive man, but they are not '*aka mainya*' – 'of evil mind'. By the time of the Younger Avesta, the daevas were thought of as hostile. In the Vendidad, a collection of later texts concerned solely with defeating and banishing the daevas, the three divinities of the Vedic pantheon, Indra, Shiva and Nasatya, become part of the line-up of Angra Mainyu's six demonic henchmen, who rather neatly represented the opposite negative qualities of the Amesha Spentas. The Vendidad was always recited between sunset and sunrise as, surprisingly enough, the daevas were usually active in darkness and this was the only time you could actually zap them.

It was the later religious cult followers of Zoroaster, the Zurvanists, who split the divine, not Zoroaster. But whether they did it truly in his name, or to sort out inconsistencies in the original Gathas, is not known. It is likely the changes began during the second half of the Achaemenid period, between about 400 and 330 BCE, and later sanctioned during the Sassaniad period of 220–665 CE. In the Zurvan doctrine, the eternal struggle was between the Truth or Spenta Mainyu of Ahura Mazda, and the Lies or Evil Thoughts of Ahriman. The myth holds that Truth will conquer Lies, with the help of the saviour, Saoshyant, born to a virgin, a familiar motif from mother-son-lover mythology that reached its peak in Judaeo-Christianity.

Squished out of all recognition, the free will of Zoroaster's original philosophy became the dualistic, fated choice of Zurvanism, possibly influenced also by the fatedness of Chaldean astrology and the inclusion of Aristotle's theory of chance. Whatever the case, it was here, in the hotchpotch, melting pot of Babylonian belief and changes in consciousness that the Jewish people were exposed to Zoroastrianism. It was to change their whole religious cosmology and set the course for the development of Judaeo-Christianity as a major world religion. And the angels followed in their wake.

Zoroaster in later history

By the twelfth century, Ahriman, the middle Persian equivalent of Angra Mainyu, created hordes of 'dews' or demons, to counter the forces of Ahura Mazda, developing the complete cosmogenic drama to include six arch-demons from Ahriman's destructive juice. The dews did not exist physically, but they were psychologically present as invisible spirits. Developed in the Bundahishn – a later text that grew from the Zoroastrian archive – the six arch-demons had a whole posse of lesser demons created by the sins that people commit, including Varun, unnatural lust; Uta, bringer of sickness through food and water; Az, the cause of heresy, which blinds man's wisdom and prevents him seeing truth from lies; Buht, idolatry; Eshm, wrath; and Rashk, envy.

Our friend Plutarch, the Greek-Roman philosopher and historian who lived around 46–120, also had something useful to say on Zoroaster:

It is not one Dispenser that like a retail dealer mixes together things for us out of two vessels and distributes the same, but it is from *two opposite Principles* and *two antagonistic Powers* . . . For if nothing can happen without cause, and good cannot furnish cause for evil, it follows that the

nature of Evil, as of Good, must have an origin and principle of its own . . . And this is the opinion of most men,
and those the wisest, for they believe, some that there are
Two Gods, as it were of opposite trades – one the creator
of good, the other of bad things; others call the better one
'God', the other 'Dæmon', as did Zoroaster the Magian.

It is interesting that Plutarch used the term 'daemon' to translate
daeva. Could it be that our friend Plutarch was more responsible
for the later association of daimon with the demonic forces than
he could imagine? But this was several hundred years later. First,
we need to see how the old Hebrew gods, goddess and assorted
spirits became assimilated into the pre-exilic texts of the Jews,
and how the desolate world of 'sheol', a lifers' prison, permanent
and no way out, was abandoned during their exile in Babylon for
something better, as were so many other spiritual messages.

PART 2:

RELIGION AND BELIEF

5

FROM 'MESSENGER OF THE GODS' TO 'GOD'S MANY MESSENGERS'

'Now it was from this very creed of Zoroaster that the Jews derived all the angelology of their religion.'

Charles W. King, *The Gnostics and Their Remains*

In a lofty turret, hidden amid the lapis-studded walls of the labyrinth that was Babylon, a scribe, a Chaldean by birth and an astrologer by trade, drew up a horoscope of the forthcoming eclipses for the year 538–539 BCE. King Nabonidus, the last of the Assyrian rulers, had resigned himself to the new prediction that the great Persian king, Cyrus, would conquer Babylon and transform most of the eastern world as he knew it. The exiled Jews would be allowed to return to their homelands, taking with them not only the mythic imagery and beliefs of ancient Mesopotamian worship, but also the symbol of the moon god, 'Sin' – a god close to his own heart, and a daily worship that Nabonidus had hoped none other would discover.

The month's lunar eclipse revealed that Cyrus would honour the Jewish people's god, Yahweh, and that he would set them free. Yet this Persian Cyrus, would he condemn or honour the Apkallu, the winged spirits who tended the sacred tree of life; would he give grace to those spirits who eternally revealed the secrets of the new arts and divine wisdom to mankind?

The soothsayer, as if he could read the king's mind, whispered in his ear, 'My own trade may prosper, but Marduk will perish.'

Nabonidus nodded, 'Tell me all that you see.'

The astrologer looked up to the stars, spread his arms out to the constellations and said, 'In the times to come, our sacred messengers will no longer be for all the gods, they will be ranked beneath one greater god. But the Persian king will know that unless his religious power is upheld, the people will return to the old gods, spirit world and beliefs. They must now look to the Persian king's one god. Some of those who are on the side of good will fall from grace. Evil will become the realm of another god, one who will oppose all goodness.'

Nabonidus nodded, then turned to the astrologer, his last messenger, and said, 'Now, go and tell this to the Jews.'

And so, as predicted, Cyrus the Great, Emperor of Persia, conquered Babylon in 539 BCE. During the final years of the exile, a man who later became known as the great prophet Isaiah wrote (Isaiah 45: 1–3)*:

[And Yahweh] says to his anointed,
    to Cyrus, whose right hand I take hold of
to subdue nations before him
    and to strip kings of their armor,

---

* All biblical quotes are from the New International Version of the Bible, 2011.

to open doors before him
   so that gates will not be shut:
 I will go before you
   and will level the mountains
I will break down gates of bronze
   and cut through bars of iron.
I will give you hidden treasures,
   riches stored in secret places

Yahweh gets rich

The extraordinary admiration for Cyrus – who, after all, was fairly benevolent as warring kings go – and the influence of his Zoroastrian monotheism, compelled the Jews to augment their own god, Yahweh, making him into a force never to be reckoned with. Along with the prevailing ideology of championing one god with his entourage of spiritual aids and guides, Jewish writers incorporated some of this ordered, hierarchical dogma, as well as the winged messengers of Sumerian and Akkadian mythology, into their own monotheism.

Monotheism was a cultural reflection of man's growing sense of self as separate, the psychological evolution of individual ego, spirit, desire and conquest, separate from the divine cosmos. The split was well under way.

Currently, there is still an ongoing heated debate about the time-line of the Old Testament and Hebrew Bible. Along with many biblical and historical scholars, including Lawrence Boadt, John T. Willis and James Kugel, this book tends to side with the argument that the Book of Isaiah, or rather the prophetic claims of a man who was said to live around 740 BCE, and thought to be the first of the biblical scribes to put pen to paper, was written at a much, much later date. The evidence suggests that the first thirty-nine chapters of Isaiah may well have been orally transmitted from the eighth century BCE, but the work had only just begun to be written at the end of the Jewish Babylonian exile, around 560 BCE, and continued to be developed by anonymous disciples of Isaiah well after their return to Israel.

As the Babylonian gods and goddesses were replaced by Ahura Mazda, the Apkallu by the Spentas, and the other spirits and gods lumped under the umbrella term of 'daevas', the post-exilic Jewish writers scribbled away at their Isaiah texts.

As in any mythology, the Jewish people's own Canaanite history, beliefs and stories had been passed down orally, so there was a big history to write about – the Egyptian exodus, and the star of the show, Moses (of no one quite knows when); the building of Solomon's Temple in 960 BCE; the split between Israel and Judah in 920 BCE; and Jerusalem's fall to Nebuchadnezzar in 586 BCE. In fact, there was an abyss-load of bloody history to talk and write about. Around 450 BCE, well after the Jews returned from their exile in Babylon, it's suggested some kind of redactor emerged, who saw the need for revival and consolidation of all the stories in one hit. And it was a hit bigger than anyone ever imagined.

Another theory, known as the Documentary Hypothesis, suggests a weaving of four narrations, which probably took place by a group of editors around the second century BCE.

Imagine Babylon. Here was a new city under the power of Persian kings, authoritarian priests and various hierarchies. Cyrus had kindly paid homage to the great Marduk, and various peoples continued to worship the old pagan gods alongside the increasingly popular Ahura Mazda. This was civilization at its best; no need for tribal acceptance through worship of the ancestors or propitiating a local sky-god to win battles. Babylon itself must have seemed like a mirror image of Ahura Mazda's heavenly realm, a perfect structure that various followers of Zoroaster had probably masterminded to promote the power of Persian rule. First, there was a kind god, like their king – a god who fought against the evils of the world, and taught people that the dead would one day be resurrected when Good won over Evil. This god had spirit messengers, angels and guardian angels, and there was light at the end of the tunnel, there was a part of man that lived forever, his soul, and there was hope.

Before the exile, the Canaanite Yahweh was a warring sky-god, and along with Anath, the daughter of Asherah, who was also identified with Astarte (Hebrew, Ashtoreth), was part of a normal dysfunctional mythological family. The patriarchal religious leaders had already divided up the original Great Mother Goddess into Anath, Astarte and Asherah, while Israelites worshipped a goddess whose spouse was Baal, sometimes called Yehouah or Yahweh. Then Yahweh got rich.

Post exile, Yahweh had messengers but ruled alone. If the ancient Sumerians, Aryans and the Babylonians had divine intermediaries, then why not develop this breathtakingly simple mythos? If Zoroaster had female guardian spirits and messengers sent by Ahura Mazda, then why not Yahweh? Before the exile, Yahweh was a tribal god of fear. After, he's squeaky clean, the universal love god, just like Ahura Mazda with his own spiritual army.

Mal'ak

Mal'ak, or *Mal'akh*, is an ancient Hebrew word for 'one going' or 'one sent' as a messenger, but also means 'reign', 'consult' or 'to make king or queen'. The word is used in the Hebrew Bible to denote both a divine and a human messenger. The translators of the Septuagint, the third to second century BCE Greek version of the Hebrew Bible, used the Greek word for messenger, *angelos*, for *mal'ak*. The later Latin version of this Greek version of the Hebrew Bible distinguishes the divine or spirit messenger from a human one; the divine messenger was called *angelus*, and the human messenger, *legatus* or *nuntius*.

In fact, the word *mal'ak*, the characterless, faceless messenger of Hebrew mythology, is used only two hundred times in the Old Testament, mostly referring to spiritual messengers sent by

God (Genesis 32: 1–2), human messengers sent by Jacob (Genesis 32: 3) and various kings (1 Samuel 19: 11–12) as well as post-exilic priests (Malachi 2: 7).

Mal'ak Yahweh, the messenger of God, is translated as angel of God or angel of the Lord, but without doubt is God himself, appearing as messenger – rather like many other mythological deities, God comes down to earth in disguise to commune with the mortal world. The 'angel of the Lord' is frequently mentioned in historical references to Israel's history, for example in Genesis (16: 7–14 and 21: 14–20), Isaiah and Ezekiel. In Exodus (3: 2–4), Moses is approached by the angel of the Lord, who:

> Appeared to him in flames of fire from within a bush . . .
> When the LORD saw that he had gone over to look, God called to him from within the bush, 'Moses! Moses!'
>
> And Moses said, 'Here I am.'

The 'angel' of the Lord is plainly God himself.

Throughout the Old Testament, writers attempted to make it clear that Yahweh had a heavenly double, like Ahura Mazda's Fravashi. After all, if human beings were forbidden to look on the face of Yahweh, they could at least have a chat with his Fravashi without pain of death. For example, in Isaiah the Fravashi of Yahweh is described as the 'angel of his presence'. In the Old Testament, the *mal'ak* were apparently created by God. However, there was never any specific time assigned to their creation, apart from observing they must have popped up when God created the heavens, as according to Job, 'the sons of God shouted for joy when he laid the foundations of the earth.'

Cherubim

The cherubim, our friends the Apkallu, also known as the Karibu in Akkadian mythology (and an obvious transliteration in name), appear in their new guise in Genesis (3: 24):

So he drove out the man; and he placed at the east of the garden of Eden Cherubims, and a flaming sword which turned every way, to keep the way of the tree of life.

The cherubim were utterly Akkadian in name and concept. The word *karibu* means 'one who intercedes', or 'one who prays', and the Karibu were originally intermediaries between the gods and men, semi-divine beings who presented mankind's prayers of worship to the gods, aka the daimon. Their similarity to the Babylonian Apkallu, and their role in worship and in mythology, are identical.

The protective Karibu statues that were placed at entrances to temples often had winged bodies of bulls or eagles, or were sphinx-like females. Archaeological examples – such as the ninth century BCE ivory and stone plaque from the Palace of King Ahab of Israel, carved with a pair of winged females protecting the tree of life – are curiously reminiscent of the guardians of the Ark in the desert tabernacle, and the Egyptian goddesses Isis and Nephythys, who guarded the sarcophagus of Tutankahmun.

In the desert tabernacle, twelve pairs of winged cherubim, made of beaten gold, beat their wings in praise and in protection of the Ark of the Covenant, and in the early Solomon's Temple, a pair of cherubim, made of olive wood covered in gold leaf, over four metres (13 feet) high with a wingspan of around nine metres (29½ feet), hovered over many a priest. By about the third century BCE, according to Jewish historian Raphael Patai, the cherubim's adrogynous imagery was replaced by a female personification of the state of Israel, opposite a male figure, Yahweh. In the Bible, it is also reported that Yahweh rode on the cherubim as if on 'the wings of the wind' (Psalms 18: 10). Ezekiel saw winged figures supporting Yahweh's throne, just like the lamassu, or winged beasts, in Assyrian art.

A passage from Ezekiel (28: 14–16) in the *God's Word Translation of the Old Testament* (World Bible Publishers Inc., April 1995) describes how a guardian cherub drove out the

King of Tyre, who was later to become wrongly identified as Lucifer or Satan. In the King James version, and most other later translations of the Bible, the King of Tyre is in fact appointed as cherub, then driven out by God for his sins. The ambiguity of translation can change one's perception of fallen angels, as it can change one's perception of kings and even God himself.

> I appointed an angel [of the cherubim] to guard you.
>> You were on God's holy mountain.
>> You walked among fiery stones.
> Your behavior was perfect from the time you were created,
>> until evil was found in you.
> You traded far and wide. You learned to be violent, and you sinned.
> So I threw you down from God's mountain in disgrace.
> The guardian angel [cherub] forced you out from the fiery stones.

This passage from the New International Version, 2011 reads:

> You were anointed as a guardian cherub,
>> for so I ordained you.
> You were on the holy mount of God;
>> you walked among the fiery stones.
> You were blameless in your ways
>> from the day you were created
>> till wickedness was found in you.
> Through your widespread trade
>> you were filled with violence,
>> and you sinned.
> So I drove you in disgrace from the mount of God,
>> and I expelled you, guardian cherub,
>> from among the fiery stones.

Whatever the case, it seems that whether the King of Tyre is cast from heaven in angelic guise, or thrown out by a cherub,

Ezekiel's message was to become confused with Isaiah's description of the fall of the morning star.

Named angels, and even choirs of angels in the earliest Hebrew Bible, are rare. They exist to fill the realm between visible and invisible, and are there to perform specific duties. The hierarchy was to come later. There were no evil angels, nor fallen ones. Isaiah sings the song of the fall of the morning star (14: 12–15) more as a satirical record of the fall of our friend Nobindus, not Lucifer, as later Christian writers believed.

> How you have fallen from heaven,
>   morning star, son of the dawn!
> You have been cast down to the earth,
>   you who once laid low the nations!
> You said in your heart,
>   'I will ascend to the heavens;
> I will raise my throne
>   above the stars of God;
> I will sit enthroned on the mount of assembly,
>   on the utmost heights of Mount Zaphon.
> I will ascend above the tops of the clouds;
>   I will make myself like the Most High.'
> But you are brought down to the realm of the dead,
>   to the depths of the pit.

The Seraphim

The Seraphim, the 'burning ones', were originally fiery serpents in the Old Testament, but were also described as frightening winged messengers, as in the verses often known as 'Isaiah's Commission' (Isaiah 6: 2–7):

> 1 In the year that King Uzziah died, I saw the Lord seated on a throne, high and exalted, and the train of his robe filled the temple.

2 Above him were seraphs, each with six wings: With two
wings they covered their faces, with two they covered their
feet, and with two they were flying.

Seraph is the name of the bronze serpent that Moses apparently
gave to the Israelites to worship. According to the scriptures,
King Hezekiah (716–687 BCE) suppressed the worship of the
snake god in favour of Yahweh. In the Christian Gnostic text,
On the Origin of the World, the seraph are described as 'dragon-
shaped angels'. Sephiphon, according to *A Biblical and
Theological Dictionary of the History, Manners and Customs of
the Jews and Neighbouring Nations* by Richard Watson,
published in 1837, is the name of a particularly pernicious,
sandy coloured snake, indigenous to the Arabian desert and
Egypt. Similarly, the Hebrew word for 'to burn', *seraph*, was
the name given to another serpent, one that had wing-like
cartilage along its rippling edges, which enabled it to rise up
from the sand and bite the odd passing horse, or maybe the odd
passing Christian.

ANGELS IN THE OLD TESTAMENT
In the Old Testament, spirit messengers were personified
according to the nature of the mission to be fulfilled. They bear
drawn swords or unleash divine weaponry and ride on horses
(Numbers 22: 23; Joshua 5: 13; Ezekiel 9: 2; Zechariah 1: 8). A
more fearsome angel appears in I Chronicles (21: 15), described
as standing 'between the earth and the heaven, having a drawn
sword in his hand'.

The author of the Book of Daniel, around 165 BCE, makes the
first attempt to personify and clothe an angel at the same time
(Daniel 10: 5–6):

I looked up and there before me was a man dressed in
linen, with a belt of fine gold from Uphaz around his waist.
His body was like topaz, his face like lightning, his eyes

like flaming torches, his arms and legs like the gleam of burnished bronze, and his voice like the sound of a multitude ...

Throughout the Old Testament, angels appear as the instrument of God's power, they come down to earth and do God's will, or reveal themselves to individuals as well as to the nation. They are event promoters, news presenters. God's faceless messengers foretell the birth of Isaac to Abraham, the birth of Samson to Manoah's wife, vaguely referred to by the Babylonian rabbis as Zlelponi, and the destruction of Sodom to Abraham.

Messengers were protective and militant, or worse still, avenging. A whole Assyrian army of 185,000 men is wiped out by an angel, and messengers go forth from God 'in ships to make the careless Ethiopians afraid' (Ezekiel 30: 9). The odd avenging angel pops up, such as the one in II Samuel (24: 16), and annihilates thousands:

And when the angel stretched out his hand upon Jerusalem to destroy it, the Lord repented him of the evil, and said to the angel that destroyed the people, It is enough: stay now thine hand.

Although evil spirits, known as the *se'irim* and the *shedim*, appear in the Old Testament, they are merely aspects of God's own wrath. There is no supernatural power beyond God in Judaism and his messengers and evil spirits are simply aspects of himself (Deuteronomy 4: 35). Influenced by the seven storm spirits of Chaldean mythology, the original *shedim* were originally evil, yet also protective spirits, and usually depicted as bull statues in royal temples, or in Babylonian magic literature.

With the Book of Revelation conceived and written, around the end of the first century(although no one is really sure by whom), the fantasy of millions of angels challenged not only

Zoroaster's Amesha Spentas, but the vast array of pagan gods, spirits and deities, all now considered to be evil.

> Then I looked, and I heard the voice of many angels around the throne, the living creatures, and the elders; and the number of them was ten thousand times ten thousand, and thousands of thousands, saying with a loud voice: Worthy is the Lamb who was slain To receive power and riches and wisdom, And strength and honor and glory and blessing! (Revelation 5:11–12)

The Septuagint

Alexander the Great's extraordinary conquest of Egypt and Mesopotamia, around 330 BCE, was the catalyst for an exciting culture diffusion across the whole of the Middle East as far as India. Against the backdrop of the Hellenistic period, until around 30 BCE, the daimon became diffuse, abused and elusive.

Besides Athens, Alexandria was one of the most important centres of Greek learning. The city represented a cultural melting pot of every Greek, Egyptian or Persian metropolis, and its library had more than 700,000 volumes. This was where the first translation of the Hebrew Bible, or written Torah, into Koine Greek was made during the second to third century BCE. This translation, known as the Septuagint, is where the confusion and, perhaps, the costly loss of the daimon to the demon really began.

Currently known as the LXX and, as legend has it, mostly the work of Philo of Alexandria, the Torah was translated by seventy-odd translators (hence the name Septuagint) who were kept in seventy individual chambers. After seventy days, they had all produced identical versions of the text, confirming a correct translation. During this translation, it seems that the word *mal'ak* was translated by the Greek word *angelos*, and all the assorted bad spirits, alien and rejected gods were grouped together under the Greek word *daimon*. According to Karen H. Jobes and Moises Silva in *Invitation to the Septuagint* (Grand Rapids, Michigan; Baker Academic, 2000):

> The noun αγγελος in classical Greek meant 'messenger' in a fairly general sense. When the LXX translators used it to represent a 'superhuman messenger sent by God' a new definition was created. The use of this specialised Greek term in the New Testament doubtlessly reflects the strong influence of the LXX.

With the Greek *angelos* fixed in the scholarly eye as 'God's messenger', what had been going on in the heads of our seventy-odd bright sparks that meant they chose the Greek word *daimon* to represent the assorted bag of evil bits and bobs?

ALL CHANGE

The four hundred or so years between 200 BCE and 200 CE was an exciting period of development in writing, language, writing tools and imagination. Throughout the Mediterranean world, apocryphal and pseudepigraphic (works pretending to be earlier works) texts flourished from Babylon to Alexandria. The hot sands and rocky wastelands were vibrant with an obsessive fascination for religious quests and fantastical answers. The more astute observers, such as the writers of Macabees, Jubilees and the Testament of Job, for reasons of political or material power, built on ancient myths and beliefs to develop cults and further their own standing or that of those who paid for their papyrus.

The Persians refined the use of religion as a political tool; the Jews refined the power of spreading the word of Yahweh to other people by shrewdly translating their religion into Greek and later into Latin. Men from Babylon to Athens, Rome to Alexandria, fabricated writings purporting to be of an earlier date, or something that they were not, or just made up stories for the hell of it.

But the ones that did work, truly worked the stage, such as the tracts of the Christian fathers and gospellers. Eschatology (from the Greek meaning 'last' and 'study') is the study of the end of things, whether the end of an age, or the end of the world; it was, and still is, in vogue. Devious, diverting, intriguing and seductive, this was the time when the first angels became God's aids, and demons became the devil's.

The highly important messenger of the gods had evolved into God's 'many messengers'. And in a few hundred years of frantic patriarchal fascination for religious order, the 'angel and demon' became well and truly polarized in our consciousness.

The daimon was now responsible for everything unsavoury or wicked, including all spirit possession and evil behaviour. A curious cast list emerged from the Old Testament writings, profoundly influenced, as we have seen, by Babylon, Sumerian mythology and, of course, Zoroaster. This in turn was to affect emerging Christianity. Once the old gods of polytheism were considered to be daevas, or daimons, it wasn't long before the later Christian apologists, not unlike the Harpies themselves, snatched at anything they could from the table of the blind kings of old, to take a new advantage.

6

BETTER THE DEVIL YOU KNOW

*'No one heard the devil's side of the story, because God
wrote all the books.'*

Samuel Butler (1835–1902)

SATAN

Who is Satan? Where did he come from, and why has the image
of him as the devil stuck like glue in our minds?

Satan's roots lie in the ancient archetype of phallic regener-
ative power. If we delve back into the mists of the pre-dynastic
Egyptian past, we come across a serpent god called Sata. Reborn
every day in the Earth Goddess's womb, he was later known as
Set, the phallic consort of the ancient goddess Sati, one-time
ruler of Upper Egypt.

In most ancient mythologies, the serpent was considered to
be a symbol of the sun god's alter ego, symbolizing dormant
sexual potency and the renewal aspect of his night phase.
Similarly, sun and serpent god pairings occurred throughout

ancient mythology, such as the Sanskrit 'nagas' and Baal and Yam in Canaanite mythology. This dark phase of the sun god was considered the sun's 'adversary', not because he was intrinsically evil, but as the sleeping phallus, the restorative night-time energy of the god was sent to test the light side of himself. In Tantric mythology, the male erection at dawn is represented by the upright serpent who rises with the sun.

In the Hebrew Bible's Book of Job, we first meet 'the Satan' – *ha-Satan*, meaning 'the adversary' or 'accuser'. In the original language, Satan was one of the 'sons of the gods', and note 'gods' plural, the *bene ha-elohim*. The many gods were sneakily singularized to 'the sons of one God' to get out of the tricky problem of referring to a pantheon of ancient gods at the root of this newly 're-visioned' monotheistic religion.

Not particularly evil, Satan was God's agent, who posed awkward questions to test the faith of the individual, like the night-time serpent phallic god tests his own power at dawn. Satan is the dark aspect of God. He first appears in Job (1: 7) when God says to him, 'From where have you come?' Satan answered the Lord, 'From going to and fro on the earth, and from walking up and down on it.'

Satan is given permission to test Job's faith, and in Balaam's story (Numbers 22: 22) he is authorized to block human action. Here, the Angel of the Lord (aka God) is Satan himself, literally there to stop Balaam in his tracks.

> But God's anger was kindled because he went, and the angel of the Lord took his stand in the way as his adversary. Now he was riding on the donkey, and his two servants were with him. And the donkey saw the angel of the Lord standing in the road, with a drawn sword in his hand.

So how did Satan became associated with Lucifer? First, we need to unravel the mysterious, but fascinating story of Lucifer.

LUCIFER

Lucifer, well-known from legend and literature, and brought to prominence in Dante's 'Inferno', was considered the leader of the fallen angels. According to St Augustine and to St Jerome's translation of the Bible, known as the Latin Vulgate, these angels rebelled against God and were cast out of heaven.

Like Satan, Lucifer's story is rooted in ancient mythology – the rebellion of the 'dark phase' god against the 'solar phase' of himself. The morning and evening star, i.e. the planet Venus, had long been identified as both 'light bringer' and 'dark bringer' to the ancient people, appearing in the sky early in the morning or late in the evening, according to the planet's astronomical cycle. Thus Venus's appearance represented the last light of the day, or heralded first light.

'Lucifer' is a late Latin word for the Greek personification of the morning star, Phosphorus, the 'light bearer'. In Assyrian–Babylonian mythology, the light-bringing god – also the god of lightning, Zu (a sky-god pre-dating Zeus) – was both storm-bird and 'seraph', a fiery serpent, the personification of lightning itself, who came down from the heavens to fertilize his mother, the earth. Our bolt of lightning, Zu, wanted the infamous Tablets of Destiny for himself – the *Me* stolen by Inanna – and shouted, 'I will direct all the oracles of the gods . . . I will rule over all the spirits of Heaven!' Boastful, covetous and egotistic, he was subsequently punished.

Another source for the light-bringing Lucifer was the Egyptian serpent god, Ami-Hemf 'Dweller in his Flame'. Ami-Hemf was identified with the morning star, and lived on the Mountain of Sunrise. He was also identified as the god Bennu, the soul of Ra, in a constant process of regeneration in his efforts to shine light on the world.

A lot closer to the Hebrew home was the Canaanite myth of Shaher, the morning star god, born to Asherah, the Great Mother. Shaher, like many lesser gods, coveted not only the glory of the sun god, his father, Baal, but the exclusive love of his mother, too. While rivalling Baal for mum's sexual attention, he was cast down from heaven like the ubiquitous bolt of lightning. A seventh-century BCE Canaanite scripture recounts: 'How thou art fallen from heaven, Helel's son, Shaher!' Shaher was the personification of the morning star who tried to usurp the sun god's throne. Helel was the hell-like 'pit', an epithet for the womb aspect of his mother, Asherah. Remarkably similar are the lines in Isaiah: 'How art thou fallen from heaven, O Day Star, son of Dawn!' This is the only reference to the 'morning star' in the Old Testament, in fact a subtle reference to the fall of Babylon and its king, Nabodinus, a veritable bolt of lightning himself. No doubt the line from the Canaanite myth was worth pinching by the 'Isaiah' scribes for their own ends.

Ahriman's revolt against Ahura Mazda in Persian mythology, a myth rehashed for the Zurvanist extremists, resonates with the myth of Lucifer's fall. Ahriman, once a serpent god, gave knowledge to the first couple in the garden of 'heden', just as Prometheus stole fire from the gods to give to mankind and just as the serpent gave Adam and Eve the light of wisdom in the garden of Eden. The Magi worshipped the Great Serpent as the source of their occult knowledge, and Ahriman, was more influential in earthly events than his solar twin, Ahura Mazda.

The Church fathers accused Lucifer of 'hubris', a Greek word usually taken to mean 'excessive pride', but it also has another meaning, 'sexual passion'. The morning star, Shaher, continued to be linked with lust and lightning bolts, and identified as Satan, when according to Luke (10: 18), in the New Testament, Jesus claims to have seen the lightning serpent fall to earth: 'I beheld Satan as lightning fall from heaven.'

It was easy to see how Lucifer and Satan were muddled, and were considered to be the same 'fallen lightning bolt'. Thanks to Luke, most Church fathers, including Paul and St Augustine, quickly took up this idea, and equated Satan with the devil. On the other hand, Gnostic Christians regarded Lucifer as the saviour and protector of humanity, and God as the jealous father – jealous of his son's love for humanity, and thus of the Earth Mother – who withheld sacred knowledge from mankind in an attempt to gain power over both his son and Mother Earth. But why did fallen angels became demons?

FALLEN ANGELS AND THE MISTAKEN 'SONS OF GODS'

Fallen angels 'fell', or were pushed, about the time of the conquest of Babylon by Cyrus the Great, and it seems the fallen angels, and Lucifer himself, are a suitable metaphor for, and reflection of, this period in history. The line from Genesis (6: 2): 'the sons of God saw the daughters of men that they were fair; and they took them wives of all which they chose', was worked into a stunning piece of fiction in the apocryphal, but highly influential, Book of Enoch 1.

There has been much debate about this reference in Genesis, albeit to say that any interpretation or cultural perception can cloud, change, dilute and inflate any passage taken out of context. Translations or interpretations can alter our world view. For example, the line in which God asks Job where he was when 'the morning stars sang together and all the sons of God shouted for joy' (Job 38: 7) invites many a theologian to conclude that the morning stars and even the sons of God are most likely to be the angels.

The line from Genesis was itself taken out of context, then developed in the Pseudepigraphic Book of Jubilees (5: 1), dated by scholars from the study of the Dead Sea Scrolls to around 160 BCE.

And it came to pass when the children of men began to multiply on the face of the earth and daughters were born unto them, that the angels of God saw them on a certain

year of this jubilee, that they were beautiful to look upon;
and they took themselves wives of all whom they chose,
and they bare unto them sons and they were giants.

But it was Enoch 1 that turned the simple line of Genesis text
into a complex and dramatic mythology of fallen angels. Enoch
himself gets his first mention in Genesis (5: 21–24). As grand-
father of Noah, he apparently lived for 365 years and 'walked
with God', and 'he was no more, because God took him',
inferring that he didn't die but went off to become an angel.
From these few lines, apocryphal stories arose about Enoch's
transformation from mortal to the archangel, Metatron.

During his apparent grand tour of heaven, Enoch is shown the
Tablets of Heaven, aka the Tablets of Destiny, aka the *Me*.
(Handily, God seems to have snatched them back from Inanna.)
God allows Enoch to copy some of the tablets' secrets as a gift for
humanity, and these copies are commonly known as the Books
of Enoch. According to legend, he passed the books on to Noah,
and they were subsequently lost in the flood. Later, they were
found by King Solomon, and lost again when he fell from power.
Throughout later history, mystics have tried to discover both the
actual Tablets of Heaven, and the lost Books of Enoch. Enoch 1
(Book 2 is now confirmed to have been written post Jesus)
describes in great detail the Watchers as fallen angels who visited
earth, mated with women and created a race of half-human, half-
spirit beings known as the Nephilim, or Giants, as they were also
known in the Book of Jubilees (Book of Enoch 1 7: 2).

And they became pregnant, and they bare great giants,
whose height was three thousand ells. Who consumed all
the acquisitions of men. And when men could no longer
sustain them, the giants turned against them and devoured
mankind. And they began to sin against birds, and beasts,
and reptiles, and fish, and to devour one another's flesh,
and drink the blood.

Fallen angel Azazel was particularly spectacular (Book of Enoch 1 8: 1):

> [He] taught men to make swords, and knives . . . bracelets, and ornaments, and the use of antimony, and the beautifying of the eyelids . . . And there arose much godlessness, and they committed fornication, and they were led astray, and became corrupt in all their ways. Semjâzâ taught enchantments, and root-cuttings, Armârôs the resolving of enchantments, Barâqîjâl taught astrology, Kôkabêl the constellations, Ezêqêêl the knowledge of the clouds, Araqiêl the signs of the earth, Shamsiêl the signs of the sun, and Sariêl the course of the moon.

The four archangels, Michael, Uriel, Gabriel and Raphael, appeal to God to judge the inhabitants of the world and the fallen angels. Uriel is sent by God to tell Noah of the coming apocalypse and what he needs to do (Book of Enoch 1 10: 2):

> Tell him in my name 'Hide thyself!' and reveal to him the end that is approaching: that the whole earth will be destroyed, and a deluge is about to come upon the whole earth, and will destroy all that is on it. And now instruct him that he may escape and his seed may be preserved for all the generations of the world.

God sends Raphael to (Book of Enoch 1 10: 4):

> Bind Azâzêl hand and foot, and cast him into the darkness . . . And on the day of the great judgement he shall be cast into the fire. And heal the earth which the angels have corrupted, and proclaim the healing of the earth, that they may heal the plague, and that all the children of men may not perish through all the secret things that the Watchers have disclosed and have taught their sons.

It is only in the Book of Enoch 2 (post Jesus) that we first hear of various ranks of angels, which by all accounts is a complete crib of Zoroaster's hierarchy. Some scholars believe Enoch 2 dates from the late first century CE, others that it is possibly as late as medieval in origin. Whatever the case, along comes Satanail, the chief archangel and leader of the Watchers. Cast from heaven on the second day of creation, he is eventually imprisoned in the fifth heaven along with the Nephilim. God, no doubt with a very large tongue in his cheek, says to Enoch (Book of Enoch 2 29: 4–5):

> He [Satanail] thought up the impossible idea that he might place his throne higher in the clouds which are above the earth, and that he might become equal to my power. And I hurled him from out of the height, together with his angels. And he was flying around in the air, ceaselessly, above the Bottomless.

Later Church fathers, such as Clement of Alexandria, Origen, Justin Martyr, Esubius and the author of the Pseudepigraphic Epistle of Barnabas (4: 3), all accepted Enoch's creative work of fiction. Meanwhile, a certain Rabbi Shimeon bed Yochai put a curse on any Jew teaching the Enochian work. By the first and third centuries, both Julius Africanus and St Augustine in his *City of God*, argued that the sons of God were the descendants of Seth (Adam's pure line) and the daughters of men were the descendants of Cain.

There are some occasions in the New Testament where Satan is synonymous with the devil. For example, when Luke states Satan entered Judas to induce him to betray Jesus, and in the gospel of John, where Satan is described as a 'man-killer'. St Paul considered demons to be 'dead idols' of the pagan world, and it was this pagan world he zealously attempted to stamp out. Paul, perhaps more than any other writer, prophet or

Christian father, was instrumental in encouraging the belief that Satan was the leader of the fallen angels, and that angels could also be the devil in disguise. In letters to the Corinthians (II Corinthians 11: 14), Paul warns that 'Satan himself is transformed into an angel of light', and to the Ephesians (6: 11–12), he comments:

> Put on the whole armour of God, that ye may be able to stand against the wiles of the devil. For we wrestle not against flesh and blood, but against principalities, against powers, against the rulers of darkness of this world, against spiritual wickedness in high places.

If Paul wasn't sure about angels, nor of his own conversion from persecutor to saint, then it would take a long time before anyone else could clarify it, either. The Church fathers continued to mould Satan into the role of the devil, merging him with Lucifer and the serpent of the garden of Eden. Other Church fathers, such as Justin Martyr, also returned to the well-known Isaiah passage, linking Satan with the Watchers, and Augustine and Jerome equated Satan with Lucifer and the devil, reinforced in the literary works of fourteenth-century Dante and seventeenth-century Milton.

The Devil
The word 'devil' is rooted in the Greek word *diabolus*, which means literally 'hurling across'. That is not so far removed from the word *s'atan*, which means 'slanderer' or 'accuser'. In the New Testament, the word *diabolus* occurs alongside *s'atan* over thirty times, referring to the same deity. In the popularist and expanding Christian mythology, as in many before, the trickster, tester, tempter and rebellious god, half-god, half-human, became a named individual in his own right. In mainstream Judaism, there is no devil as such, but in the

apocryphal books, such as Enoch 2 and the Book of Wisdom, the devil raises his head and becomes not only an accuser and adversary of man, but also that of God. Whether known as the Devil, Satan, Lucifer, Beelzebub, Antichrist or Mephistopheles, the 'evil' urge in humanity had created its very own divine representations, accompanied by an army of malevolent spirits.

Beelzebub

Beelzebub is probably one of the most well-known names for the devil and Satan, originating as 'Baal-zebub' meaning 'prince of devils' and 'lord of the flies'. Baal-zebub was orginally a Canaanite or Phoenician god, who, like Hermes the Psychopomp, led souls on their journey to the afterlife. In mythology, flies, as well as birds, were often considered to be the vehicle needed to transcend the soul in search of its new incarnation. During the first century, the Pharisees accused Jesus of exorcising demons in Beelzebub's name. They believed that the power to expel demons could only come from making a pact with an evil spirit. Since Baal-zebub was the prince of devils, this together with several passing references to him in the New Testament, was enough to equate him with both Satan and the devil, or vice versa.

In the Pseudepigraphic 'Testament of Solomon', Beelzebub is empowered by Solomon's ring. He tells Solomon he lives in the evening star (Venus, Hesperus, and so on) and was once the highest ranking angel in heaven, choosing to live on Venus when all the other Watchers fell. He tells Solomon he destroys tyrants, causes wars and arouses sexual desire in holy men, but will disappear if anyone cries *'elo-i'* ('my god'), just as Jesus did on the cross. Looks like Jesus had a pact with Beelzebub after all.

By medieval times, Beelzebub had risen to the status of a demon with extraordinary powers. He was said to copulate with witches, and his name was chanted at high society black masses, which were popular in European courts of the seventeenth century. He was also named in demonic possession cases, such as the Loudun and Aix-en-Provence possessions of the sixteenth and seventeenth centuries respectively, and as late as the 1930s Earling possession case in the USA.

A growing amount of literature, both orthodox and heretical, was being produced, whether on papyrus or clay. Fiction writers, philosophers, religious scholars, Church fathers and a growing bevy of theologians all worked feverishly to put their message across. These were the real 'angels and demons'. These were the new messengers for developing religious beliefs, whether right or wrong, for political power-mongering, or for the evolving individual consciousness. As the conquering Romans subdued the Greeks and Jews, it was inevitable that orthodox Christian fathers, such as St Paul, promoting his cynical belief that every angel was possibly Satan until proven otherwise, would try to put their crowd-pulling messages across. Whether believable or not, the story of Jesus and his resurrection provided a new mythology of atonement and salvation, not forgetting a useful band of angels, ready to fight against evil.

Evil angels

Philo of Alexandria, one of the influential philosophers of the middle Platonic school of thought, was a contemporary of Jesus's. Born in the year 2 BCE, and passing on to higher things around 50 CE, Philo merged Hellenistic philosophy with Jewish biblical belief. Convinced that Moses was the patriarch of all ancient Greek religion, as well as influencing both Homer and Hesiod, Philo had a considerable effect on later Christian writers, such as Plutarch, the Greek historian, and second-century theologian Origen.

Philo divided the cosmos into three types of being – pure intellectual souls, the first to be created by God; the animals; and finally man. He considered man to be a mixture of the other two, and posited that pure intellectual souls aid humanity, providing guidance to man, but can fall into vice themselves, and thus tempt or lead man astray.

Philo made it very clear that these souls were called angels or *mal'ak* by the Hebrew scriptures, and *daimones* by the Greeks. Not agreeing with the Hebrew perception that the pagan gods were evil *daimones*, he attached goodness to them, and considered them to be intermediaries with the ascending and descending spirits of Jacob's dream ladder (Genesis 28: 11–13). Philo equated the *angelos* of the LXX Greek translation of the Hebrew Bible, with the *daimones* of ancient Greek religion. In *On the Giants* (2: 6–9), Philo's commentary on Genesis 6, he writes:

> It is Moses' custom to give the name of angels to those whom other philosophers call [daimons] (or spirits), souls that is, which fly and hover in the air.

He pointed out that angels could be evil, too (*On the Giants* 4: 16).

> If, therefore, you consider that souls, and demons, and angels are things differing indeed in name, but not identical in reality, you will then be able to discard that most heavy burden, superstition. But as men in general speak of good and evil demons, and in like manner of good and evil souls, so also do they speak of angels, looking upon some as worthy of a good appellation, and calling them ambassadors of man to God, and of God to man . . . the following verse testifies to the truth of my assertion, for he says, 'He sent upon them the fury of His wrath, anger, and rage, and affliction, and he sent evil angels among them.'

As late as the sixteenth century, there was still confusion about whether angels were daimons and whether daimons were devils, awkwardly put by the theologian Robert Burton in 1621

(*Anatomy of Melancholy*). Across a goblet of wine and flickering candlelight, Burton managed to put quill to paper to write (in Part 1 Section 2):

> *Substantiae separatae* and intelligences are the same which Christians call angels, the Platonists devils, for they name the spirits *daemones,* be they good or bad angels.

Confusing indeed on first reading, but therein lies a nugget of pure gold.

7

THE GOSPEL TRUTH

'*Great good and great evil are born in one breast.*
Love horns us and hoofs us – or gives us our wings,
And the best could be worst, as the worst could be best.
You must thank your own worth for what I grew to be,
For the demon lurked under the angel in me.'
Ella Wheeler Wilcox (1850–1919)

Around 35 CE, somewhere on a dusty road to Damascus, a dazzling light, blinding yet illuminating, brought a man not only to his knees, but apparently to his senses. His apparent revelation was to influence Christian religious belief for several thousand years. This messenger, no mounted courier, no intermediary spirit, no goddess, no Isis, Iris or Hermes, was just another man, and one with a missionary vocation. A bad guy and persecutor in the early Christian evangelists' eyes, Saul of Tarsus was soon to become the darling angel of the very movement he despised. Could it be that his own words – 'for Satan himself masquerades as an angel of light' (II Corinthians 11:14) – were possibly an unconscious revelation about himself? The evil oppressor transformed into a do-gooding Christian messenger? Or was he a double agent, acting for the devil himself?

At around the time Philo of Alexandria was interpreting Hebrew scripture along Platonic lines, Paul of Tarsus (c. 5–67 CE) was scribbling away at his epistles. Also known as Paul the Apostle, both a Roman citizen and a Hellenistic Jew, he proudly announced himself as the Apostle of the Gentiles. One of the most influential Christian fathers throughout the Mediterranean world, his conversion to Jesus has been attributed to the beginnings of the early rift between Judaism and Christianity.

Before his conversion, Paul violently vicitimized the early Christians, but after his 'trip' on the road to Damascus, he believed Jesus's resurrection proved him to be not only the Son of God, but the Messiah. In what manner this revelation or vision of the resurrected Jesus occurred, or whatever kind of trip he was on, is still under much debate, but it certainly had the desired effect on future writers, theologians and Church leaders.

Paul's approach to angels, from various differing translations, appears ambiguous, sometimes erring on the side of caution. Angels could at any moment be the devil in disguise, and mostly liable to seduce you into some cultish religion (Colossians 2: 18):

> Do not let anyone who delights in false humility and the worship of angels disqualify you. Such a person also goes into great detail about what they have seen; they are puffed up with idle notions by their unspiritual mind.

He also refers to them as man's protectors: 'Be not forgetful to entertain strangers: for thereby some have entertained angels unawares' (Hebrews 13:2). Although believed to be written by Paul, the author of the anonymous Book of Hebrews is still under hot debate.

St Paul, for all his ambivalence about angels, spirits and himself, had a few profound truths to say about love. In one of his most famous quotes, he says that if he could speak the language of angels, or move mountains, what would be the point of such power, if he had no love? Without love, he would be nothing – a profound truth that redeemed him at least in his own eyes (I Corinthians 13 1:6):

> Though I speak with the tongues of men and angels,
> And have not love,
> I am no better than a clanging gong or a brass bell.
> And though I have the gift of prophecy, and know every hidden mystery; and though I have faith enough to move mountains,
> And have not love,
> I am nothing.

THE BOOK OF TOBIT

If guardian spirits had been hovering around for thousands of years in some form or other as Ba, daimon, Fravashi, Amesha Spentas or Apkallu, in terms of Christian angelology, the first biblical story of a guardian angel appears in the Book of Tobit, in the LXX.

The story, supposedly set in the eighth century BCE, concerned an exiled Jewish family. The myth tells of the blind Tobit's son, Tobias, who sets off on a journey to collect a debt on behalf of his father. At the start of the journey, the family are visited by a stranger, who offers to help Tobias on his way. At the end, in a revelation, the stranger identifies himself as the angel Raphael. Tobias, unaware the stranger is a guardian angel, is also accompanied by his dog, who becomes a key character in St Jerome's later translation from Greek to Latin. Tobias then frees Sarah from the curse of the demon Asmodeus, who was particularly obsessed with strangling every man she was about to marry before their wedding night. Eventually, thanks to Tobias and the stranger, Asmodeus is cursed, flees to Egypt and Sarah marries Tobias. A wonderful Judaeo-Christian tale of morality if ever there was one.

However, a rival to the vivid mythology of orthodox Christianity, now labelled Gnosticism, was growing to be more than a thorn in Christianity's side.

GNOSTICISM

Ascetic and God-fearing as they were, radical, heretical offshoots and cult movements developed, known today under the umbrella term of Gnosticism. This included mystical or pagan religions adapted to merge with monotheistic ideas, which had been around long before the rise of Christianity. Throughout the first few centuries CE, gospel writers, evangelists, Christian fathers, scholars, philosophers, poets and biographers were able to circulate their work more freely than before thanks to the development of a new type of book production, called the codex. Codices were waxed wooden tablets, tied together like a ring file. This welcome invention was the precursor of later codices made with papyrus, parchment or paper. Scrolls were still used by the more elite or scholarly writers, while papyrus sheets were the common writing material in Egypt.

The majority of Gnostic texts were written on huge papyrus sheets, cut up to make a stack of leaves for the codex.

Gnōsis means a form of revealed esoteric knowledge. In other words, Gnostics actively sought immediate knowledge of God and the divine, and creation was seen as an unfoldment of emanations from a primal source, resulting in the material universe.

Some Gnostics used the term 'Archon' to refer to the messengers or spiritual envoys of the demi-urge, the fashioner of the universe, who was also an emanation of the initial creator. The archons, like the rapidly developing angelic hierarchy of orthodox

Christianity, roamed the material realms, and like *sa'tan*, created obstacles to the soul who sought ascension to higher realms.

Gnosticism includes what is called the pre-Christian Eastern-Persian schools, which essentially came out of Zoroastrianism, such as Maniasm, and well-known movements such as the Syrian-Egyptian schools, influenced by Platonic ideas.

Many of these early Gnostic writings were translated from Greek into Coptic and were hidden in the fourth century. They were discovered in the 1960s and together are known as the Nag Hammadi Library. Gnosticism, although basically Christian in spirit, drew on other traditions as well, such as Hermetic, Zoroastrian and Platonic thought. Syncretic and radical, Gnosticism rivalled orthodox Christianity.

The gradual split of Judaism from Christianity may have been due to a melange of political warmongering, the destruction of Jerusalem in 70 CE, the long-term influence of St Paul, or the conversion of the Roman Empire to Christianity. Whatever the cause, Gnosticism was seen as heretical by both Jew and Christian alike, and its various cults went underground.

Nag Hammadi

Angels and demons appear in many of the Nag Hammadi texts. For example, the text known as 'On the Origin of the World' (II: 5 and XIII: 2) whips together Christian and Greek myth and philosophy, plus a spoonful of Egyptian thought. In the origin of the angels, the author comments:

> By that throne he created other serpent-like angels, called 'Seraphin' which praise him at all times. Thereafter he created a congregation (*ekklesia*) of angels, thousands and myriads, numberless.

In the well-known Hermetic text, the 'Asclepius' (21–29, VI: 8), a dialogue takes place between initiate Asclepius and Trismegistus, aka Hermes. Trismegistus explains to a fearful Asclepius what happens to the soul after the death of the body. He describes the great daimon, whom God has sent to judge the soul of man, and 'when the soul comes forth from the body, it is necessary that it meet this daimon'. If the soul is judged to be good, then it will 'come and go in the air'. However, if the soul is judged to be evil, it will be 'put in the places of the daimons which are filled with pain', and 'the ones who are called stranglers'. How nice.

One of the longest works in the Nag Hammadi Library is 'Zostrianos' (VIII: 1). Drawing on Platonic thought, it fuses mythology and philosophy, and is written as an autobiographical account of Zostrianos's journey to the heavens to discover 'gnosis' or divine knowledge. With the help of a series of angel guides, he makes a grand tour of the 'aeons' or heavenly realms, and with a splattering of knowledge returns to earth to help others leave the material world and become enlightened. Zostrianos poses question after question to the angels during his 'baptism' into each aeon, until he 'became a holy angel' himself. He does find the answer, and it's worth reading.

Mystery cults, such as Mithraism, added to Judaism, heretics, Christians, Gnostics and pagans, to make the Mediterranean world a hotchpotch of fertile and radical ideology. Some religious groups maintained their Jewish roots and understanding, others their Greek, Egyptian or pagan beliefs, and many others based their religious faith on a hybrid of them all. But then Christianity began to 'apologize'.

JUSTIN MARTYR

One of the earliest apologists was Justin Martyr, a pagan Roman who converted to Christianity around 130, and was martyred in 165. He wrote his 'apologist' letters around 150, describing Jesus as 'King, and Priest, and God, and Lord, and angel, and man'. Justin wrote his apologies to the Roman Emperor, not only in defence of Christianity, considered by pagans, such as

Plutarch, to be a 'pernicious superstition', but also to argue that Christians were neither savage nor evil. Turning the tables, he said the blame lay with the very gods and spirits that the Roman Emperor worshipped and respected.

From the translation of the Torah, all spirits, whether specific gods, goddesses, spirits of water, illness or good luck, were lumped together under the Latin translation of daimons as 'daemons', and any pagan or alien god or spirit became associated by Christian followers with evil. On the other hand, Justin welcomed the 'host of "good angels" who were held in the greatest veneration' ('First Apology', chapter 6). Justin's contemporary, Athenagoras, another apologist, refers to the 'duties of angels whom God appointed to their several posts, to occupy themselves about the elements, and the heavens, and the world' (*A Plea for Christians*, 10). There was also a general concensus of agreement with Athenogoras's take on evil that 'Satan is a created being like the other angels and is opposed to Good in God and it is the demons who incite men to worship images.'(Apology 24.)

In his 'First Apology' (chapter 5), Justin, a well-trained debating philosopher, blamed the 'daemons' for the persecution of the Christians, cleverly equating their persecution with that suffered by Socrates:

[The Greeks] called them [daemons] 'gods', and gave to each the name which of the daemons chose for himself. And when Socrates endeavoured by true reason and examination, to bring these things to light, and deliver men from the demons, then the demons themselves, by means of men who rejoiced in iniquity, compassed his death.

He also accused Jupiter of being controlled or possessed by demons and of 'being overcome by the love of base and shameful pleasures . . . ' while 'wicked devils perpetrated these things'.

If the ordinary man in the street converted to Christianity out of fear, rather than anything else, the Apologists did nothing except pour scorn upon themselves in more intellectual circles. With platonic and esoteric sub-culture rife, the Christian apologists had more to contend with than they expected.

MIDDLE PLATONISTS

> *'The Greeks, a certain scholar has told me, considered that myths are the activities of the Daimons, and the Daimons shape our characters and our lives. I have often had the fancy that there is some one myth for every man, which if we but knew it, would make us understand all he did and thought.'*
>
> W. B. Yeats, *At Stratford-on-Avon*, 1901

To the followers of Plato, the daimon denoted a personal guiding spirit who had a certain amount of say in a man's fate and the fulfilment of his destiny. The daimon also guided the soul of the deceased 'to where it belonged'. The Middle Platonists, active during the first few centuries CE, crossed over into the esoteric systems of the Gnostics, the *Corpus Hermeticum* and the Chaldean Oracles. All of these involved the idea of planetary powers and intra-cosmic 'daimones' mediating between humanity and the cosmic forces. It is easy to see how the mediating daimon of the Platonists, was adopted in the Christian ranks as their very own guardian angel.

In those first few centuries, a growing following of Platonists picked their fellow Platonists' brains over daimons, either as guardian spirit, messenger, good or bad and sometimes both. But we cannot overlook the extraordinary brain of Plutarch.

Plutarch

Greek historian and biographer, Plutarch wielded his codex, papyrus or scroll some time between 46 and 120 CE. Known as the sage of Chaeronea, Plutarch was admired from the Renaissance onwards for his moral treatises and characterful biographical tales. Even in his own era, he was immensely popular because he was able to explain convoluted philosophical theories to the layman. His books brought him a certain international fame, and his home became a private school for young philosophers. A wealthy traveller, he was also visited by the emperor Trajan, who honoured him with the regalia of an ambassador. From then on, he swept around Athens, Rome and Alexandria, wearing a golden ring and a white toga with a purple border.

Plutarch's philosophy professor, Ammonies, had posed an interesting question in Plutarch's days of scholarly learning in Alexandria: 'Are the daimones anything else than souls that make their way in mist apparelled, as Hesiod says?' It seems Plutarch was desperate to find out, and tried to prove they were much more.

Plutarch sought to show that the daimons bridged the gap between man and the divine, helped prevent the universe from falling apart, lived for over nine thousand years and shared the characteristics of man's passions and the immortality of the gods. In 'Morals: Theosophical Essays' on Isis and Osiris, he has a lot to say about the daimon/daemon. On one level he agreed with Homer's epithets for daemons, who 'had a mixed and inconsistent nature and disposition', and Plato's and Xenocrates's negative theory that 'the unlucky days of the month . . . abusive or obscene language' are due to 'malignant and ill-tempered' daemons. 'The good ones, on the contrary', Hesiod styled 'pure daemons' and 'guardians of men'.

In 'The Daimonion of Socrates', he talks of 'daimonic time' as not being eternity, but belonging to souls liberated from corporeal bodies, united with 'nous' and free of mortal attachments; or at least the 'daimons who watch over men' belong to this category.

In 'The Cessation of Oracles', he notes that Hesiod:

> Was the first clearly and distinctly to make four species of
> rational beings – gods, then daemons 'numerous and benef-
> icent', then heroes, lastly men, the demigods being ranged in
> the class of heroes. Others make out a change in the bodies
> equally with the souls, in the same way as water is seen to be
> produced from earth, air from water, fire from air, in conse-
> quence of the essence tending upwards, so from men to
> heroes, from heroes to daemons, souls of the better kind go
> through a transition. Of daemons, some few in long process
> of time, having been thoroughly purified by means of virtue,
> become partakers of divinity.

Yet it is Plutarch's own ambivalence about the daimon, perhaps
more an expression of his own psychology than anything else,
which added a sea of confusion to the daimon's very nature and
meaning. He at times equated the daimon with Tyche (the
ancient Greek goddess of fortune), but also attempted to give
the daimon separate status. In Greek magic, *tyche* and daimon
had often been partnered up as expressions of the nature of fate
when casting a spell. One taken from Betz's *The Greek Magical
Papyrii in Translation* reads: 'Hail Tyche, and you, the daimon
of this place, and you the present hour, and you, the present day
– and every day as well. Hail Universe, that is, heaven and
earth . . . ' There was little chance of getting your spell wrong if
you hailed *tyche* and the daimons in one hit.

As a historian, Plutarch was confounded by the contemporary notion that the '*tyche*' of a man, or a country's fate, was
set in stone. Yet he often lurched happily towards Empedocles'
proposition that the flow of fortune was inconsistent and often
moved from good to bad, then bad to good. In his work *In Mist
Appareled: Religious Themes in Plutarch's Morals and Lives*,
Frederick E. Brenk refers to an example of Plutarch's very

dichotomy in his biography of Marius, where the dying, drunken Marius flays around on his deathbed, commanding troops into an imaginary battle.

In a magnificent piece of philosophical-literary moralizing on the use of one's own tyche, Plutarch comments that, the wretched Marius, though showered with many opportunities and blessings in his life, lamented his tyche to the end, but the noble Plato on his deathbed thanked his daimon and his tyche that he had been a Greek and not a barbarian and that he had lived at the time of Socrates.

The ambiguous use of 'daimon' appears to depend on what Plutarch was writing about and for which audience. In his writing, we see the philosopher who longed to meet his own Platonic daimon, and also one who had little choice but to agree that one's fortune and destiny were entangled in the arms of Tyche. But for the most part he veered unsteadily towards the idea that the daimon was not so much 'tyche', but a divine interloper who steered the soul along, while in fact it was Tyche who went along for the ride. Plutarch had an obsessive, life-long fascination for the daimon, and yet he never really quite managed to pin this deity down.

Epictetus (55–135 CE)

A Greek Stoic philosopher, Epictetus was also in tune with Platonic thought. He believed that all external events are determined by fate, and suggested that we must learn to accept whatever happens, whether good or bad, and always with a calm mind. As individuals, however, we are responsible for our own actions, which we can control through rigorous self-discipline. His most famous dictum was that we can never fail to be happy if we learn to desire that things should be exactly as they are. Epictetus considered that 'Zeus has placed by every man a guardian, every man a daimon, to whom he has committed the care of the man; a guardian who never sleeps, is never deceived.'(Dissertation 1 chapter 14, 12) He also said (in Dissertation 1 chapter 14, 14) that 'God is with in, and your daimon is with in.'

Apuleius (125–180)

Another influential philosopher, a back-packing Berber of the Mediterranean world, Apuleius, studied Platonic philosophy in Athens and was an initiate in several mystery cults, including that of Isis.

He is most famous for his Latin novel entitled *The Golden Ass* or *Metamorphoses*, but it was his work *On the God of Socrates*, a treatise on the existence and nature of daimones, that was later mercilessly attacked by St Augustine. In it, Apuleius tried to explain the substance of the daimon:

> There are certain divine middle powers, situated in this interval of the air, between the highest ether and earth, which is in the lowest place, through whom our desires and our deserts pass to the Gods. These are called by a Greek name daimones, who, being placed between the terrestrial and celestial inhabitants, transmit prayers from the one, and gifts from the other . . . But if the clouds fly loftily, all of which originate from, and again flow downward to, the earth, what should you at length think of the bodies of daemons [daimons], which are much less dense, and therefore so much more attenuated than clouds? . . . The human soul, therefore, even when situated in the present body, is called, according to a certain signification, a daimon.

The second-century Greek rhetorician, Maximus of Tyre, also agreed the existence of intermediary daimons between God and man, dwelling on the edges of heaven and earth. He commented:

The soul in many ways bears a great resemblance to the divinity; it is partly mortal, partly immortal, and, when freed from the fetters of the body, becomes a daimon. Life is the sleep of the soul, from which it awakes at death.

Celsus

Celsus, another second-century Greek philosopher, was known for his work *The True Word*, an early attack on Christianity. He portrayed daimons as the caretakers of men with the power to heal humans and predict the future. They are not the Christian 'enemies of man'. He was one of the first early sources to say that Jesus was the illegitimate son of a Roman soldier, and due to the reported resurrection of Jesus by an hysterical woman, Jesus's followers quickly promoted the myth to impress those who wanted to believe in such magical powers.

Celsus put it clearly, but controversially in *On the True Doctrine: A Discourse Against the Christians*:

That life is under the control of gods one can see from the writings of the Egyptians. They say that a man's body is under the power of thirty-six demons [daimons] who divide it among themselves . . . By invoking these names, they heal the appropriate part of the body. In any case, what is to prevent someone from paying homage to these and other gods, if he so choses – so that at least one can be healthy and not ill, have good luck rather than bad, and be delivered from misfortunes of all sorts. Instead the Christians make ridiculous claims for themselves . . . At the name of Jesus every knee in heaven and earth, and those under the earth, and every tongue confesses Jesus is Lord . . . I am not making the case for invoking demons, however; I am merely trying to show that the Christians do the same things that the Egyptians do in memorizing the names of thirty-six demons, only they choose to invoke but one.

That 'one daimon', Jesus, had already become the maestro of popular awe and fear, and of priestly power.

NEO-PLATONISTS

In the third century, a new wave of Plato followers emerged. The founder was the pioneering Plotinus (204–270). In this new Platonic perception, the daimon originates from Plato's *Symposium* (202d-e), where Plato not only refers to Eros as a daimon but argues that every daimon is the mouthpiece for God.

From Plato's *Republic*, *Phaedo* and *Timaeus*, the Neo-Platonists developed the idea of the personal daimon, guiding the soul ever on through each of its succeeding lives. Plotinus expresses the difference between daimons and gods in his treatise *On Love*:

Now we speak and think of the race of gods as without affections or passions, but we attribute affections and passions to the daimons; we say that they are eternal next after the gods, but already inclining towards us, between gods and our race.

Plotinus viewed daimons as 'bodies of air or fire'; he also believed they spoke, had magical powers and that 'daimons and gods are beautiful' (*Enneads*, Treatise I.6).

He equated daimons with human beings who were actively 'daimonic' in their lives; in other words, with those people who could communicate or converse with the gods, such as shaman, mystic, poet, or writer, not unlike our old friend and philosopher, Empedocles, four hundred years earlier (*Enneads*, Treatise III.4 chapter 2):

Who, then, becomes a daimon? He who was one here too. And who a god? Certainly he who was one here. For what worked in a man leads him [after death]. Since it was his ruler and guide here too.

To Plotinus, the daimon, whether a higher spiritual principle of oneself or an inner psychological dynamic, was mostly a friend, but also a god.

In Porphyry's biography of Plotinus (*Vita Plotini*, chapter 10) is a fascinating account of an Egyptian priest who visited Plotinus in Rome. The priest challenged Plotinus to test his powers by conjuring up his personal daimon. Off they went to the Temple of Isis, the only pure place in Rome according to the Egyptian, and Plotinus set to work. Whether he scryed, prayed or cast a personal spell, Porphyry is not clear, but rather than a mere daimon appearing, Plotinus conjured up a god. The priest marvelled at the apparition and exclaimed, 'Blessed are you, because a god is by you as your daimon and not some low class daimon!' Unfortunately, there was no chance to communicate with the god. Several of the onlookers strangled the temple hens of sanctity in an attempt to abort the magical invocation, and the daiman vanished in a puff of smoke.

Plotinus may not have been a great supporter of magical conjurations for contacting the divine – theurgy (magical ritual) became the backbone of most scholarly fascination in the occult in the later Middle Ages – but he was certainly curious to know if a man's daimon could be a god, and why not? 'It is better not to call any being in the intelligible world a daimon, but, even if there is an idea of a daimon, we should call this a god.'

Iamblichus (234–305) developed the concept that the daimon has its own separate character, as we do. Also that the daimon is assigned to us *before* birth, directing us through our lives from the place of the divine from which we came, and back again. This premise comes from the graphically detailed account of the myth of Er, recounted in Plato's *Republic* and probably the basis for ALL Westernized guardian-angel philosophy.

A certain man called Er had been killed on the battlefield. On being brought back to life, he brought news of what happened after death, but also what happened before birth, having had a sort of 'in-between lives' experience.

According to Er, the soul chooses the life it wishes to lead. With the help of the Fates, the soul is alloted a daimon to guide it through life. This personal daimon is our inner voice, our guardian angel, our sense of vocation, the 'divine sense' within, which drives us on, the blueprint of ourselves that we were born into. So 'in an instant they [the souls] were driven upwards in all manner of ways to their birth, like stars shooting'. Likewise, we are catapulted into life, along with our divine companion.

Archetypal psychotherapist James Hillman, in *The Soul's Code*, and writer and scholar Patrick Harpur, in *A Complete Guide to the Soul*, agree that during our life we will encounter this sense of ourselves in many guises, but most commonly through external relationships. However, our guardian angel is both the daimon and the guardian of our soul. It calls us to live out our character and our destiny. We respond to something, such as a vocation, a lover or soul-mate, and feel drawn to follow that pathway. Unlike the *tabula rasa*, 'you are born a blank slate', dictum of Aristotle, developed by the eleventh-century Islamic philosopher Avicenna, and by Thomas Aquinas and John Locke, where experience and environment build or formulate our character, Plato's daimonic life is to do with becoming who we already are. Our daimon is our destiny, and destiny is our daimon.

Iamblichus developed an array of intermediate spiritual beings between the lower souls and the intelligible real. This included daimones, the souls of heroes and spiritual angels of all sorts. Iamblichus was the first to introduce the idea of an angelic hierarchy. As the divine stretched down to the material world and the basics of nature, the souls became embodied as human beings. This hierarchy was ruled by a complete mathematical form, and Iamblichus's cosmology included the belief that embodied souls are both divine and imperfect. The origin of evil is that the personal soul has lost touch with its deeper divine nature and alienated itself.

Fusing the ideas of Plato, Pythagorus and Hermeticism into one system, Iamblichus developed an extraordinary hierarchy that was to be cribbed by the mysterious, yet at the time believable, master of all hierarchies, Pseudo-Dionysius.

Neo-Platonist Porphyry (234–305) drew on astrological hierarchy, and man's ascent through the Virtues, to prove the validity of the daimon. Known as a violent opponent of Christianity and defender of all things pagan, he famously said, 'The Gods have proclaimed Christ to have been most pious, but the Christians are a confused and vicious sect.'

Proclus (412–485) was one of the last classical Neo-Platonists to have a great influence on medieval Western philosophy. He was a staunch vegetarian dedicated to the goddess Athena, magic and the supernatural. His biographer Marinus reported that when Christians removed the statue of the goddess from the Parthenon, a beautiful woman appeared to Proclus in a dream and announced that the 'Athenian Lady' wished to stay at his home. Proclus believed that 'all daimons come from one mother, that is, they have a common daimon-comprehending source', which he refers to later in his commentary on *Alcibiades* (68.5) as either Rhea or Hecate. In his commentary *On Parmenides* (829), he reveals the following about the daimon and mankind's individual talent or creative urge. Interestingly, we have already encountered Hecate and Athene as dark queens of the daimones.

It is not surprising that their [the talents of man] causes are thought to reside among the daemons, who are said to have given them to men ... For example, the art of Bronze-working may be said to have its patron in the daemon

Hephaestus who possesses the Idea of the Art, while the Great Hephaestus could be said only symbolically to have forged the vault of heaven.

THE ANGELS FIGHT BACK

As philosophers wracked their brains over soul and daimon during the first few centuries CE, Christianity steadily gained momentum, split with Judaism and burned a good few pagan temples in the process. Commentators, apologists and leaders attacked everything pagan under the sun in an attempt to convince the heads of state, particularly the Romans, to convert. But why didn't the early orthodox Christian writers market their spiritual messengers? If Zoroastrianism had placed heavy emphasis on the female Fravashis, the early Christian fathers placed emphasis on the one and only God and his redeemer Son. Honouring a host of numinous spirits would have aligned to polytheistic pagan worship, and worse, worshipping spirits would only encourage their rising status, equal to Jesus or God. A belief in the one and only God with his hosts of angelic messengers was one thing, but no angel could be a rival for God's power. It was the growing angel cults that began to give orthodox ascetic Christianity a run for its money. Evil personification was a different matter, and then there were the veritable Church fathers to consider, too.

Origen

'You yourself are even another little world and have within you the sun and the moon and also the stars.'

Origen (185–254)

One of the early great Christian philosophers, Origen was born in Egypt at a time of passionate Christian persecution and pagan suppression, and became a controversial figure in later orthodox Christian circles. As a child, he wanted to martyr himself after his father's death, and was only stopped from running out into the streets to do so by his mother hiding his clothes. Ascetic to the point of self-castration, Origen's early views on angels, demons and men acquired a cult following among sixth-century Palestinian religious sects. His belief that 'fallen angels may become men or demons, and from the latter may rise to be men or angels' (in a fragment from the first book of *De Principiis*, translated by Jerome in his epistle to Avitus) was stopped in its tracks by anti-Origenist Jerusalem monks in the sixth century.

Conspiring with a Roman deacon, Palagius, the monks convinced the powerful Byzantine emperor Justinian to curse Origen's teachings and anyone who subsequently followed them. The Church was essentially powerless to resist Justinian's imperial decrees. Along with his power-mad wife, ex-prostitute Theodora, Justinian believed God had entrusted the entire Empire, including Rome, to him. It was little surprise that the idea of angels trespassing on his patch, and his own growing identification with the Godhead, got him worried. Perhaps Origen's controversial doctrines would sow provocative seeds in the heads of many a Christian. Could Justinian be a fallen angel himself?

Origen had posited that wherever angels fall, which they could do at any time, depending on their own free will, they walk the earth as men. If they persist in their evil ways, they ultimately become demons, which have, according to Origen, 'cold and obscure bodies . . . in whom the divine love had grown cold'. He states that these demons could have been 'hidden in gross bodies such as ours, and have been called men'.

Three of the fifteen anathemas (Christian-type curses) against Origen damn his teaching on the incarnations of fallen spirits and angels becoming men. All Christian churches in the Byzantine Empire under the power of Justinian (Rome included) forbade Origen's controversial teachings, particularly his belief in the pre-existence of souls and the controversy over fallen angels

becoming men. In the centuries that followed, these doctrines
were, however, actively taught among Cathars, Hermetic philosophers, alchemists, Rosicrucians and Christian cabalists.

Socrates had been quite positive about the benefits of sipping
small quantities of wine, which 'commits no rape upon our
reason, but pleasantly invites us to agreeable mirth', and
between several glasses of something resembling a sweet
Sauternes, Origen argued that Ezekiel's description of the
Prince of Tyre (28: 12–19) was 'a certain angel who received the
office of governing the nation of the Tyrians'. Not just any old
prince of darkness, this was some kind of superior divine power
fallen from a higher position, now reduced to a lower one. But
Origen was convinced that good angels could also become
human. In his *Commentary on the Gospel of John*, he posited
that John the Baptist was an angel who chose to become a man
so he could worship Jesus:

> From the beginning, those who have occupied the most
> eminent positions among men and been markedly superior
> to others have been angels in human form. This explains
> the passage in Scripture which says that John was one of
> God's messengers, or angels, who came in the body to bear
> witness to the light.

Yet the Second Council of Constantinople in 553 pronounced
the following anathema against Origen's teaching:

> If anyone shall say that a psychic condition has come from
> an angelic or archangelic state, and moreover that a
> demoniac and a human condition has come from a psychic
> condition, and that from a human state they may become
> again angels and demons, and that each order of heavenly
> virtues is either all from those below or from those above,
> or from those above and below: let him be anathema.

After so many curses against Origen, or anyone else foolishly following in his angelic footsteps, it's hardly surprising that few even dreamt of entertaining angels unawares, let alone imagining they might be one.

Origen was also responsible for a corrected translation of the earlier Septuagint version of the Hebrew Bible. The confusion of *angelos* as *mal'ak*, referring to both God's messenger and God himself in his guise as messenger, gave him much to mull over. In his treatise *Against Celcus* (5: 4) he says:

> In the Bible angels are sometime called 'God' because of their divine character. But this does not mean we are supposed to worship and honour them instead of God, to whom alone, all prayers and supplications should be directed.

Very few of Origen's six thousand or so recorded works remain, most of which are in fragments. Yet long into their dark nights of austerity, Church fathers continued to fret about angels infiltrating the ranks of mankind, such as the fifth-century Gallic writer, Vincent of Lerins, who, legend has it, described Origen as an extraordinary teacher who became a misleading light.

St John of Chrysostom

A misleading teacher who became an extraordinary light was St John of Chrysostom, Archbishop of Constantinople, born around the same time as St Augustine, who also had explicit views on angels. The 'golden-mouthed' ascetic, John, was born in Antioch in 349, and famously led a mob in 401 to destroy the Temple of Artemis at Ephesus. Artemis had once been dubbed the '*Angelos* of Syracuse', so it was no surprise that St John wanted to destroy her worship and put an end to her association, as a pagan goddess, with angel messengers. A known persecutor of pagan symbols and temples, St John was one of the Mafioso-type church leaders who converted many (or victimized many) to take up the ascetic and self-denying chains of the new Christianity.

By 313, the Church's power swept throughout the Roman empire. St John, while trying to convert the Anomoeans, followers of Arius (a devoted exponent of exposing the true relationship between God and Christ, and a bit of a Gnostic to boot), drafted his famous set of writings, *Homilies*, taken from his public speeches. These claimed mostly that God was incomprehensible, and angels were a power to be reckoned with. His whole argument rested on the fact that Arius's gnostic followers believed that God could be 'experienced within'.

In *On the Incomprehensible Nature of God*, St John argued that not only is the essence of God hidden and unknowable to man, but even to the angels. Quoting Isaiah's lines where the seraphim covered their faces with their wings, he argues this was because they could not bear the 'lightning which shines from the throne'. The seraphim may be physically nearer God, but God is still beyond their intellectual grasp. However, the seraphim's angelic incomprehension was a step nearer to an understanding or experience of God than man's, especially as 'a man cannot look upon the essence of an angel without fear and trembling'. Hierarchy was beginning to be a useful tool in the defence of Christianity. St John quoted various lines from the Book of Daniel to prove the power of angels over men. 'The Angel is called by that name because he announces to men the things of God. The Archangel is called by that name because he rules the Angels.'

Disclaiming any alliance of the angels with earlier pagan winged spirits or deities, he puts forward one of his best and memorable sales pitches:

> Gabriel is shown as flying not because angels have wings, but so that you may know that he comes down to human beings from places that are lofty . . . the wings then reveal the lofty nature of the powers above.

He makes it clear that God is incomprehensible not only to the cherubim and seraphim, but also to the principalities, the powers and any other created power.

And if the angel, like a human being, couldn't quite get the hang of God, nor comprehend Him, that meant angels had something in common with mankind, and man could identify with the angels. Around this time, the earliest known depiction of Christian angels with wings appeared on the Prince's Sarcophagus in Sariguzel, near Istanbul, attributed to around 379–395. Wings were back in vogue. And whether wings were merely a symbol of St John's 'loftiness' or a lingering pagan symbol of the bird goddess or shaman, they were also a symbol of the individual's own 'comprehensible experience' of winging its way to encounter the divine. But then, no good heretic was about to reveal that particular secret.

It seemed with wings, halos and a hefty dose of St John's incomprehensible manifesto, the angel had been wrapped up in pretty packaging for many happy Christmas days to come.

St Augustine (354–430)

'Every visible thing in the world is put under the charge of an angel.'

St Augustine of Hippo

St Augustine had both Manichaean and Platonic roots when he converted to Christianity. He later admitted that it was easier to describe the function of angels and demons than to explain what they are. In discussing dreams of the dead, he attempts to explain that the living or dead person of the dream doesn't actually materialize, but is brought into view

by angelical operations, then, I should think it is effected, whether permitted from above, or commanded, that they seem in dreams to say something . . . just as angels have direct contact with man's psyche and present their messages before the inner eye, so also do demons . . . They persuade [men], however, in marvellous and unseen ways, entering by means of that subtlety of their own bodies into the bodies of men who are unaware, and through certain imaginary visions mingling themselves with men's thoughts whether they are awake or asleep.

In his best known work, *City of God*, demons or the fallen angels were deceitful, wicked sinners and were lower than the lowest of humans. He clearly metamorphosizes the daimon of Apuleius's theory into an evil demon.

We can by no means accept the theory which Apuleius does his best to prove . . . namely that demons are situated midway between gods and men and serve as interpreters and intermediaries . . . on the contrary we should believe that they are spirits fanatically bent on doing harm, completely at odds with justice, swollen with pride, green with envy, and well practised in deceit, who live, it is true, in our air, but do so because they were cast out from the lofty regions of the higher heavens.

Augustine's work was another nail in the coffin for the pagan world, especially when he also commented:

Hence a devout Christian must avoid astrologers and all impious southsayers, especially when they tell you the truth, for fear of leading his soul into error by consorting with demons.

He wasn't exactly enamoured with unorthodox Christian sects either, such as that founded in the second century by Montanus, a priest of Cybele, who identified Attis with Christ. Montanus claimed that women were agents of the goddess herself and could preach and prophesy just as well as men. This contradicted the orthodox Pauline belief that women must never speak publicly on holy subjects, let alone pagan ones, nor uncover their hair in church, 'in case of the angels' (I Corinthians, chapter 2) – another ambiguous St Paul phrase if ever there was one. In the fourth century, angelic worship was declared a heresy and many angel followers were quietly bumped off, locked in their monastries or burnt. Meanwhile, St Augustine chose to remind us that Cybele was 'the mother, not of the gods, but of the demons'.

But one clever soothsayer, a pagan masquerading as a devout Christian, was to change the whole course of angel and demon history. Now known as pseudo Dionysus the Aeropagate, his perfect choirs and battalions of angels were to become an awesome influence both on the collective and individual psyche.

8

ANGELS GROW WINGS

'God committed the care of men and all things under heaven to angels.'

Justin Martyr (103–165)

Around 250, the head-count for Christian converts in Rome numbered around one hundred thousand, albeit mostly riffraff or slaves. However, the Romans were still a pagan and superstitious lot. They stuck pins in wax models to seduce their amours, cut out the genitalia of hares to prevent infertility and thought nothing of lining their marble shelves with a fascinating selection of magical potions and fatal poisons. In 313, Rome officially adopted Christianity along with its more ascetic Pauline values. An empowering mix of Hellenistic and Jewish tradition, plus two magic ingredients – Roman order, and the useful archetype of redemption – ensured poverty-loving Christianity was on to a winner.

Gradually, ancient pagan religions not so much went underground as became the empire's greatest heresy, and it was the darker deceits of the emerging Christian powers that rose to majesty for the next thousand years or so. Much-loved pagan gods became quickly assimilated as saints or consorts of the devil. Angels fluttered by the popular imagination, and cults developed.

Simon Magus

Gnosticism still had its influence, but most writings were suppressed or burnt by the second-century Bishop Irenaeus. One of the earlier Gnostics, and often called the father of all heretics, Simon Magus, a contemporary of Jesus himself, lived around 35 CE. He was one of the first to propose on paper, according to Hippolytus, that divine truth could be found within oneself and that within each individual 'dwells an infinite power, the root of the universe'. Renowned for his magic tricks, illusions and levitation, accomplished with the help of angels in front of Emperor Nero, Simon Magus was one of the many dissident mystics and writers responsible for the cultish worship of angels.

Angel cults were pervasive in Phrygia and Pisidia up to the time of Theodoret's rule at the end of the fifth century. An influential bishop and theologian, Theodoret was also prickly, and quick to attack Simon Magus's beliefs. Among these were the fact that Simon was the Messiah returned to earth to save mankind, and the world was actually created by angels, not God. Simon Magus equated himself with Jupiter and his prostitute lover, Helena, whom he believed was the mother of all angels, with Minerva.

While performing his levitation stunt, with accompanying invisible angels, Simon dropped like a stone to the ground, and died a few days later in a rage. According to the apocryphal texts, Simon's death so upset Nero that he ordered the arrest and martyrdom of the apostles Peter and Paul, who had tried to prove that Simon Magus was in league with the devil. Maybe Simon Magus's angels had just had enough of his antics. The whole image is magnificently depicted in a fourteenth-century painting by Jacobello del Fiore, 'The Fall of Simon Magus'. A wonderful piece of Christian propaganda (the angels supporting Simon in his flying act are shown as demons), it served as a moral lesson to anyone who considered heresy a fascinating diversion.

Irenaeus (c.115–202), yet another fervent orthodox bishop, decreed not only that all gnostic writings were heretical, but also that the church must be catholic (universal) and angel worship banned, commenting, 'a Christian does nothing by their invocation'.

Eusebius (263–339), bishop of Ceasarea, condemned the worship rendered to angels as heretical. He decreed that pagan polytheistic worship was echoed in the popular worship of angels and was thus a threat to the worship of Christ and God.

However, later Christian fathers were in disagreement. St Ambrose (340–397) explicitly supported the worship and invocation of angels, while St Augustine of Hippo (354–430) was resolutely against their veneration.

According to Christian historian Sozomen (400–450), the Emperor Constantine erected a church not far from Constantinople dedicated to Michael the Archangel, who apparently had appeared on the very spot in all his flaming angelic glory. Theodoret had also noted an inscription in probably the same city, dedicated to Michael: 'Archangel Michael, have mercy on thy city and deliver it from evil'. Towns and villages often came under the patronage of angels according to Didymus the Blind, and pilgrims came from far and wide for their worship.

PSEUDO ANGELS

From the end of the fourth century, churches were frequently dedicated to angels, and with Christianity granted freedom from persecution after the edict of Constantine in 313, Byzantine artists indulged their religious imagination. To keep in line with the patriarchal biblical stories, not forgetting 'the sons of God' myth, early angel iconography depicted wingless males. Marketing angels as good Christian men meant they were distinguishable from their pagan antecedents, such as the winged Apkallu, the Greek daimones, Harpies and Egyptian goddesses.

But as Christianity grew, so did the imagination of artists, who reverted to the ancient archetype of winged spirits. Glamourized angels maintained their human form, but were now draped in flowing robes, halos and all-encompassing wings.

Then around the end of the fifth century, a mysterious messenger, wearing an intellectual hat and flapping his own religious wings, alighted on earth. With mystical knowledge, mostly gleaned from Neoplatonic thought and almost certainly a complete rip-off of both Hermetic and Iamblichus's cosmic hierarchies, Pseudo-Dionysius, as he is now known, threw a very large angelic cat among the religious pigeons.

Whomever he really was, Pseudo-D wrote under the pen-name of St Dionysius the Areopagite, taking his name from a real Athenian member of the judicial council, named in Acts 17: 34. This character pops up in a scene where Paul, preaching his heart out in Athens about the resurrection of Jesus, gets booed and jeered by the Greek philosophers, although a few, including the Areopagite, were apparently converted:

> But some men joined him and believed, among whom also were Dionysius the Areopagite and a woman named Damaris and others with them.

The work, assumed to have been written by Dionysius himself, over two centuries before the rise of Neoplatonic mysticism, gave our mysterious messenger impeccable Christian credentials. So successful was his work, that Pseudo-D acquired star status as an apostle capable of extraordinary divine revelation, and his influence in the Middle Ages and the Renaissance was surpassed only by Thomas Aquinas himself.

In 1457, almost two centuries after the death of Aquinas, Lorenzo Valla, an Italian humanist, exposed Pseudo-D's writings as fake. According to Yale theologian Jaroslav Pelikan (1923–2006), Thomas Aquinas is said to have quoted Pseudo-Dionysius over a thousand times. Ironically, the original Neo-Platonic stairway to heaven had become a core tenet of the Catholic faith, and the angels that St Paul seemingly so mistrusted had become the trusty mediators between God and man. Paul's belief that the only mediator between God and man was Jesus, was being usurped by the very daimons themselves.

Pseudo-Dionysius's work *The Celestial Hierarchy* describes the hierarchy of spiritual beings from the highest of the high down to the material low. There are intermediaries for every level of reality, which he equates to the steps of a ladder. On the question of illumination – in other words, spiritual oneness with God, or 'divine comprehension' as St John might describe it – the higher hierarchies received a more direct illumination, and were thus able to transmit the light to the lower hierarchies. The closer a hierarchy is to the source of divine light, the greater the degree of purity and spirituality.

Whether he was a sneaky Neo-Platonist or a Gnostic disguised as a full-blown Christian, Pseudo-D agreed with the Church fathers, including St John, that no human being can directly comprehend God. He maintained that even Moses did not have a direct vision of God but rather a vision adapted to his level of perception. He went on to show how Christ's incarnation was in accord with the hierarchical order of angels, and why the word 'angel' is used generically to cover all subdivisions between God and man.

The hierarchies that appear in the scriptures are divided into three groups of three each:

- First hierarchy – seraphim, cherubim and thrones
- Second hierarchy – dominions, virtues and powers
- Third hierarchy – principalities, archangels and angels

The meanings are as follows:

- Seraphim – fire, 'those who burn'
- Cherubim – messengers of knowledge, wisdom
- Thrones – the seat of God
- Dominions – justice
- Virtues – courage, virility
- Powers – order, harmony
- Principalities – authority
- Archangels – unity
- Angels – revelation, messengers

Pseudo-D argued that priests could also be called angels, because the illumination of the higher orders radiates all the way through to the lowest orders with gradually decreasing brightness. To get round the sticky problem of how the seraphim had purified the prophet Isaiah, he argued that the illuminating powers of the order of the seraphim had descended through the lesser orders. Light can pass through substances depending on its degree of translucency. This analogy applied to human consciousness and an individual's ability to glimpse divine light. Concerning numbers, he argued that there are an infinite number of angels acting in the innumerable planes of the universe.

The Christian doctrine of guardian angels (not to be confused with the Neo-Platonic one) had already been posited by a rather obscure second-century Christian writer, Hermas. Along with most of the Apocrypha, Hermas's book *The Shepherd* was included with the New Testament as part of the whole Christian package, and his work continued to be highly respected by the Church fathers. Hermas believed that each individual has two guardian angels, one of righteousness and one of wickedness. Gregory of Nyssa agreed with him when he wrote:

Our human weakness is protected by the assistance of the
Angels and . . . in all our perils, provided faith remain with
us, we are defended by the aid of spiritual powers.

Meanwhile, Origen had suggested that nations had guardian
angels, and each individual was assigned a personal guardian
angel at baptism. However, if individuals sinned, they would
come under the power of an evil spirit. Whatever the case, this
angel was not to be worshipped or invoked. The outstanding
Roman writer, Tertullian (160–220), also agreed that an individual would be purified by the angel spirit's presence, described
as 'angelus baptismi arbiter'.

The actual nature and substance of angels was, and still is,
controversial. Some, such as Tertullian, believed angels and
demons were winged, invisible and ubiquitous. St Jerome
(347–420) believed that they manifested as physical entities, St
Ambrose (340–397) that they were ephemeral and incorporeal, St Augustine (354–430) that all descend and ascend
from the heavenly city of God, and are incorporeal in
substance. He declined to comment on their hierarchy,
avoided the subject of guardian angels for individuals but
agreed on their status for nations. He was resolute, however,
that they should not be worshipped.

Finally, at the second Council of Nicaea in 787, the depiction
and veneration of angels was sanctioned by the Church. By the
end of the ninth century, there was a general agreement on
the nature of Christian angels, as previously clarified by one of
the last Greek fathers in the seventh century, John of Damascus:

An angel, then, is an intellectual substance, always mobile,
endowed with free will, incorporeal, serving God, having
received, according to grace, immortality in its nature, the
form and character of whose substance God alone, who
created it, knows.

Archangels

Once an angelic hierarchy was firmly established in the Christian Church's psyche, it was the archangels and their specific functions who became the most popularized of all the angels both in art and in literature.

The seven angels who stood before God in Revelation are considered to be the archangels. However, they are inter-changeable, depending on different religions. Interestingly, of all angels mentioned in the Old Testament, only Michael is referred to as the 'archangel'. According to Pseudo-Dionysius, the seven archangels are Michael, Jophiel, Chamuel, Gabriel, Raphael, Uriel and Zadkiel. The most popular, however, were Gabriel, Michael, Raphael and Uriel, and the remaining three of the seven were often picked from among others not mentioned by Pseudo-D, such as Raguel, Metatron, Sariel, Ramiel, Raziel and Anael.

By the fifteenth century, Italian writer Dante had poetically formulated his own hierarchy, based very much on Pseudo-D's ('Paradiso', Canto XXVIII):

The three Divine are in this hierarchy,
First the Dominions,
and the Virtues next;
And the third order is that of the Powers.
The in the dances twain penultimate
The Principalities and Archangels wheel;
The last is wholly of angelic sports.
These orders upward all of them are gazing,
And downward so prevail, that unto God
They all attracted are and all attract.

Michael

Michael, known as God's champion, is usually depicted with sword in hand and sometimes armoured. He defeated the serpent, or Mother Goddess, by hurling him, or her, out of the heavens to be forever confined to hell. Michael is God's henchman, the only archangel mentioned as such in the early Hebrew Bible, and likely to be a reinterpretation of the pagan archetypal warring gods, such as Ashur, Indra, Ares and Mars. Michael appeared in the Book of Daniel in the Hebrew Bible and was leader of the angelic army in Revelations. In Hebrew, Michael means 'who is like God', usually interpreted as a rhetorical question: 'Who is like God?' This implies that *no one* is like God, and so Michael is interpreted as a symbol of humility before God.

Michael, interestingly, has had more sightings than the other archangels. He's said to have appeared to Emperor Constantine at Sosthenion, a random place fifty miles south of Constantinople. The dying or ill would assemble there and sleep in the church sanctuary, known as the *Michaelion*, in the hope of his manifestation and a subsequent cure. Feasts were celebrated throughout the Greek, Syrian, Armenian and Coptic churches in Michael's name. His apparition also appeared, according to legend, in 530, on top of Monte Gargano, and holding a feast in honour of this became a widespread practice in the Latin church. From the time of Pius V such an occasion was called the 'Apparitio St Michaelis', referring to the actual apparition. In fact, it was the Lombards victory over the Greeks, with Michael's aid, that was being celebrated.

According to another legend, Michael appeared on top of Hadrian's mausoleum during a procession led by Pope Gregory to invoke divine help against the plague. Weirdly, in the presence of Michael, the plague ended. In honour of the archangel, the church was turned into a fortress known as the Castel di Saint Angelo. Our ubiquitous Michael also descended to earth in 708 on a visit to St Aubert, bishop of Avranches, to inspire the construction of the famous sanctuary at Mont St-Michel in Normandy, France.

Gabriel

Although mentioned just twice in the New Testament, Gabriel is probably one of the most popularized angels in the Christian tradition. Gabriel is considered to be the angel of mercy, Michael the angel of judgement. This is contrary to the Jewish canon, which considers Gabriel to work with judgement, Michael with mercy.

Gabriel is well-known for being a bit of a fortune-teller. He announces the birth of John the Baptist to Zachary, and the birth of Jesus to the Virgin Mary. Usually depicted as androgynous, winged and often carrying a lily, which he presents to Mary, late nineteenth-century artists, such as James Tissot, depicted Gabriel with a female face, radiating divine light and attached to a pair of beautiful wings.

A set of magical Jewish bowls inscribed with Hebrew and Syriac incantations, which include the names of Michael, Raphael and Gabriel, have been found on the site of ancient Babylon, now known as Hillah. These bowls, currently in the British Museum, date from the Jewish exile, suggesting that although angels weren't a high priority in the Hebrew Bible, nor in subsequent Judaic religion, they were at one time considered to have mystical powers known only to *Elohim* himself. Our divine messengers grew their wings in response to the growing cultural need for some kind of sense of unity with the divine, now so apparently cut off by one God and his only intermediary, Jesus. Wings meant they weren't just lofty, they could come down to earth, too.

Raphael

Raphael is the angel of healing and travelling. He eased Abraham's pain after his circumcision, and, disguised as a man, he escorted Tobias on his debt-collecting voyage (but where did he hide those huge wings?) He then helped Sarah free herself from the wicked demon, Asmodeus, and led her up the aisle to marry Tobias. Raphael's worship was widespread in the eastern Mediterranean. Although mentioned only in the Book of Tobias, he taught Solomon how to capture demons and put them to use as slave labour while the temple was being rebuilt, and he taught Tobias how to exorcise demons. In fact, Raphael was a thoroughly good 'chap' to have around.

Uriel

There is much debate over the other archangels. In 745, a Roman Council under Pope Zachary ordered seven angels to be removed from the recognized ranks, including Raguel, whose name, ironically, means 'friend of God'. According to the pope, Raguel was a demon who 'passed himself off as a saint'. Uriel's fate was no happier. His name means 'God is my light', and according to apocryphal writing, he was the fifth angel, who brought alchemy, astral knowledge, divine magic and the Cabala. In the Book of Enoch he was called the angel who 'watches over thunder and terror'. In the Bible, he originally warned Noah of the impending flood, and escorted young John the Baptist into the wilderness. His worship was widespread in Ambrose's time, but the Council of Auchen in 789 excluded him from any Christian worship, and like many of the other named angels, his cult following went underground.

BYZANTIUM

By the beginning of the seventh century, the Roman Empire was split into the East and West regions of the Mediterranean. The West was ruled from Rome, the East from Constantinople, and the eastern Byzantine Empire, ruled by Heracles between 610–641, was growing in power. The Byzantine Christians saw themselves not only as the natural inheritors of the faith of the apostles, but also of the Christian martyrs who had been executed by the Roman state. They believed themselves to be the people of God, the true Israel, those who had followed

God's promises and saw those promises fulfilled in the Messiah. But Christianity had other, more worrying rivals for religious power to contend with. Would Michael and his army of angels save Byzantium, just as he had driven the serpent to hell? Another tricky problem was that angels now had about as much free will as man. Someone was about to put a stop to that.

ISLAM

'The house which contains pictures will not be entered by angels.'

Qur'an

On 6 April 610, a divine messenger descended to earth, in a cave on Mount Hira, not far from Mecca, to make a world-changing announcement. The archangel Gabriel (on call as usual), known in Islam as Jabra'il, announced not a literal birth but a symbolic one, the revelation of the Qur'an. Whether in a vision or apparition, Jabra'il appeared to the holy prophet Muhammad, instructing him to recite the book, verse by verse, in the name of Allah. The book was the mouthpiece of God (Sura 2: 97):

Say, 'Anyone who opposes Gabriel should know that he has brought down this (the Qur'an) into your heart, in accordance with God's will, confirming previous scriptures, and providing guidance and good news for the believers.'

Across the Persian Empire, Byzantine Christianity and the old world of Zoroastrian cosmology, Islamic rule took over from 642. Islam claimed the names and stories about angels and adapted them to Arabic traditions and gave them new interpretations. Jesus, or Isa in the Qur'an, became a semi-angelic character in the company of angels, nearest to God. Belief in angels is an article of faith for Islam. Known as 'malaikah', a word similar to the 'mal'ak' of Hebrew tradition, they are messengers of God, have no free will, and can do only what God tells them to do. Besides Jabra'il, the angel of revelation, the other protagonists are Mika'il (Michael) and Israfil (Raphael).

Mika'il represents mercy, and nourishment for body and soul. Israfil is the angel of judgement and will blow his trumpet twice at the end of time; the first blow will destroy everything, the second will resurrect the dead to meet the Lord. The only other 'useful' angel is Izra'il, the angel of death, referred to in the Qur'an as 'mal'ak al-maut'. The Qur'an also mentions angels who punish the sinful in hell. Numbers of angels are anything from nineteen angels of fire and brimstone to thousands everywhere. Islam rejects the idea of fallen angels, and Iblis, or Shaitan, is a 'jinn' – an invisible spirit who can be good or bad – not a fallen angel.

Muslims also believe in guardian angels. Every Muslim has a pair of angels watching over him or her through his or her life. One angel watches by day, the other at night. The angels have an irritating habit of writing down every good and bad deed a person commits, ready for Judgement Day; these angels are referred to as Kiraman Katibin, or 'honourable scribes'. Other angels include the eight who will carry the Throne of Allah; those who will bear the Ark; those who come to earth and attend religious gatherings; those who blow souls into human foetuses; those who govern the wind, thunder, lightning, seas, mountains and other aspects of nature; and those whose sole purpose is to worship Allah. Angels, without free will, are characterless. Similar to Jewish angels, they are useful, perform a role, work hard at their jobs, and do not have the choice to lead a merry dance.

Yet the jinn, a like the fallen angels of Christianity, did have free will, and lived alongside mankind in a parallel invisible world, according to the Qur'an. The origins of the jinn are as cryptic as the jinn themselves.

The etymology of 'jinn' is rooted in the Arabic word meaning 'to hide' or 'be hidden'. The nomadic Bedouins were often associated with the jinn. These people, considered antisocial outcasts, lived in the desert and had little contact with civilization. There was nothing supernatural about the Bedouins, but they were super self-contained.

In pre-Islamic Persian mythology, the jinn were inferior spirits with human traits. Often left-handed, they were considered to be not so much evil, more of a bother, similar to the sprites and leprechauns of Western mythology. Pre-Islamic mythology was filled with storm gods, personified stars and thousands of lesser spirits, and the jinn were thought to live on the mystical Emerald mountain of Kaf. In Islam, the jinn were made from smokeless fire by Allah, thousands of years before he made Adam, but were inferior to the angels. Their gift of free will was abused by Iblis, and, subsequently, the jinn became more evil than indifferent, suffering the same fate as the impartial Greek daimon.

And then there were the Essenes.

ESSENES

'Thou hast purified my body to join the army of angels on earth and my spirit to reach the congregation of the heavenly angels.'

Thanksgiving Psalm, Dead Sea Scrolls, VI

On a hot, windy day in the Judean Desert in 1946, a Bedouin shepherd discovered a stone cave not far from the settlement now known as Qumran, on a barren plateau not far from the Dead Sea. In the cave he found ancient scrolls, which eventually became one of the most important finds in religious history, alongside the Nag Hammadi Library.

Known as the Dead Sea Scrolls, scholars believe that the collection of texts belonged to an ancient Hebrew sect known as the Essenes. Dating back to between 150 BCE and 70 CE, the

Essenes's mystical beliefs burst into life after two thousand years of silence, disturbing rather more Judaic–Christian dust than had been bargained for.

There has been much controversy over the original authorship of the scrolls. Many scholars, such as Professor Rachel Elior, Israeli professor of Jewish philosophy, argue that the scrolls were written by Jewish temple priests in Jerusalem, who, after the destruction of the temple in 70 CE, fled to Qumran and hid the scrolls in the caves. Professor Elior believes that the Essenes, as a people or sect, were invented by Roman historian Josephus, and commented that it's 'a history of errors which is simply nonsense'. Professor Elior concluded that the true authors of the scrolls were the Sadducees, a sect descended from the high priest Zadok, who anointed Solomon.

Early sources in favour of the Essenes theory include Pliny, the Elder, who died in 79 CE. He commented that the sect had existed for thousands of generations, and Philo believed they were spread across the whole of Israel. Josephus gave far more details about their habits, celebrations, prayers and ascetic life-style, which included the huge importance of their communion with 'angels'. The Essenes developed a complex angelology, while the Sadducees denied the existence of angels. From our 'daimonic' powers of deduction, the likelihood of these texts being written by the Sadducees seems unlikely.

The Essenes believed in the immortality of the soul and that the 'physical body was the temple of the soul'. They already practised baptism, and shared wine long before Jesus or John took to the bottle. In the original Hebrew texts of these writings, the word 'mal'ak' is used to designate 'spirits' or 'angels'. To the Essenes, it meant an 'emanation of God', the energy of the divine. The Essenes had a complex understanding of astrology, revered the Book of Enoch and developed a programme of communing with the 'angels', as well as the invisible and visible forces of the universe, later developed in the Cabala.

Their angelology centred around the mystical number seven and the ancient symbol of the Tree of Life. Seven of the angelic 'forces' were of a heavenly nature. These included the Heavenly Father, and the angels of Eternal Life, Peace, Love, Wisdom, Power and Creative Work. Seven other angelic forces were of an earthly nature – the Earthly Mother, and the angels of Earth, Life, Joy, Sun, Water and Air. These were in symbolic resonance with the seven branches (heavenly forces) and the seven roots (earthly forces) of the Tree of Life.

Man, symbolically in the centre of the Tree, was seen to be surrounded by cosmic forces, in contact with heaven and earth. Specific communions with each 'angel' or 'energy' were dependent on the day of the week and the time of day – 'With the coming of day I embrace my Mother, with the coming of night, I embrace my Father' (Manual of Discipline, Dead Sea Scrolls).

Qumran Cave 5, as it is known, contained fragments of hymns or songs dating back to 75–50 BCE. The thirteen compositions invoke angelic praise and describe the thirteen Sabbath communions, the angelic priesthood and the heavenly temple. The recital of these songs was a major vehicle for the experience of communion with 'angels'. Jewish rather than Christian in origin, the angels are called, literally 'spirits of knowledge'.

The Essene believer in contact with the angels comprehends God. The individual discovers the divine within himself, already 'above' as he is 'below'. The Essenes, whoever they really were, drew on a hybrid of varying faiths. They must certainly have been a threat to both Christian and Judaic monotheistic teachings. Perhaps they were one of the reasons behind Paul's insistence that angel worship should be outlawed. It's hardly surprising that the best-kept secret remained that way for over two thousand years.

TALMUD

The Talmud is the core text of mainstream Judaism. Compiled in two parts around the third and sixth centuries, it developed the oral traditions of earlier Hebrew beliefs and attempted to contain the tenets and doctrine of orthodox Jewish belief.

Judaism never really developed its own hierarchy of angels. With fanciful apocrypha, Pseudepigrapha, mysticism and Christianity all around, angels became merely Rabbinic literary embellishments. For example, in the story of Esther, angels raise up her head and invest her with grace, and another hands her the King's sceptre. Hosts of unnamed angels appear in the Talmud as justified representatives of God's council. It was generally agreed that they were created by God either on the second or fifth day, a fanciful addition perhaps to preserve the monotheistic creator as the only one worthy of worship.

The Babylonian winged spirits, influential during the exile, had been the first 'mal'aks' of the Old Testament. In the last-written books of the Old Testament, such as Daniel, Chronicles and Ezekiel, angels became more prominent but remained unnamed and without distinctive identities. It is only in the Book of Daniel that Michael and Gabriel are specifically named, and described as 'watchers'. Raphael was accepted in the Catholic Bible, but considered apocryphal by Protestants and Jews.

During the Rabbinic period – roughly 100 BC to 200 CE – angels were named and described and tales were elaborated about them. Such stories often paralleled pagan myths or offered between-the-lines fillers for the adapted Bible texts. Michael overthrew mountains, Gabriel bore Abraham to Babylon, the voice of Hadraniel penetrated through the firmaments, and Ataphiel kept heaven from falling down by balancing it on three fingers. Atlas was, indeed, a patient soul.

PART 3:

CULTURE, FEAR AND SALVATION

9

ALL AN ANGEL IS

'The sin, both of men and angels, was rendered possible by the fact that God gave them free will.'

C. S. Lewis (1898–1963)

THE DARK AGES

If the Jewish and Islamic religions resisted the temptation to give free will to their angels, Christianity accepted that like man, angels are born essentially good, but some fell into evil ways. The added benefit was that angels became useful intermediaries between God and man. The archangel Michael had proved he could take on all the characteristics of the pagan gods of war. An alpha-male representation was essential to the neurotic world of spiritual self-denialists.

Set against the backdrop of war-torn, erratic and bloody centuries, the spread of Christianity throughout Western Europe between the sixth century and first millenium was as catching as the plague of Justinian's time (540). The dark ages were inevitably bleak for most people, but an attempt was made to shine a light at one end of a particular tunnel. In 835, the Roman Catholic Church generously made the first day of November a holiday to honour all the saints; it was known as All Hallows. The all-purpose saints were made up of a hotchpotch of pagan gods and spirits in an attempt to assimilate all the old favourites of Europe into the 'universal' or new Catholic religion.

In northern Europe, as in the Mediterranean, war, conquering heroes, rape and pillage continued to express patriarchal virility and power. Vikings settled in Ireland in 840, and by the end of the ninth century, Alfred the Great reigned in Saxon England. The Roman and Orthodox churches split decisively in the eleventh century. William the Conqueror appeared on the English scene, and Westminster Abbey opened in 1066. With the crusading Richard Coeur de Lion in the twelfth century and his victory over the Saracens, the dark ages began to head towards the light again. Pagan deities were still the undermining power of the northern European popular imagination, and yet the pressure to convert was immense; being forgiven for your sins to save your soul from being punished in hell was becoming alarmingly fashionable.

For the next several centuries, scholars of all religious faiths identified, wrote about, denounced or classified angels. Angels were embraced, heretics persecuted, and pagan beliefs survived underground. Christian clergy and theologians did all in their power to persuade the people that their only hope for salvation was to convert to Christianity. Whether because of human fear, or a need to find a reason for sin and salvation, the quest was on to find another scapegoat. Projecting patriarchal darkness onto a people, a sect, a lifestyle or even the 'fairest of them all', had never been so easy.

Angel names were invented by putting Hebrew letters or old pagan words before 'el', meaning 'of God', or adding '-irion' to the end. Thus Hod, 'splendour', became Hodiel, 'Splendour of

God'. Gevurah, 'strength', became Gevurael; Cherubiel became the eponymous leader of the order of cherubim and Seraphiel ditto of the seraphim. The names of thousands of angels were created in this fashion. Greek, Babylonian, Persian and Roman gods and heroes became angels. The Greek god Hermes became the holy Hemesiel, and Nergal, the Akkadian lord of the underworld, became the angel Nasargiel. Angels began to appear in religious and secular literature, and some achieved canonical status.

Isaac de Acco was a fourteenth-century disciple of Nahmnaides (1194–1270), who was a leading medieval Jewish cabalist. According to A. E. Waite, founder of the late nineteenth-century mystical sect known as The Order of the Golden Dawn, de Acco 'laid claim to the performance of miracles by a transposition of Hebrew letters according to a system he pretended to have learned from the angels.' Shortly, we shall see how this ancient Jewish mystical system, known as the Cabala, became one of the most powerful secret angelic traditions incorporated into Christian and Neoplatonic mysticism in the Renaissance. It was this revival of pre-Christian thought that gave the Catholic church and its over-idealized band of angels a run for their money.

THE SEVEN DEADLY SINFUL 'DEMONS'

The Middle Ages was also a time when the idea of the seven deadly sins flourished. But where did the seven deadly sins originate? According to most Christian scholars, the first scribbling of any specific order of sins was by John Cassian (360–435), a Christian theologian known as one of the 'desert fathers'. However, it seems that he pinched the idea from his mentor, Evagrius the Solitary (345–399), a highly esteemed classical scholar, polished writer and monk, who wrote a key work entitled *Antirrehtikos*, in which he discussed the habits and personal problems encountered in the disciplined monastic life.

Cassian's *The Institutions* was commissioned by the Bishop of Apt, and was probably based on Evagrius's work, which already had said much on the subject of monkish temptation – 'Because we are human beings and wrestlers with demons, we cannot always keep the proper thought uncorrupted.'

Earlier in his life, Evagrius of Pontus, an Egyptian, had fallen madly in love with a married woman, and experienced all the usual sexual corruptions and temptations of Constantinople city life. Eventually, he ended up in a small community of less educated monks in a desert monastery. From his cell, he set out to 'cure' others in their daily fight against 'demons', whether real or of the mind.

> I write of the reasoning nature [that fights] beneath heaven: first, what it battles against; second, what assists it in the battle; and [finally] what the fighter keeping valiant watch must confront. Those who fight are human beings; those assisting them are the angels of God; and those opposing them are the evil demons.

In the introduction to his book *Talking Back: A Monastic Handbook for Combating Demons*, Professor David Brakke explains how Evagrius provided remedies to help a monk resist eight specific temptations. Complete manuscripts of Evagrius's book exist only in Armenian and Syriac, and Brakke's translation is the first contemporary English version of the entire text. The eight titles include such mouthwatering subjects as 'Combating the Thoughts of the Demon of Anger' and 'Against the Cursed Thought of Pride'. Evagrius's cures are made up from various excerpts from the Bible. These gems of literature are to be repeated aloud to combat evil thoughts or their accompanying demons. The four hundred or so biblical excerpts were collected in response to a letter from a monk,

Loukious, whose pleas for help against the demonic thoughts (we can imagine which ones) infesting his monastery obviously had the desired effect.

Referring to the Demon of Lust, no doubt the most difficult to avoid from any monkish cell, Evagrius may well have been talking from his own experience.

> 2.25 To the Lord, on account of the unclean demon of lust that approaches the thighs of those who strive to keep themselves far from him; by which he suddenly carries off the soul in insanity, in which he places it through a multitude of pleasure-loving thoughts. But it is very good when we are tempted by this demon to leap up and immediately forsake our cells with hasty and speedy footsteps.

> 2.29 Against the thoughts that threaten me: another devil of lust, even worse and more savage than the first will be sent to you who will easily do violence to your soul and draw your soul to sin which comes about through idleness.

The remedy was to recite a line from Psalms 34: 5:

> They will be like chaff before the wind; and the angel of the Lord will pursue them. Their way will be dark, and slippery, and the angel of the Lord will pursue them.

Say no more.

Evagrius's spell-book of instruction became popular among ancient classical authors. The habit of consulting ritualistic, magical handbooks to ward off evil powers and encourage good ones was common from the fifth century right up until the rise of the witch-hunt at the end of the Middle Ages. Using powerful incantations was considered normal, whether to invoke the help of angels or of God, to exorcise demons or call on the planets. Creating a neat and impressionable kind of demonology,

Evagrius was apparently influenced by the heretical Origen, and Didymus the Blind's adaptations of the Stoic philosophers' idea of the 'first movement'.

The 'first movement' refers to our basic instincts, feelings and passions, such as lust and anger, which, with conscious effort, we can learn to control. Adapted to a Christian viewpoint, and noted by Gennadius of Marseille in the fifth century, Evagrius's eight principle vices became lodged in many a theologian's conscience with Satan, the champion of these sins. With the inclusion of the individual's judgement, the soul had the choice to resist or control the initial passion, or to express it as a sin. These thoughts, according to Evagrius, were:

> The tricks of mocking demons, which imitate both perception and memory in order to deceive the rational soul that strives for the knowledge of Christ.

When Evagrius was talking demons, he was talking in Greek. But with many of the original works lost, most were translated into Syriac and, according to Professor Brakke, as well as the word 'daimon', Evagrius also used the word 'pneuma' or 'pneumata', which meant 'evil spirit(s)'. The equivalent word for 'daimon' in Syriac is 'dywh', transliterated as 'dyw'' – the apostrophe is important here – and according to the Standard Syriac Dictionary by Payne Smith, the word is related to the Persian 'dew'. 'Dew' means, of course, the epitome of evil, the demon. Again, it was easy to see how the innocent 'daimon' was becoming, in translation, evil.

SINS AND DEMONS

Ambivalent Greek 'daimons' or not, demons in the bright, new Christianized world had become sins, and sins were demons. Evagrius listed eight human passions in ascending order of gravity – gluttony, lust, avarice, sadness, anger, acedia (spiritual sloth), vainglory and pride. Evagrius believed pride or 'hubris', excessive pride, was the most dangerous of sins. But his accompanying development of some of Origen's more esoteric teachings, particularly the pre-existence of the human soul, led his work to be declared heretical by the Second Council of Constantinople in 553.

In the late sixth century, Pope Gregory the Great revised Evagrius's original list and came up with his own 'seven sins'. Knowingly or not, he opted for a number riddled with mystical connotations. He merged vainglory with pride, acedia with sadness, which later became simply known as sloth, and added a little envy. His order of ranking was based on the amount each sin offended against love. The top-ranking sin was still considered self-love or hubris/pride, the number-one sin according to Evagrius, followed by envy, anger, sadness (sloth), avarice, gluttony and lust. Lust was later changed to extravagance ('luxur'), at the time implying excessive desire for anything.

According to the Venerable Bede (673–735), English church historian, poet and translator of many natural science works, Pope Gregory is purported to have said the famous line, *'Non Angli, sed angeli'* – 'they are not Angles but angels' – when he first encountered fair-haired slaves at a market, and sent St Augustine to convert the English. Bede himself was not short of legendary status, either. He'd gone through a near-death experience and seen angels himself. He was given his title, 'Venerable', by a frustrated monk, who was attempting to write an epitaph for Bede. The monk left a blank space, went to bed with the line unfinished and the next morning discovered the word *venerabilis* inserted into his text. The only possible explanation he could give was that an angel had added the word. From then on, Bede was considered, well, Venerable.

Later theologians, including Thomas Aquinas, questioned Gregory's method of ranking, and by the seventeenth century, the Church had replaced sadness with sloth.

As the artistic and literary imagination flourished through the Middle Ages, iconography associated with each sin depicted specific punishments that were believed to await the perpetrator in hell. The penalty for pride was to be broken on a wheel; for envy, to be forever entombed in freezing water; boiling in oil was favoured for avarice; and being torn apart, limb from limb, for wrath or anger. Highly recommended for lust was to be roasted by fire and brimstone. The gluttonous would be forced to eat rats, snakes, spiders and toads, while the slothful paid the penalty of being thrown into a snake pit.

However, with the Christian world so biased towards duality, heavenly virtues were needed to compensate for the dreaded sins. The first recorded virtues were those known as the Cardinal Virtues, as posited by Plato and Aristotle, later taken up by Aquinas. The seven virtues were derived from 'Psychomachia' ('Contest of the Soul'), an epic poem written by the Roman poet, Aurelius Clemens Prudentius (c. 410), describing the battle between virtues and vices.

The great popularity of this work in the Middle Ages helped to spread the concept of holy virtue. To protect one against temptation from the seven deadly sins, it was important to follow the accompanying virtue, or contrary virtue. The first three of these virtues were the theological virtues, faith, hope and charity, followed by fortitude, justice, temperance and prudence.

In 1589, the same year Galileo was beginning his revolutionary experiments on bodies in motion, Peter Binsfield (1545/6–98), a German theologian, published an authoritative list of demons and their associated sins. Lucifer as pride, followed by greedy Mammon, lusting Asmodeus, envious Leviathan, gluttonous Beelzebub, wrathful Satan and slothful Belphegor.

MEDIEVAL GOINGS ON
Meanwhile, in the forests and apple groves of northern Europe, Cernunnos, the horned god, was still being worshipped, and the

list of injunctions against so called 'demonic' worshippers began to gain momentum. The devil was a rival in the political eyes of the Church. Back in the seventh century, the Archbishop of Canterbury prohibited eating and drinking in heathen temples, and cross-dressing as an animal (rather than the opposite sex) incurred a penance of three years, 'because it is devilish'.

A ninth-century injunction from Rome was proclaimed against 'certain wicked women reverting to Satan and seduced by the illusions and phantasms of demons'. Yet meanwhile, in the cold cloisters of every monastery, in the ascetic values of every churchman, the Christian faith was growing a more distorted form of canker than any diseased rose. The Pope, literally, ruled one's body and soul, while the Church's obsession with heretics became the foundation of all power plays.

The first thousand years or so of the Christian era were pretty dirty – dirty money, dirty people and grubby politics. Christianity was not only depressing – its main assertion that the only sure thing after death was hell's eternal fire unless you were a saint or pope or sin-free – but also a useful weapon in both war and politics. The end of the world was deemed to be nigh by many a prophet, poser or theologian. People sought salvation, and turned to the Church, apparently their last chance to be at peace. Visions of angels were numerous, particularly among the clergy, nuns and priests. The Venerable Bede revealed that St Cuthbert could converse with angels, and St Columba was said to have received many 'sweet angel visits'. Female mystics, such as St Cecilia and Hildegarde of Bingen, testified to visions of Jesus, God and the Virgin Mary, all accompanied by angels.

In medieval art, the good soul, resembling a dove, was carried to paradise by angels, while demons carried sinners to hell. Pope Gregory commented on visions claimed by the dying and death-bed companions. When the vision was angelic, the room filled with light and perfume, and the music of heaven was heard. When sinners died, the visions were horrifying. Demons, crows, vultures and beastly faces breathed fire, and dragons and serpents entered the dying sinner's mouth.

To most of the European population, ravaged by centuries of war, poverty and ascetic principles, it seemed indeed that God was punishing the world for its sins. Of course, there was no shortage of preachers ready to suggest extreme measures for humanity to atone for its transgressions. Fasting, prayer, penitence, absolution or wearing a hair shirt were particularly recommended. Later, in the mid-thirteenth century, self-flagellation became a cult in itself, already common among the more ascetic religious orders, such as the Dominican monks.

TURNING POINT

In the medieval world, spirits, prophecy, apocalypse and the possessed took hold of the imagination. But then, after the desperation of the Dark Ages and its obsession with the masturbatory, as opposed to fashionable, habits of monks, it was hardly surprising.

The medieval Russian Bishop of Novgorod was almost initiated into demonic ways himself when a young monk in the Kiev Caves monastery in the late eleventh century. More commonly known in Russian Orthodox circles as St Nikita the Recluse, as a novice he decided to retreat to a cave. Headstrong and ambitious for miraculous powers like Jesus, he was determined to pray his way to success. Maybe that was a sin in itself, and his first error.

Down in the squalid cave, a sweet fragrance filled the air and he heard a voice. Convinced it was an angel, since no demon would surely risk speaking prayers to the Lord, he demanded proof all the same, and the voice said, 'When the angel comes to you, do everything he says you must do.' A demon appeared as an angel and told him to read the Old Testament and nothing but, until he had learnt it off by heart; meanwhile the angel would continue saying his prayers for him. The angel/demon began to recount all that was happening in the world, and Nikita found that he, too, became clairvoyant – certainly a short-cut to miracle working, if ever there was one. He no longer wanted to read or hear the Gospels, and the other monks dragged Nikita from his cave, exorcised the demon and Nikita finally repented. Thankfully, Jesus forgave him, and he was granted the power of miracle-working.

So what is the true value of this story? What does this demon disguised as an angel tell us, other than that fear had always been the driving force behind Christianity? But if you couldn't trust even an angel to be an angel, how could anyone trust a bishop clothed in a white frock with purple bits and bobs hanging about him?

The medieval, predominantly Christian, world view through-out Europe came to a turning point when cultural ideas and activity developed after years of savage wars and insular thinking. The pagan past came alive through education, and contact with neighbouring cultures. The first university was founded in Paris in 1170, setting the stage for Europe's redis-covery of Aristotle's writings, preserved in Arabic and readily available in Latin. Philosophy and theology attempted to merge, as did nature with reason, and behind the religious glamour of it all, Christian spirit and pagan soul found a common bond. This was the beginning of thought based not just on theological spec-ulation, but also on a scientific one. And who better laboriously to spout it all out for the rest of Europe, than Thomas Aquinas.

Thomas Aquinas (1225–74)
Thomas Aquinas's lectures in 1259, according to Christian sources, set down everything known about angels. His lengthy reasonings were primarily taken from biblical and extra-scriptural sources. Aquinas concluded that angels were intellect, not matter; they could assume bodies at will, and ate, drank and appeared among mankind. Aquinas also fixed the hierarchy of angels, and

his pronouncements prevailed in Christianity for three-quarters of a millennium. A few decades after Aquinias died, around 1320, the Italian poet Dante Alighieri followed on from the hierarchy set forth by both Pseudo-D and Aquinas in his 'Divine Comedy', which included definitive rankings and poetic descriptions of all the heavenly creatures, both good and evil. Dante mostly wrote of angels as transcendent beings of light and song.

Known as the 'angelic doctor', Thomas Aquinas was one of the most influential theologians and philosophers in Western Europe. Swayed by the ideas of Aristotle, Aquinas created his own, ponderously dull, school of 'Thomistic' thought. Determined to become a celibate, self-flagellating Dominican monk at a young age, his family forcibly prevented him from joining the order. Kidnapped, he was held hostage in their château. One night his brothers sent a prostitute to seduce him out of his ascetic ways. According to legend, two angels appeared instead, confirming his determination to join the order and remain celibate.

Of his many sleep-inducing works, *Summa Theologica* is his best known. Here he speculates long and hard on the nature, substance, number and creation of angels. Drawing on Aristotle's notion of the intelligences that move the spheres, he also refers to biblical accounts of angels and demons, as well as possible objections and questions from heretics and Christian alike, and even Neo-Platonic ideas on the intermediaries between God and man.

'It must be affirmed that angels and everything existing, except God, were made by God,' he wrote. He argued that angels were pure in spirit, incorporeal, with no bodies of any kind except those they chose to assume when appearing to ordinary mortals:

Although air as long as it is in a state of rarefaction has neither shape nor colour, yet when condensed it can both be shaped and coloured as appears in the clouds. Even so the angels assume bodies of air, condensing it by the Divine power in so far as is needful for forming the assumed body.

He wrote extensive arguments about the whys and wherefores of fallen angels, and whether evil existed simultaneously with good at the moment of creation. Most medieval Christian theologians agreed with Aquinas that the world was created by one God, and when it was created it was very Good indeed. The devil and his demons, or fallen angels, had been created Good, but through their own ability to 'sin' they became evil. For this ascetic Christian world, there was no original powerful opponent to God; and certainly not as the duo of Ahura Mazda and Ahriman of Zoroastrianism. The Creed of Lateran IV (from the Ecumenical Council of 1215) stated:

> The Devil and other demons were indeed created by God good by nature but they became bad through themselves; human beings, however, sinned at the suggestion of the Devil.

Aquinas also argued that angels were faced with a choice at the moment of creation, either in favour of God's commands or independent of their creator.

> It would seem that there can be other sins in the angels besides those of pride and envy. Because whosoever can delight in any kind of sin, can fall into the sin itself.

Aquinas prevaricated over the question of whether it was the highest angel who sinned, leading the rest to tumble down after him, and whether the highest angel was a cherubim or a seraphim. But he managed to get himself out of his logical knot by deciding that it was sin itself, rather than a persuasive angel, that led to the fall:

The sin of the highest angel was the cause of the others sinning; not as compelling them, but as inducing them by a kind of exhortation. A token thereof appears in this, that all the demons are subjects of that highest one; as is evident from our Lord's words: 'Go you cursed, into everlasting fire, which was prepared for the devil and his angels.'

On the number of angels, Aquinas dodged any specific number, by saying:

Hence it must be said that the angels, even inasmuch as they are immaterial substances, exist in exceeding great number, far beyond all material multitude.

But why was Aquinas so at pains to explain lengthily, and reason the case for angels and demons? Was it the fear that unless the Church put its stamp, and the authority of God, as above and higher than angels, the angels would begin to run amok? Angels had been carefully threaded into the tapestry of Christianity with golden threads; now there was a chance that the needlepoint would be unpicked and the whole tapestry fall apart. Needlepoint, however, is far from fragile.

Was Aquinas, like many theologians, flexing his intellectual muscles, or simply trying to free himself from the curse of the contradictory back catalogue of Christian gospellers, writers and even heretics? Perhaps, on a darker note, he was actually one of the few twelfth-century Christian theologians and philosophers who sensed that the flourishing new wave of European scholarship, plus the foundation of the first university and the revival of pagan heritage, would be the biggest challenge to Christianity for over a thousand years.

PINS, NEEDLES AND POINTS

Talking of needles and universities, the extraordinary influence of a late thirteenth/early fourteenth-century mystic may have

been something Aquinas had sniffed out in the changing intellectual wind.

Aquinas had questioned whether an angel moving from A to
B passed through the points in between. He also then asked
himself, rather than anyone else, whether a dozen or more
angels could all be in the same place at once. From this he
surmised the deeply revealing answer that there was no answer.

Since then, many have lampooned and derided Aquinas for
his silliness, and a catchphrase, 'how many angels can dance on
the head of a pin?', was attributed to Aquinas's silken bed of
wisdom. But for all his pointless ponderings about whether
angels know more things in the morning than they do in the
evening, or whether they wore nightshirts in bed, he never did
say anything about them dancing on pinheads.

Where angels and 'needle' heads are first mentioned is in a
fourteenth-century treatise attributed to the German-born
mystic and philosopher, Meister Eckhart, known as the
Schwester Katrei tract, or the *Sister Catherine Treatise*. There is
debate about its authorship, and scholars currently believe it
was probably written by a woman, due to its style and language.
However, the tract is positively bulging with Eckhart's
philosophy and mystical beliefs.

First a Dominican monk, then theological and philosophical
professor at the University of Paris in the late thirteenth and
early fourteenth century, Meister Eckhart was not only famous
for successfully defending himself against the Inquisition, but
also for his paradoxes, psychological insight and metaphors,
and the creative word play in his writings.

Eckhart believed that the divine flowed through the world
and the individual. He believed that we can open ourselves to
receive the 'Son of God' in our soul, and thus become One with
God. His doctrines were inspired by the French mystic
Marguerite Porete. She was the author of a spiritual work
entitled *The Mirror of Simple Souls*, and was burnt at the stake

in 1310 for heresy and for refusing to remove her book from circulation. Both Porete and Eckhart were considered to be the 'founders' of the 'Heresy of the Free Spirit' cults that developed in the fourteenth century. These cults were based on Sufism and its beliefs that all is divine, there is no afterlife, heaven and hell are states of being, and the individual is united with God, and is above all laws, church or sin.

In the *Sister Catherine Treatise*, the dialogue between Sister Catherine, who was a Béguine, that is a member of a lay religious community, and her father confessor includes hefty chunks of Eckhart's belief system. For example, Catherine says:

> I am as I was before I was created; just God and God . . . Eight heavens are often spoken of and nine choirs or angels; there is nothing of that where I am.

The heretical tract reveals how Catherine, respectful of her confessor, returns from an ecstatic spiritual union with God. On her return, she looks more like an 'angel' than a woman, and ends up as the spiritual teacher of her father confessor. The confessor asks:

> Tell me daughter, doctors declare that in heaven a thousand angels can stand on the point of a needle, now rede [sic] me the meaning of this?

She replies:

> The doctors are right. The soul that enters into God owns neither time nor space, nor anything nameable . . . God might make heavens and earths galore, yet these together with the multiplicity of creatures he has already made, would be of less extent than a single needle tip, compared with the standpoint of a soul atoned in God.

With artful needle-point analogies, the tract shows how the Béguine's soulful experience of God is so vast that the whole universe and its choirs of angels wouldn't even cover the tip of a needle in comparison to the enormity of the soul's experience.

The other point is that as far as mystics such as Eckhart or Sister Catherine were concerned, the doctors of the theological world were talking out of their biblical passages, and Aquinas's ponderous logic about why 'angels do this and why angels can't do that' is irrelevant to true spiritual union with God. After all, if 'man can transcend the angels and receive all things from the source of divine truth', what was the point of angels at all?

Eckhart was a volatile fuse among the dead sparks of the time. He reminded those who knew that angels were perhaps not all they seemed that hell was simply one's memories and attachments. If you can't let go of those attachments, you'll see demons pulling you down to hell; but if you've made your peace with yourself and life, they are no longer demons but angels, freeing your soul, letting you leave the trap that is life.

Although Eckhart's philosophy sounded a jolly good idea across his fourteenth-century university coffee table, it was probably of little comfort to students, women or theologians when the devilish angel, the Black Death, swept across Europe in 1349–51. Even worse, the innumerable guardian angels that medieval theologians, such as Aquinas, had insisted protected, helped and healed mankind, or put us one step nearer to God, weren't exactly winging their way to help. On a lighter note, perhaps the 'freeing' of so many souls into the universe had a positive knock-on effect, as we shall see.

THE DAWNING OF THE RENAISSANCE
Angels and demons, kept alive in the mystical, magical nature of the supernatural occultists, meant grimoires, or books of magic, flourished, and Europe became a microcosm of the blessed and the cursed. Thanks to the Florentine ruler Cosimo Medici's

fascination for the treasure trove brought to his court by a Byzantine magician, Gemistos Plethon, in 1439, ancient traditions, pagan messengers and gods alike animated the Renaissance world. After the rediscovery of original works by Plato, the Neo-Platonists, such as Plotinus, Porphyry and Iamblichus, were revived by Marsilio Ficino and Giovanni Pico della Mirandola. These two were responsible for the school of thought known as the Renaissance Humanists.

Humanism was a response to the scholastic educationalists of the medieval period. They sought to revive the study of the humanities, such as history, grammar, rhetoric, poetry and philosophy, and in doing so bring to life the culture of classic antiquity. They also revived the Zoroastrian or Chaldean Oracles, the Hermetic works believed then to date back to the time of Moses, as well as the Hebrew Cabala and the Egyptian mystery religions. Like the Greco-Romans, they embraced the cycles of the universe, and oversaw a rebirth of the Golden Age, a reawakening of the notion of potential divinity to be found within oneself, as well as without – the same one that Eckhart had so beautifully championed.

Humanists blossomed in the royal courts of Florence and the Vatican, working with archetypal symbols and metaphors, incorporating the old arts of astrology and its pantheon of planetary deities and correspondences. Even though God now reigned supreme, other gods were given value, and mythology or pagan beliefs infused art with a different religious truth. Angels became reunited with ancient classical deities, stylized and sensuous, whether the winged Hermes, Nike herself, Victory or Iris. Greek daimons were converted to angelic status, and renewed veneration of Venus, Hermes, Saturn or any god with charisma became apparent. Angels were contacted or summoned, demons packed the latest grimoires, exorcisms outnumbered marriages, witch-hunting became a serious business, and conversing with angels a dangerous pastime.

Ramon Lull (1232/1233 – 1315/16)

The writings of Spanish fourteenth-century mystic and philosopher Ramon Lull had a huge influence on the Renaissance mindset. Lull was born at a time when Spain had a huge Jewish population, was still dominated by the Catholic Church and yet was partly under Moslem Arabic rule. The Jews had brought their own brand of mysticism with them to Spain, and the Cabala was the generator of Lull's Art – a synthesis of the three religions, Jewish, Moslem and Christian – through which he attempted to convert Jews and Moslems to Christianity.

The Jewish mystical Cabala dated back to the first century, and re-emerged during the twelfth century to become the basis for many European occult traditions. The core tenet of the Cabala is based on the belief that God gave Moses the secrets of the universe. (Inanna's secrets lived on.) This esoteric knowledge was passed down orally by initiates, and a mystical cult developed believing the secret of God's words was coded in the text of the Old Testament. Using elaborate manipulations of the Hebrew alphabet, this was religious magic or 'theurgy' at its best. The Cabalistic doctrine was also centred around the powerful emanations of God, the Sephiroth, usually described as angelic forces. These angelic qualities were part of the Cabala's mystical synthesis to enable man to ascend the heights and discover the words of God.

Lull believed that, although all three religions had their differences, they would agree that God was good, true, virtuous and so on. Lull's Nine Dignities corresponded to the nine planets that were known at the time, and nine qualities, such as Bonitas (goodness), Veritas (truth) and Gloria (Glory). Using highly complex geometry, he implied that each manifestation of God could appear on any level of creation, whether with the angels in the celestial sphere, or with man on the terrestrial one. Symbolic, yet mystical, he based this on both the Cabala and its Sephiroth – the ten names most common to God – as well as the coded

Hebrew alphabet. The Sephiroth are known as Gloria, Veritas, Bonitas, Potestas, Virtus, Eternituas, Sapientia, Splendor, Fundamentum and Voluntus. The similarity to Lull's nine manifestations is no coincidence. In his attempt to convert Jews and Moslems to Christianity, Lull used the allegory of a wandering artist who climbed the ladder of creation to reach the angelic heights. In his work, *Ars Generalis* (Part 9 Section 2), he attempted to prove the true nature of angels:

> An angel has virtue with which it is naturally active in its principles inasmuch as they are virtuous in virtue; and it has virtuous acts that are good in goodness, great in greatness, etc. But the intellect wonders: what mode does an angel have for acquiring accidental virtues? And then it remembers that an angel has virtuous habits as it objectifies objects through virtuous understanding and loving and through just, prudent and charitable action, as angels help us to resist sin and oppose the evil angels by transmitting messages to us from the supreme principle, by bringing our prayers into God's presence, and by praying for us . . . An angel is not composed of contraries for it naturally stands outside the elements just as it stands outside of points, numbers, figures and things like these. Now the intellect wonders: if good and evil angels are not composed of contraries, then what causes them to oppose each other? Until it remembers that a good angel is habituated with the prime end, whereas an evil angel is empty of it. And here the intellect realizes how awesome this opposition is in the *sempiternal aevum*.

The 'eternally forever' Constantinople was taken by the Turks in 1453. With the influx of Greek refugees into Europe, followed by the discovery of mystical works and the arrival of Jews in Florence in 1492, the second half of the fifteenth century was poised for the rebirth of the classical past.

Hermetic occult philosophy, alchemy and Cabala merged in the Medici courts of Florence, thanks mostly to Pico della Mirandola and Ficino.

Giovanni Pico Della Mirandola (1463–94)

Pico was born into one of the most powerful dynasties of the Italian fifteenth century. His family were distinguished in the arts and scholarship of the time. Renowned for his amazing memory, and a precocious child prodigy, Pico was proficient in Greek, Latin, Hebrew and Arabic. In 1486, at the age of twenty-three, he proposed to defend nine hundred theses he'd written on religion, philosophy, natural philosophy, humanities and magic. Against all-comers, he wrote the famous *Oration on the Dignity of Man*, which became a key text of Renaissance humanism. Supporting the branch of Cabala devoted to the harnessing of the powers of spirits and angels to commune with God, he maintained that if magic was performed in the holiest way, it had nothing to do with devil or demon worship.

In the *11th Cabalistic Conclusion*, he describes a trance-like state in which the soul communicates with God via the archangels. The soul transcends the body, rising to the mystical realms on naming the ten Sephiroth, who correspond to the ten spheres of the universe. The system of ascending the cosmic ladder is aided by naming specific angels, such as Michael, Raphael and Gabriel.

Pico was influenced by Hermetic magic and the Chaldean Oracles. In Perugia *c.* 1484–5, recovering from injuries sustained during a fight involving the husband of his secret lover, he wrote to Ficino:

> Divine Providence . . . caused certain books to fall into my hands. They are Chaldean books . . . of Esdras, of Zoroaster and of Melchior, oracles of the magi, which contain a brief

and dry interpretation of Chaldean philosophy, but full of mystery.

In 1487, Pope Innocent VIII condemned Pico's theses and his *Apologia*:

> In part heretical, in part the flower of heresy; several are scandalous and offensive to pious ears; most do nothing but reproduce the errors of pagan philosophers . . . others are capable of inflaming the impertinence of the Jews; a number of them, finally, under the pretext of 'natural philosophy', favour arts that are enemies to the Catholic faith and to the human race.

Pico died under mysterious circumstances. It is believed he was poisoned for his disloyalty to the Medici family, and his dabblings with the anti-humanist monk Savonarola, a lifelong friend. Savonarola, who was invited to Florence by Pico, repeatedly preached against the Medicis, urging Florentines to reject the excesses of the Renaissance. Works by Botticelli and Michelangelo were burned during the 'Bonfire of the Vanities' in 1497, when the monk's followers set fire to lavish furniture, mirrors, pagan books and erotic sculptures in the Piazza della Signora.

German scholar Johannes Reuchlin (1455–1522) was inspired by Pico. In his work *De verbo mirifico* (1494), he praises both the Cabala, as a divine science, and the Hebrew language, as the language spoken by God to the angels. Reuchlin took a great interest in summoning angels, and believed cabalistic magic was safe because the inclusion of naming angels purified the old magic of any evil intent.

His later work, *De arte cabalistica*, was to become the bible of the Christian cabalists. Here, the names of God, the Sephiroth, the Hebrew alphabet and the names of angels were all expressed in numerical values.

Zorzi and beyond

Francisco Giorgi (1466–1540), also known as Zorzi, was a Franciscan friar living in Venice, who fused the Neoplatonic and Hermetic teachings with Cabala. Giorgi also developed the angelic connections between angel hierarchies and the planetary spheres, based on the secrets of numerology. His important work *De harmonia mundi* influenced Elizabethan philosopher Dr John Dee (1527–1608/9). Giorgi's Christian version of the Cabala connected Pseudo-Dionysius's angels with the Sephiroth, pouring goodness down through the stars. He believed that the planetary influences are all wholly good, because they are already affected by the angels passing through them, so that astrology is essentially made up of goodness, and the planets, such as Saturn, are not malefic as believed. He also theorized that if Christian angels protect the magus in his workings, surely the magus is angelic, not demonic.

One late fifteenth, early sixteenth-century Renaissance magus was not so lucky in getting away with his heretical thoughts, and his far from angelic reputation continued up until the twentieth century. Dubbed the *archimagus*, the very personification of black magic itself, by Jesuit Martin del Rio, Henry Cornelius Agrippa (1486–1535) was considered to be a sorcerer in league with the Devil, and throughout his life was hounded by the Inquisition. Yet Agrippa's view on magic was to be the catalyst for both the growing witch-hunt obsession and the rise of late Renaissance Neo-Platonism and its associated occult traditions.

The hound of demonic possession and angelic summoning was stirring from his kennel.

10

THE VAIN BABBLINGS OF IDLE MEN

'Sit, Jessica. Look how the floor of heaven
Is thick inlaid with patines of bright gold.
There's not the smallest orb that thou beholdest
But in his motion like an angel sings,
Still quiring to the young-eyed cherubins.'
William Shakespeare, *The Merchant of Venice*,
Act V, Scene I

Was spiritual asceticism finally losing its appeal in the dawning of the second millenium CE? After a thousand years or more of sexual repression and misogyny in the cloisters of religious power, the collective psyche was ready to restore its lost sensuality.

As long-forgotten Eastern delights crossed borders, and lush areas of Europe, such as the Languedoc in southern France, drew on cultural self-indulgence rather than self-denial, taste buds and pleasurable delights were evoked. The troubadours sang of unrequited love – a contrived romancing of man's sexual frustration if ever – and although women had been tar-brushed as demonic or siding with the devil, the monkish disdain for all things to do with the flesh was growing wearisome. Angels couldn't quite reach the parts women could reach, and scandals concerning the cloistered ones, such as eleventh/twelfth century French theologian Peter Abelard and his affair with Heloise, created newsworthy love stories. The mystical, ecstatic visions of holy women, such as Hildegarde of Bingen, and the genre of courtly love blended in the words of Chretien de Troyes and Dante, and in the oils of Boticelli and Da Vinci .

Old pagan religions still survived underground in Europe, and with a growing mistrust in Christianity and its angelic realms, plus the emerging new wave of intellectual interest in mystery religions, it's hardly surprising that people turned to esoteric traditions to find some kind of hope, joy or solace. Ficino and other Renaissance Neo-Platonists believed that if you truly merged with the stars, angels and the gods, you too could let the power of the universe flow through you. Renaissance artists, such as Michelangelo and Raphael, believed the ancient mysteries were already inherent within themselves, and they were just now discovering the hidden truths.

The idea of the daimon re-emerged, both as the genius of the artist and the working of the spiritual force within. Raphael believed he was directly inspired by the archangel Raphael, and that God worked through him. Like Empedocles, over fifteen hundred years earlier, these were the new *daimonic* men. Charismatic characters emerged, such as Shakespeare and Spenser in literature; Agrippa, John Dee, Ficino and Pico in the esoteric arts; and Copernicus, Galileo, Newton and Descartes in science and philosophy. The scientific revolution, perhaps initiated by Nicolaus Copernicus in 1543, wasn't so much a rebirth of old ideas as rebirth of old ideas put in new ways. Yet whether in philosophy, science or mysticism, this period of European history stands out for its remarkable achievements, the change in cultural and religious thinking and, of course, the dawning of the scientific age.

A few stood out where angels and demons were concerned, too.

JOHANNES TRITHEMIUS (1462–1516)

One winter's night in the frozen North, as snow fell heavily in huge drifts throughout the forested hills of Germany, a bright young student on his journey from the University of Heidelberg to his home in Trittenheim on the Moselle, took shelter in a Benedictine Abbey near Sponheim. When he was fifteen, Johannes had had a dream of two angels holding out a tablet, one inscribed with text, the other with pictures. Asked to choose between them, he chose the writing, because of his 'longing for knowledge'. And knowledge was certainly his passion for the rest of his life. For some reason unknown to anyone except himself, Trithemius decided to stay on with the community of monks, and by 1483 he had become its abbot at the age of twenty-one.

With education his priority, Trithemius developed a vast library, restored the crumbling abbey, and decorated the walls with verses from poetry and classical prose. His library, containing more than two thousand books, became renowned throughout Europe as a centre for scholars on any subject. Not only influential as a great historian and lexicographer, Trithemius was acclaimed as an occultist. Fascinated by the Cabala, he had a profound influence on the mystic scholars of the sixteenth century, particularly his pupils Agrippa and Paracelsus, and later, the English magician and Queen Elizabeth's astrologer, John Dee.

As counsellor to Emperor Maximilian I, Trithemius is said to have conjured up the emperor's recently passed-away bride so he could see her one more time, and was subsequently accused of being in league with the devil.

Trithemius is best known for his work the *Steganographia* (*c.*1499), a three-volume book filled with practical exercises for magical communication with spirits and angels, and, of course, banned by the Catholic Church. The word 'steganographia' means 'concealed writing', and it is subtly different from cryptography because it reveals a way of writing hidden messages, known only to the sender and receiver. Cryptography, on the other hand, is the art of concealing information, not necessarily the sending of messages from sender to recipient. The message could be hidden in a list of things to do, a journal, a receipt, or the words of a hymn.

During the 1990s, attention was drawn to Trithemius's work by linguistic Professor Thomas Ernst at La Roche College, Philadelphia, USA, who sought to prove that Trithemius's invocation of angels was merely a clever device to cover up his encryption techniques, consisting of numerological and alphabetical values of angels and planetary positions. These techniques were similar to the enigma device used by the Germans to encrypt messages in the Second World War. Coincidentally, Jim Reeds, a mathematician with the Cryptography Research Department of American Telephone and Telegraph Inc., also analysed Trithemius's work, and came to the same conclusion, that this was a work not of magic, but of cryptography.

Ostensibly, *Stegnographia* is a book of angelic magic. Not only does Trithemius devise a hierarchy of angels and spirits who rule places, people, time and cosmos, but he uses the angels as a means of sending secret messages to a recipient. His other work, *De Septum Secundeis*, a history of the world based on astrology, also employs the method of angelic text messaging. The one who wishes to send a message must first find the right angel by a specific magical incantation and write a message to summon that angel. Then while the message is being sent by the angel, the recipient must also summon the right angel to bring the message. Takeaway angel pizzas never tasted better.

But perhaps there is more to Trithemius's book than just a clever way of revealing how to send secret messages. It may be

that his angelic sorcery works on both an espionage and spiri
-tual level. Trithemius commented, 'The word magic is the
Persian term for what is the Latin for wisdom, on which account
magicians are called wise men.'

Whether the book is magic pretending to be cryptography, or
just inspirational cryptography disguised as a magic book, or
maybe both, is irrelevant, but interesting. What is important is
that it had such an affect on John Dee. Deciphering codes and
inventing new ones was part of the glamorous political goings-
on in sixteenth-century Europe. Intrigue, treachery, betrayal
and 'the powers behind many a throne and its downfall',
propelled the angel towards a dodgy future, and ironically, the
demon to greater things.

Trithemius wrote a letter to his friend, Arnoldus Bostius, a
Carmelite monk in Ghent, excited about his new angel work,
boasting that it would be 'a great work, that if it should ever be
published (God forbid) the whole world will wonder at it'.
Bostius, unfortunately, died before receiving the letter (obviously angels weren't employed for a quick delivery), which was
then circulated among his horrified Carmelite brothers, who
tried to discredit Trithemius. Magical elements of the book
were described in the letter, including over a hundred kinds of
secret writing, incantations and spells for teaching Latin and
Greek, plus methods for reading someone else's thoughts,
which we now call telepathy.

In 1509, French mathematician Charles de Bovelles (1475–
1567), an officious type by all accounts, describes his visit to
Trithemius. Shocked by the magical incantations and
summoning of angels and spirits, Bovelles decreed the book
should be burnt, and asserted that Trithemius was in league
with demons. By 1510, after the publication of the letter,
Trithemius's reputation was demoted to that of heretic and
magician, and the *Steganographia*, although passed around in
manuscript form, was not formally published until 1606.

But why did Trithemius use angelic magic to hide his cryptography? Some scholars suggest it was a kind of rhetorical strategy to sustain the reader's interest. By its own disclosure, in the title, it was a work that revealed different ways to write and send codes. Trithemius added in his text that he wanted to use this angelic network to know more about every working of the world, and that:

> To men of learning and men deeply engaged in the study of magic, it might, by the Grace of God, be in some degree intelligible, while on the other hand, to the thick skinned turnip heads, it might for all time remain a hidden secret and be to their dull intellects a sealed book forever.

In 1508, Trithemius also wrote *De Septem Secundeis*, proposing that seven archangels rule historical cycles of 'approximately' 354 years and four months each. Each archangel corresponded to one of the seven planetary forces used in astrology, Orifiel to Saturn, Anael to Venus, Zachariel to Jupiter, Raphael to Mercury, Samuel or Kamael to Mars, Gabriel to the Moon and Michael to the Sun. We are currently in the age of Raphael, an era every bit as glib and unpredictable as Mercurius himself.

Whatever the double messages, or triple double messages, hidden in Trithemius's work may have been, it was to have a profound influence on both Cornelius Agrippa and John Dee, who took the art of angelic magic to its most dazzling heights and into the royal courts of a Renaissance Europe, where the Catholic Church had began to lose not only its angels, but its head.

CORNELIUS AGRIPPA

A genuine entrepreneur, profiteer and practitioner of the magic arts, and notoriously but wrongly associated with the Devil, was Cornelius Agrippa (1486–1535), a native of Cologne. Influenced by Reuchlin and Trithemius, Agrippa went to

England after penning *De Occulta Philosophia* in 1533, a work describing at length the operation of ceremonial, natural magic and the summoning of angels. A relentless, restless traveller, follower of Dutch humanist Erasmus (1466–1536) and the whole Humanist movement, he studied both Hermetic mysticism and the Cabala in Italy, where he became acquainted with the Chaldean Oracles and most of the Egyptian esoteric arts. At one point, he contradicted his own work by writing *De Vanitate Scientiarum*, an ostensibly sceptical work, slating human intellect and the 'vain sciences', which included Cabala, magic, geometry, alchemy and astrology, the very subjects that he so championed. However, this was likely to have been a useful defence against weighty Christian opposition if he was ever accused of heresy.

In *De Occulta Philosophia*, he writes on the virtues of magic:

Magic is a faculty of wonderful virtue, full of most high mysteries, containing the most profound contemplation of most secret things, together with the nature, power, quality, substance and virtues thereof, as also the knowledge of whole Nature, and it doth instruct us concerning the differing and agreement of things amongst themselves, whence it produceth its wonderful effects, by uniting the virtues of things through the application of them one to the other.

The sixteenth/seventeenth-century German biographer and historian Melchior Adam described Agrippa as '*Ipse Philosophus, daemon, heros, Deus et omnia*'. Roughly translated, that means 'He/himself was a philosopher, daimon, hero [as in demi-god], divine/God and everything.' According to Lynn Thorndyke's *History of Magic and Experimental Science*, published in 1941, Agrippa was a fifteenth-century intellectual vagabond and wayward genius. He practised alchemy and astrology, dallied in medicine, and as well as practising as an illicit physician, was the fount of all knowledge when it came to anything occult. Thorndyke also treats his magic and beliefs with a large dose of disdain. Yet fashion and its historians change with the wind, and now, thanks to the research of historian Dame Frances Yates, Agrippa has had his status restored, and been given fresh credibility as an influential astrologer and occultist of his time.

De Occulta Philosophia is an encyclopedia of cosmic magic. It describes, in graphic detail, how through each plane or level of the universe, the virtues of the creator manifest, through the angels, the intellect, the stars, the elements and the world. He describes natural magic, the power of sympathetic magic – how like attracts like – and the influences of the stars, numerology and ceremonial magic and ritual directed towards the angelic spirits, heavily laden with incantations, spells and talismans.

Drawn heavily from the *Asclepius* – the bible of Hermeticism, erroneously thought at the time to have been written by Hermes Trismegistus, the Egyptian magus living at the time of Moses – *De Occulta Philosophia* simply confirms Hermes's words:

> O Son, how many bodies we have to pass through, how many bands of demons [daimons], through how many series of repetitions and cycles of stars, before we hasten to the One alone?

The *Asclepius* pointed out that the early Egyptian priests and sorcerers cast spells to imbue the statues of their gods with divine power, and that angels, gods, 'elementals' and the stars were all one.

Agrippa combined Cabala and Hermetic occultism with the power of Hebrew words. The inclusion of Hebrew, and the 'goody-goody' reputation and quality of angels, guaranteed the safety of the magus in his work, preventing evil influence. Demons, or rather daimons, become confused yet again in translation and easily misinterpreted with evil in Agrippa's three orders of intelligences, which he called 'demons' – the super-celestial demons, who are just part of the divine; the celestial demons, who belong to the stars, planets and zodiac signs, and have names, characters and can be summoned; and the lower world of demons of fire, earth, air and water. Fusing the angelic hierarchy of Pseudo-Dionysius with the Hebrew orders of angels, and adding his own twist to the tail, Agrippa's angels and demons certainly brought more than the Christian Church down upon him– it brought him a long-term reputation as a sorcerer, or even Satan himself.

Agrippa believed that 'all things which are similar and therefore connected, are drawn to each other's power'. He concluded that the naming of angels gave one the power to elevate oneself nearer to the divine.

THE GRIMOIRE

A majority of sixteenth-century mystical texts were magical handbooks called grimoires. The word 'grimoire' derives from the French word *grammaire*, which referred to books specifi- cally written in Latin (and from which we have derived the word 'grammar'). The term was used exclusively for spell- books among English-speaking occultists in the early nine- teenth century, after the publication of a handbook of occult and ceremonial magic in 1801, entitled *The Magus, or Celestial Intelligencer*. This had been compiled by Francis Barrett, who gathered his spells, demonology, angelelogy, talismans and ceremonial bits and bobs from older, or ancient, occult hand- books. In the preface, Barrett says:

> We have collected out of the works of the most famous magicians, such as Zoroaster, Hermes, Apollonius, Simon

of the Temple, Trithemius, Agrippa, Porta (the Neapolitan),
Dee, Paracelsus, Roger Bacon and a great many others . . .

In fact, most of the material comes from Agrippa's three books
of occult philosophy and Pietro d'Abano's *Heptameron*. The
Heptameron involved the summoning of seven specific arch-
angels, corresponding to the seven planets, which was not far
removed from Trithemius's classification. D'Abano named
Cassiel as the angel of Saturn, Sachiel the angel of Jupiter,
Camael the angel of Mars, Michael the angel of the Sun,
Anael the angel of Venus, Raphael the angel of Mercury, and
Gabriel the angel of the Moon.

Meanwhile, for the Catholic Church, naming and trying
witches was to become as vicious as the feeding frenzy of a shark
attack. If the Church's darling angels were being hijacked by the
esoteric avant-garde, then the Devil and his billions of demons
were becoming a powerful marketing tool for the Roman
Catholic mission. A kind of reverse, perverse psychology was in
play. Fear the Devil and God will protect you; join the Devil and
God will punish you. Who needs angels when the torture rack
and the stake were deterrents, ridding the populace of all its evil
associates? In the revival of intellectual curiosity and interest in
the occult mysteries, Christianity had a new threat to its power.

There were others, too, in the shape of self-professed
reformers. The first Protestants had already emerged at the end
of the fifteenth century, and the structure, questionable
doctrines and papal corruption of the Catholic Church left the
way open for reformation. There was only one way to contain it
all – 'Burn the witch'.

Malleus Maleficarum

Such demonic forces were at work on behalf of the Church when
the first edition of the *Malleus Maleficarum* was published in
Germany in 1487. It became the leading reference for witch trials
and procedures for the next two hundred years or so, the

rapid development of printing at the time helping to elevate it to the bestseller ranks of the day. Protestants and Catholics alike adopted its rules and judgements, although currently, scholars believe it had less influence than was previously thought. But then the times are always changing.

The authors, two Dominican inquisitors, Heinrich Kramer and James Sprenger, were hired by Pope Innocent VIII in 1484 to prosecute witches in Germany. The zealous, fanatical misogynist Kramer was apparently the key author. Kramer appears to have been a particularly nasty piece of work, and was intent on proving all women were evil. Witchcraft had already been renounced as a pagan pastime and therefore nothing to do with God. God, after all, allowed the Devil to tempt men and test their faith, but the *Malleus Maleficarum* sought to prove that witches were directly in league with the devil and his demons and therefore a visible threat. All of this could well have been a reaction to the growing influence of mystical, holy women, such as the influential Catherine of Siena, who seemed to hold more sway over the royal courts than many a bishop.

The *Malleus Maleficarum* was hardly an original text. It drew most of its ideas from Johannes Nider's *Formicarius* of 1435, but Kramer was particularly obsessed with the sexual lustings of women, the ultimate working of Satan. Kramer, with the permission of God, believed that the Devil's power was greatest in human sexuality, and that women were more sexual than men. Nymphomaniacs, frustrated spinsters and older women were named as having sex with the Devil in a pact to become witches. According to the *Malleus*, 'all witchcraft comes from carnal lust, which is in women insatiable'.

In the first part of the *Malleus Maleficarum*, Kramer poses the question: 'Whether Witches may work some Prestidigatory Illusion so that the Male Organ appears to be entirely removed and separate from the Body.' The answer was, of course, they can and do. We can imagine the lengths, literally, Kramer may have gone to to prove this point to himself.

In his second question, concerning women who copulate with the Devil, he backs up his argument with a few classics:

> Cicero in his second book of *The Rhetorics* says: The many lusts of men lead them into one sin, but the lust of women leads them into all sins; for the root of all woman's vices is avarice. And Seneca says in his *Tragedies:* A woman either loves or hates; there is no third grade. And the tears of woman are a deception, for they may spring from true grief, or they may be a snare. When a woman thinks alone, she thinks evil.

The *Malleus Maleficarum* is made up of three parts. The first part discusses how the Devil is under the power of God, who gives the Devil free reign to perform such evil acts. The second discusses witches, their spells, the pacts they make with the Devil, and various remedies to prevent the Devil getting under your skirts. The third part provides a whole string of abominable stories of witches' sabbats and copulations with the Devil from testimonies of women either framed or tortured by the inquisitors and Kramer himself. The trial, torture procedures, depending on the victim's response, and sentencing were all exclusively aimed at promoting the execution of every witch. The *Malleus Maleficarum* not only highlighted the power of the demon, but ironically the power of the 'demons' inside the Church.

Another work responsible for the frenzied witch-hunts and witch craze in the late sixteenth century was Jean Bodin's persecutory book *De La Demonomanie Des Sorciers*, which followed on from Kramer's work. It described not only how to try, punish and torture witches, but said that inevitably they must all be put to death. Starting with an attack on Pico and Agrippa, Bodin described them both as evil magicians, whose contact with demonic forces had provoked demons to possess women.

Another charismatic figure of the Renaissance was the fanatical Dominican friar, Giordano Bruno (1548–1600), who was burned at the stake for his esoteric beliefs based on Hermetic and alchemical philosophy. Not only did Bruno believe the heretical Copernican view that the earth revolved around the sun, but that God was immanent, there was no hierarchy between man and God, the universe was infinite, and the sun was just another of many suns and solar systems. Bruno also believed that the human soul or spirit could transcend and travel through many levels and worlds. Like Agrippa, Ficino and Giorgi, he believed that the old pagan gods, 'daimons', spirits or angels, whether good or bad, could be manipulated by man if he so chose.

No longer God's envoy, the angel seemed to be every Renaissance man's little helper in the quest for divine knowledge. But one man claimed that he would discover the secret of the universe from his contact with angels – Elizabethan philosopher, astrologer and scientist, John Dee. We need to delve a little further into this brilliant man's obsession with angels and his extraordinary relationship with skryer and alchemist Edward Kelly.

DR JOHN DEE (1527–1608/9)

Eminent historian Dame Frances Yates argued that John Dee was the ultimate 'Renaissance man', embodying everything about the Renaissance, from its esoteric and literary revival, its art, its search for the truth and divine knowledge, to the scientific revolution, which seemed to oppose all that the Renaissance truly represented, the rebirth of the Golden Age. The development of science was simply a discovery of all that was already stored in the cosmic mind, waiting to be revealed by man; and the secrets of the universe were being discovered in a variety of ways. Those who were the founders of modern science, such as Copernicus, Tycho Brahe, Johann Kepler and even Newton, also had a deep interest in the mystical world.

In the early 1570s, John Dee and Thomas Digges (1546–95), another English astronomer and mathematician, along with Danish astronomer Tycho Brahe (1546–1601), discovered a new star in the constellation of Cassiopeia. In 1573, as the star began to fade from view, the findings were published, causing panic and excitement among the European courts. The commotion surrounding this discovery was based on the fear that the universe wasn't all that it appeared to be. The old belief that the cosmos was ordered by God from the moment of Creation and therefore unchanging, was now disputable. It was hardly surprising that the sighting of a comet a few years later in 1577 sent both terror and wonder throughout the royal courts. Predictions came and went, portents of doom were interpreted, the usual soothsayers and charlatans profited from the undecipherable sky, and fears of invasion by Ottoman maurauders, or the failure of Elizabeth's reign, voiced.

In his diary, Dee noted other important astronomical and earth-shattering events around this time. In April 1580, an earthquake shook London, then another blazing comet appeared, this time in the zodiac sign of Pisces in October 1580, just as Elizabeth and the Duke of Anjou indulged in a seemingly amorous courtship, much to the disgust of the Protestant Church. Dee supposedly advised Elizabeth that the Duke of Anjou would die a violent death very soon, and therefore marriage was not advised. In fact, he died of malaria the following year. It was a turbulent time.

In 1583, another rare event took place in the heavens – the triple conjunction of Saturn and Jupiter in Pisces, that is it occurred three times in the same year. The last time this had happened was in 7 BCE, a year believed to be the true year of Jesus's birth. The phenomenon was considered to be the Star of Bethlehem. The transits of Jupiter and Saturn are still used today by astrologers who work with the stock markets and huge changes in world economic trends. For Dee, 1582–3 was to be the year that his life changed.

Although he had apparently dabbled in magic, like many other scientists and philosophers of his day, Dee was particularly interested in Cabala. He had a huge library and had sought many of the most prized esoteric books in Europe. On a visit to Antwerp, he'd heard that a rare copy of Trithemius's *Steganographia,* hunted by scholars for over fifty years, had turned up in town. Dee, who had already acquired a copy of Trithemius's earlier book, *Polygraphia,* was an advocate of cryptography, a fashionable intrigue at royal courts. At the time, the *Steganographia* was simply a work on angelic magic, revealing the mystical secrets of the divine. To someone as passionate about seeking divine knowledge as Dee, it was the road to revelation.

Dee had already used skryers – mediums or channelers – to contact spirits, but with the arrival of Edward Kelly (1555–97) in his life in 1582, the angels seemed to be more easily invoked. No one is really sure of the true relationship between Dee and Kelly, and we can of course imagine and invent what we like. But it seems that Kelly had a powerful influence over Dee, to such an extent that by the time of their final split, in 1587, Kelly had not only become a prominent alchemist in his own right, but had persuaded Dee to a 'wife swap'.

The early séances involved a host of different spirits, such as Anchor, Michael and Uriel, while wicked spirits came but were sent away. Magical talismans, incantations and various instructions were quickly revealed by the angels. Uriel was of particular interest to Dee, not only for his impressive appearance in the Pseudepigraphic book, *The Life of Adam and Eve*, but in the Book of Enoch, where Uriel reveals the secrets of the Tablets of Heaven to Enoch. Dee had also heard rumours of lost Books of Enoch that set out the divine language God had taught to Adam. Much communing with the angels led Dee to conclude that this language could surely be transmitted by an archangel, such as Uriel, and its discovery would hold the key to the secret knowledge of the universe. (If only he'd invoked Inanna instead.)

Recording the summoning of Michael and Uriel in his journal, Dee described the séances performed under the spell (literally or psychologically) of Edward Kelly. Kelly was either a good medium or a good trickster, or both. It is also possible that he was under the delusion that he really did hear spirits and angels. Whatever the case may have been, his visions were not only vivid, but often prophetic. He enchanted angels and he enchanted Dee. His ability to use complex cabalistic diagrams and spells, his sophisticated knowledge of language and his ability to call up Enochian angels into the ether, led Dee to try to convince King Stephen of Poland and Emperor Rudolph II (perhaps on the hidden political motivations of Kelly) of the importance of angelic communication.

Dee also deciphered codes in his quest to find the whereabouts of hidden treasure under Kelly's recommendations. He was contacted by another angel, namely El, who promised the lost Books of Enoch would be his very soon, and told him to dig for the lost treasure; the constant angelic dictation of the magic language meant he had barely time to transcribe it, and he and Kelly began to argue.

Kelly, disturbed and bewitched by his own demons, whether hallucinatory or real to him, began to complain of being 'filled with fire', alluding at the same time to the recent burning of an adulterous couple and his own wretched marriage. By the time the less than angelic spirit Madimi arrived on the scene, Kelly was calling on demons as well as angels. Kelly's interpretation of a vision and messages from Madimi, that the two men should wife swap, alarmed Dee, so why did Dee go ahead with the pact? Perhaps Kelly's performance was breathtaking, or perhaps philosophically and psychologically, it was what Dee wanted to believe, see and hear. Yet wife swapping was the last straw. When Dee asked why he should agree to such a pact, Madimi, the spirit, answered through Kelly: 'Your own reason riseth up against my wisdom. Behold you are become free. Do that which most pleaseth you.'

Dee realized he had offered up his soul as some kind of pawn in a very elaborate game. Was it a test of his faith, or was it all a great deception? Yet he agreed, perhaps because he had always wanted to believe that the angels were on his side. Experiential magic convinced him that he was communicating with the spirit world, and that meant involving himself in its ritual, its performance, its experiments and the sacrifices he must pay for that knowledge. This was a knowledge he wanted to introduce to the higher powers of public and royal life.

Kelly's subsequent rise to fame as an alchemist soon turned to misfortune, and his last famous sighting was reported in 1598 by the Czech alchemist, Matthias Borbonius, yet his infamous visions of angels and demons lived on.

Dee was enchanted not only by Kelly, but by the magic of the times. He'd hoped that the angels would lead him to a divine truth, the one he sought all his life, but all he discovered was that 'neither any man living, nor any book I could yet meet withal, was able to teach me those truths I desired and longed for.'

AVENGING ANGELS

If angels had become darlings of the occultist renaissance, the Devil was finding himself equally at home in the obsessive mindset of the Reformation and its later Counter Reformation backlash.

At the latter end of the fourteenth century, a major event occurred known as the papal split, and also by its grand title, 'The Great Schism of Western Christianity', which was considered to be a direct cause of the Reformation. Basically, two men claimed to be the Pope, causing a diplomatic and theological crisis that divided Europe, and led to widespread revelations of corruption in the Catholic Church. By the time it was sorted out in 1416, a new wave of thinking had emerged. Self-professed reformers, particularly in northern Europe, began to protest at the nefarious doctrines and infrastructure of the Roman Catholic Church. By the time Martin Luther (1463–1546), a German priest and professor of theology, published his controversial ninety-five theses in 1517, the warped antics of the Church were well and truly laid bare for all to see.

These reformers split from the Catholic Church and created 'protestant' churches, which later provoked a Counter Reformation, and Europe was divided into predominantly Catholic in the south, and Protestant in the north. The Protestants eventually split again into other faiths, including Calvinists, Presbyterians, Puritans, Lutherans, Anglicans and so on. Martin Luther was excommunicated by the Pope and outlawed by the Holy Roman Emperor, Charles V.

Luther believed that salvation was received by the grace of God not just for good deeds, but by utter faith in Jesus as a redeemer of sin. Apart from the tremendous work he did in reforming the Church, including setting a role model for marriage among the clergy and priesthood, translating the Bible into German and writing hymns, he was in his later years overtly anti-Semitic, believing that the Jews were entirely responsible for the murder of Jesus and probably everything else.

JOHN CALVIN (1509–64)
But what were the rebellious Protestants to do with the angels? They undoubtedly originated in the pagan past, but yet had been worthy of worship by the Catholic Church. To get round the tricky dilemma of angel worship, the subject was largely dismissed, but it was agreed that angels were 'useful' and sent by God. Luther noted that 'an angel is a spiritual creature created by God for the service of Christendom and the Church'. But another great reformer, John Calvin, the French theologian who split from Catholicism in 1530, had much more to say about angels than that.

In his work entitled *Institutes of the Christian Religion* (1536), Calvin approached the whole subject of angels with a heavy dose of disdain. Although he advises the only angels worth their salt are those mentioned in the scriptures, he warns against propitiating angels, and insists that Christ is superior to them, and that questions of rank, number and nature of angels are merely 'the vain babblings of idle men'.

However, Calvin accepted their protective attributes and commented that, 'angels are the ministers and dispensers of the divine bounty towards us. They regard our safety, undertake our defence, direct our ways, and exercise a constant solicitude that no evil befalls us.' However, he thought it highly unlikely that each individual has a personal guardian angel, because a 'fancied divinity has been assigned to angels from many an idle man'. Calvin then argued that Dionysius's angelic hierarchy was pointless and unprofitable, and dismissed the Neo-Platonists as if they were flies buzzing around his head:

> Away then, with that Platonic philosophy of seeking access to God by means of angels and courting them with the view of making God more propitious – a philosophy which presumptuous and superstitious men attempted at first to introduce into our religion, and which they persist in even this day.

The Devil, on the other, more sinister, hand, generated a flurry of writings as both Luther and Calvin took the fallen angel seriously. Calvin maintained, 'the duty of a theologian is not to tickle the ear, but confirm the conscience.'

The Protestant view of Satan followed the medieval tradition. God had created Lucifer, the highest of angels, but because of his pride, he chose to betray his creator by presuming to imitate God. Thrown out of heaven, Lucifer, eager for revenge, corrupted Adam and Eve. God then turned humanity over to the Devil, who tempts mankind daily to test individual faith, thus causing all worldly evil. To each person, he assigned an individual demon, who would test and encourage his own sins;

and the Devil and his demons can appear anywhere and in any form, even as Christ himself. In fact, all human sinners, stated Luther, are servants of the Devil.

Luther had his own personal struggle with Satan, whether the psychological demons within himself, or the apparent external one. His first ambition had been to study law, but a lightning storm terrified him into believing the Devil was out to get him, and he decided to devote his life to God. Fear and a persecution complex dominated Luther's life, and became his constant companions. He writes of the Devil pelting nuts at the roof, rolling logs down the stairway, appearing as a serpent or a star. Grunting like a pig and smelling foul, Satan lodged in Luther's bowels, appearing as faeces and flatulence. Luther believed, like the desert fathers, Evagrius and John Cassian, that the purer your faith in God, the more the Devil would try to lead you astray.

Europe was divided religiously, and the laws of science were beating their wings against many a man's soul. In the Renaissance era, more fascinating goings-on were to be discovered in the 'real, material, scientific world'. If astronomers, the new breed of astrologers, marvelled that the cosmos was not as predictable as was once thought, it meant to the greatest thinkers and theologians alike, that God's immaculate creation was now in question, too.

LOSS OF THE ANGEL

Simultaneously, Christian angels began to lose their status and power. The Catholic Church floundered, then counterattacked, and Protestants, humanists and Renaissance men found better ways to 'idle' their time away.

The child angel was born, influenced by mythological messenger spirits, the Greek Erotes, associated with Eros. Donatello (1386–1466) had been the original Renaissance inspiration behind the winged infants, later called 'putti' (little men), who became fashionable decorative motifs in both Christian and secular art throughout the next few centuries.

The sensual Renaissance gave way to a Baroque Catholic southern Europe and a Puritanical north. If the Protestants preferred secular themes, such as diligence and asceticism, the Catholic Reformation induced the expression of explicitly ornate, highly religious themes, with no sign of pagan influences. As Baroque turned to eighteenth-century rococo, artists idealized all spiritual beings, gilding their churches, furniture and homes with fashionable but dispirited angels, cherubs and putti. The divine message now was that angels were everywhere. The early messengers, reshaped by orthodox religions to meet the purpose of their religious message, were now free to be portrayed by each individual with his own message.

The eleventh-century Byzantine historian, Michael Psellus, had classified daimons as 'old gods, spirits and fallen angels' and grouped them as starry, airy, earthy, watery, fiery and subterranean. By the time of the grimoires, daimons and fallen angels were mutually exclusive. With free will, the daimon was considered a demon, without it, he/she stayed an angel. The divine messenger no longer relayed a message; he had intelligence, therefore he could manipulate his message, which is why angels in occult and religious ritual were desperately called on to 'thwart' demonic spirits. Examples of 'thwarting' angels include Raphael who binds Asmodeus, Uriel for Ornias, and Gabriel who thwarted Barsafael.

Angels had been employed as the go-betweens of God and humanity, they had fought the Devil and helped make Christianity victorious. Yet the more they became socially acceptable, let loose in the collective imagination, worshipped, indulged in the arts or summoned by magicians, the more the 'divine' was becoming a personal experience. The ego was in vogue.

This was dangerous for orthodox religion. Angels, from the point of view of both Protestant and Catholic Churches, were safer locked away in the realms of heaven, as pure abstract intellect, surrounding God's throne and having little to do with the goings-on of kings, magicians or artists. Poetry, too, had found a place for Satan, and one that was uncomfortably reminiscent of the anti-heroes of Greek mythology.

JOHN MILTON (1608–74)

While Catholic artists fell in love with their Baroque putti, Puritanism was falling out of line in mid-seventeenth-century England. The English Republic lasted from 1649 to 1660 – led by Oliver Cromwell from 1653 to 1658 – but came to an end with the restoration of the monarchy. During this purist era, a young man serving under Cromwell, a political activist who had rejected the Catholic Church and the divine ideology of kingship, revived a form of poetry, dear to the heart of Shakespeare, known as iambic pentameter, or non-rhyming verse.

Milton's 'Paradise Lost' is complex in plot with political and mythological allusions, but is ostensibly concerned with the fall of Adam and Eve and the positive outcome of negative experience. Pamphleteer and poet, Milton coined the word 'pandemonium', which literally means 'all the demons', for his Devil's assembly hall. The parallels of the fallen angels to the political uprising and overthrow of the monarchy were also a literary device. Rebel angels discuss how to overthrow heaven, and debate their tactics in Pandemonium, just as Oliver Cromwell and fellow activists had their debates in Parliament.

The angel Raphael warns Adam not to eat the fruit of the Tree of Knowledge, for

In the day thou eat'st, thou diest;
Death is the penalty imposed, beware,
And govern well thy appetite, lest Sin
Surprise thee, and her black attendant Death.

Adam asks Raphael for knowledge concerning the stars and the heavenly orders, to which Raphael replies with a warning:

> Heaven is for thee too high
> To know what passes there;
> be lowly wise.

Milton's Christian world view held that man was never going to be equal to the angels, and all pagan gods were devils, although along with its parodies of political debate and military heroism, 'Paradise Lost' portrays Satan as a sympathetic character, perhaps a quirky lampoon of Oliver Cromwell himself. Satan is both the fallen hero we love to hate, but also the dark anti-hero, or the dark side of ourselves.

Satan's words 'Better to reign in Hell, than serve in Heaven' may well have summed up Milton's own views on religious idolatry, his rejection of the Catholic Church and the divine ideology of kingship. It may also have summed up the psychic indigestion of the populace of the day. Maybe God, Christianity, the Reformation and all its spiritual strutting, had accomplished only endless war and strife with not much of an angel in sight. In a way, Milton knew what was coming. Religious power had gradually been eroded over the past few centuries, and in Europe at least, was about to be turned upside down with the coming age of enlightenment and the scientific revolution. But even the scientists had a problem with angels.

11

TRACKS OF ANGELS IN THE EARTH

'I saw the angel in the marble and carved until I set him free'

Michelangelo (1475–1564)

'The more materialistic science becomes, the more angels shall I paint: their wings are my protest in favour of the immortality of the soul.'

Edward Burne-Jones in a letter to Oscar Wilde

From the nurturing winged goddesses of Egypt, sculpted in high relief on pharaohs' tombs, to the rococo putti's puffed-up cheeks and tiny testicles, we have come a long way in the history of angels. By the nineteenth century, the angel declined in religious interest, its appearance more a literary or artistic device, which to some may have demeaned its divine connection, to others, enhanced it.

From the seventeenth century until the end of the nineteenth, apart from its exclusivity in mystical visions and art, the angel archetype became dormant, out of demand and mainly denied, repressed, projected or sublimated – as any good psychoanalyst would tell you. Yet there were some strange goings-on beneath the world of materialism, not so much in the corridors of orthodox religion but in more esoteric ones. The angel, in its true sense of the word, the 'messenger', was not so much dead but, like the Egyptian god whose sleeping phallus rises at dawn, was lying dormant, patiently awaiting its revival with one eye open. And some who professed to a scientific bent had enough curiosity to enter the realms where rationalists usually feared to tread.

THOMAS BROWNE (1605–82)

Sir Thomas Browne was one of these. A Royalist and scholarly medical doctor, he lived most of his life in Norwich, and was knighted by Charles II on the restoration of the monarchy. Like most of his contemporaries, Browne believed that Satan was the power behind the ancient pagan world's obsession with mysticism, polytheism, divination and magic. Yet he was intrigued. A sincerely orthodox medical man, he nevertheless had connections with Elias Ashmole, a celebrated officer of arms, well known for his alchemical dabblings and Hermetic beliefs. Ashmole believed the philosopher's stone was 'the food of the angels'. But getting anywhere near the banquet table was a hard task. Browne, for all his medical and Christian background, was still fascinated, and in his best-known work, *Religio Medici,* published in 1642 – not only a great work of prose, but a bestseller in its time – he says, 'the Severe Schools should never laugh me out of the philosophy of Hermes, that this visible world is but a picture of the invisible', thereby aligning with most of Hermetic and Neo-Platonic philosophy.

Something of an eclectic philosopher, Browne, forever enquiring, witty and sometimes cryptic, gathered ideas from

Greek, Christian, Jewish and Hermetic philosophy in an attempt to free the intellectual spirit as if it were an angel itself.

> Let thy studies be free as thy thoughts and contemplations, but fly not only on the wings of imagination, join sense unto reason, and experiment unto speculation, and so give life unto embryon truths, and verities yet in their chaos.

The angel of intellect was being reborn.

Browne wrote most of his works from a personal perspective, steeped in his own fascinating ventures into mysticism and alchemy. He introduced wit and humour, and spiritual depth, not forgetting his Christian conscience and upbringing, into the worlds he longed to unite – science and mysticism.

Browne worried about dreams and the influence of demons, and whether angels were actually as significant in our dreams as we thought demons to be. In *On Dreams*, he says:

> That there are demoniacal dreams we have little reason to doubt. Why may there not be angelical? If there be guardian spirits, they may not be inactively about us in sleep; but may sometimes order our dreams: and many strange hints, instigations, or discourses, which are so amazing unto us, may arise from such foundations.

In *Religio Medici*, he also wonders if the discovery of 'many secrets', whether premonitions, oracles or:

> ominous prognosticks, which forerun the ruines of States, Princes, and private persons, are the charitable premonitions of good Angels, which more careless enquiries term but the effects of chance and nature. [He continues] that mysteries ascribed to our own inventions have been the courteous revelations of Spirits. [This leads him to conclude] that not onely whole Countries, but particular

persons, have their Tutelary and Guardian Angels. It is not a new opinion of the Church of Rome, but an old one of Pythagoras and Plato; there is no heresie in it; and if not manifestly defin'd in Scripture, yet is it an opinion of a good and wholesome use in the course and actions of a man's life, and would serve as an Hypothesis to salve many doubts, whereof common Philosophy affordeth no solution.

For Browne, the guardian angel and the daimon were important intermediaries between the scientific and the religious.

On the hierarchy between God and man, he suggests that:

Between creatures of meer existence, and things of life, there is a large disproportion of nature; between plants, and animals or creatures of sense, a wider difference; between them and Man, a far greater: and if the proportion hold one, between Man and Angels there should be yet a greater. We do not comprehend their natures, who retain the first definition of Porphyry, and distinguish them from our selves by immortality; for before his Fall, 'tis thought, Man also was Immortal; yet must we needs affirm that he had a different essence from the Angels.

In the changing political and scientific development of England in the late seventeenth century, Browne kept the angel/daimon alive, as did his friend Ashmole, who patronised astrology, alchemy, antiquarian books and early Freemasonry. Browne may have not been the most pedantic of scholars, and often he wanders off into the ether himself in his writings; but he was one of many who wanted to know, wanted to believe, and wanted somehow to show that science and mysticism were not so far apart as they seemed. If only he'd met the quantum physicists of the twentieth century.

Browne was one of the few, though, who wasn't entirely convinced by the causal world of rules and measurements. Instead, it's likely he too engaged in trying to experience the 'immeasurable moment', like Newton and Ashmole. But then there was Swedenborg.

EMANUEL SWEDENBORG (1688–1772)

Scientist turned mystic, Stockholm-born Emanuel Swedenborg was anatomically savvy. Renowned for his mechanical inventions and medical research, he attempted to locate the seat of the soul in the body, with test-tube and scalpel in hand. After many a body-snatching exercise (no doubt), he decided that the soul was carried in the blood.

Noted for his research on the pituitary and pineal glands, left and right brain functions and the nervous system, there was something else going on in his own pineal gland – ironically, considered to be the 'third eye', which connects us to higher states of consciousness. In the mid-1740s, Swedenborg began to experience lucid and erotic dreams, which he recorded in a dream journal not published, due to censorship, until the nineteenth century. One entry reads:

> Afterwards during the whole night something holy was dictated to me, which ended with '*sacrarcium et sanctuarium*'. I found myself lying in bed with a woman . . . She with her hand touched my member, and it grew large, larger than it ever had been. I turned round and applied myself; it bent, yet it went in. She said it was long.

After various erotic callings, and a vision of Jesus in a London tavern in 1745, Swedenborg believed God had called him to interpret the true spiritual meaning of the biblical scriptures. The work, *Arcana Caelestia (Heavenly Secrets)*, was published in Latin in eight volumes between 1749 and 1756. Swedenborg revealed, by a series of correspondences, the symbolic nature, rather than the literal one, of the stories. His belief system hinged on Eckhart's earlier ideas, that heaven and hell were self-chosen states of consciousness in this life and the next.

Swedenborg periodically lived in London while working as a secret intelligence agent for a pro-French, pro-Jacobite party in Sweden, 'the Hats'. Known to have experimented with yogic breathing techniques to achieve altered states of consciousness, he said, 'sometimes I was reduced into a state of insensibility as to the body senses, this almost to a state of dying persons.' With knowledge of Eastern mysticism, Cabala and the erotic secrets of the Sabbatians (initiates into the cult of seventeenth-century Jewish rabbi Zabbati Zevi, who claimed to be the messiah), Swedenborg was quite the dashing young eclectic guru.

From his Tantric-cabalistic sources, coupled with his medical knowledge of every millimetre of the male genitalia, he learnt all about spiritual/psycho-sexual control of orgasm, and how to raise the act of conjugal love to cosmic significance. In 1768, he was so inspired by these revelations that he published *The Delights of Wisdom Pertaining to Conjugial Love*. Swedenborg was also familiar with the erotic spirituality of the London branch of the Moravian Church, led by Count Zizendorf, who equated the wound in Christ's body with a vagina. The Count's infamous congregations were urged to imagine, no doubt as they prostrated themselves in front of the Count himself, the spear of Longinus thrust repeatedly into the vagina. In his diaries, Swedenborg recorded many of the lurid sexual ceremonies of the Moravians, which initially attracted, but later repelled him.

So what has all this to do with angels? Swedenborg's influence on the Romantic Movement, steeped in erotic mysticism and cosmic love, was generated from his extraordinary, detailed accounts of travels and communications with angels from other planets and in other worlds. Those drunk on the milk of Swedenborg's paradise were poets and writers, such as Blake, Coleridge, Balzac and Baudelaire; musicians, such as Beethoven; artists, such as Turner and most of the pre-Raphaelite movement; and later Yeats, and Jung.

Swedenborg wrote:

> It must be known that all spirits and angels without exception were once men, for the human race is the seminary of heaven; and that spirits are altogether such as to their affections and inclinations as they had been when they lived as men in the world, for every one's life follows him. This being the case, the genius of the men of every earth may be known from the genius of the spirits who are from it.

Even the angels had something to say on Tantric philosophy and its orgasmic disciplines. In *The Delights of Wisdom Pertaining to Conjugial Love*, an angel guides Swedenborg through not only the celestial heavens, but also through the matrix of the Golden, Silver, Copper and Iron Ages of humanity to see how the ancients made love. Lengthy dialogues with angels, and particularly with the one guiding him, fill this work with a million wisdoms on the value of love, riddled with hidden allusions to the ideal of the merger of mystical and sexual union.

> I have heard from angels, that when these delights ascend from chaste partners on earth, they perceive them to be exalted from themselves and infilled. Because some of the bystanders who were unchaste, to the question of whether this applied also to the ultimate delights [sexual intercourse], they nodded assent and said tacitly, 'How can it be otherwise?'

Swedenborg goes on to discuss that angel-approved sex brings not only a greater intellectual intensity but a mind-blowing orgasm.

His justification for his travels through heaven and hell was that:

> Spirits and angels, when it pleases the Lord, can see the things in the natural world through the eyes of a man; but this is not granted by the Lord with any except those whom He permits to speak with spirits and angels.

Yet Swedenborg also recognized a more profound sense of his Neo-Platonic heritage when he said, 'heaven is within . . . and a man, also, so far as he receives heaven, is a recipient, a heaven, and an angel.'

Swedenborg, like Empedocles, John Dee and Da Vinci, was a daimonic man. But if Swedenborg romanced the angels, spirits and sex, another took the romancing of angels through into the nineteenth century and the birth of Romanticism itself. William Blake also danced with the angels.

WILLIAM BLAKE (1757–1827)

The Angel

I dreamt a dream! What can it mean?
And that I was a maiden Queen
Guarded by an Angel mild:
Witless woe was ne'er beguiled!

And I wept both night and day,
And he wiped my tears away;
And I wept both day and night,
And hid from him my heart's delight.

So he took his wings, and fled;
Then the morn blushed rosy red.

I dried my tears, and armed my fears
With ten-thousand shields and spears.

Soon my Angel came again;
I was armed, he came in vain;
For the time of youth was fled,
And grey hairs were on my head.

William Blake, poet, painter, engraver, visionary and mystic, was born in Soho, London. His father, James Blake, a successful hosier, had already dabbled in Swedenborg's work, and from an early age, William was already communicating his visions of angels, ghostly monks and apparitions of historical figures. In later life, he reportedly replied to a lady, when she asked about a vision he claimed of angels in a hayfield, and where he saw them, 'Here madam,' touching his forehead.

Blake was never particularly successful as an artist in his own day, yet he was commissioned to illustrate many works, including Thomas Butts's *The Book of Job* as well as Dante's 'Divine Comedy'.

At an early age, Blake claimed to have seen 'a tree filled with angels, bright angelic wings bespangling every bough like stars'. According to his Victorian biographer, Alexander Gilchrist, Blake reported the sightings on his return home, and was beaten by his father for telling lies until his mother intervened. Blake said he was given encouragement and support by the archangels to create his mystical art and writings. Apparently, the archangels enjoyed reading them, too. While Blake was living in Felpham, Sussex, he wrote in a letter to John Flaxman:

It [Felpham] is more spiritual than London. Heaven opens here on all sides her Golden Gates . . . voices of celestial inhabitants are more distinctly heard, and their forms more distinctly seen . . . I am more famed in Heaven for any works than I could well conceive . . . which I wrote and painted in ages of Eternity before my mortal life; and those works are the delight and study of the Archangels.

William Wordsworth, like many of his contemporaries, concluded that Blake was 'mad'. But with the publication of Alexander Gilchrist's *Life of William Blake*, his reputation grew and he was championed by both Dante Gabriel Rossetti and the poet Algernon Swinburne. Blake's paintings unveiled angels and Satan in a new light. In one of the illustrations for 'Paradise Lost' (*c*. 1808), 'Satan watching the endearments of Adam and Eve', Satan is depicted as Apollo, sensually caressing a serpent, while in 'the Angel of Revelation' the archangel exudes pure masculine power. Earlier angel imagery, such as in 'Jacob's Ladder' for the Bible series, focuses on diaphanous, fey Greek females, while for 'Paradise Lost', in 'Casting of the Rebel Angels into Hell', the fallen ones would no doubt be seducing a few of the unfallen ones in any gym, with their weight-trained sinews, nimble buttocks and ambiguous genitalia.

Blake blended sexuality, numinosity and luminosity into the human form, and the angel came alive, vivid yet somehow still divine, with rippling six-packs and character-filled eyes. Ethereal yet human, divine yet corporeal, Blake's angels are edgy. They capture human qualities in the divine, and the divine in the human. These are 'real' angels. They are both daimon and human.

ANGELIC SYMBOLISM
It wasn't until the middle to end of the nineteenth century and the evocative and provocative Pre-Raphaelite and symbolist movements in art, that the angel and daimon began to merge as one. For example, in the mystical, beautifully compelling picture by English painter G. F Watts (1817–1904), 'The Dweller in the Innermost', we see our angel and our soul. We see our daimon. If you ever have a chance to see it, don't be surprised at your reaction.

French symbolist Gustave Moreau (1826–98) had a palette of angels as vast as his palette of colours, from angels laden with symbolic red wings, who announce St Cecilia's forthcoming martyrdom, to the work entitled 'Angel Traveller', in which an angel sits on a high building above a city. The guilt of man's materialism weighs heavy in his soul. Moreau's version of 'Jacob Wrestling the Angel' (1878) depicts an androgynous angel, who looks on scathingly as Jacob wrestles with his own phantom. Here are angels who have emotions and human characteristics, and free will becomes a passion. Moreau's contemporary, Frenchman Alexander Leloir (1843–84), paints Jacob and the angel struggling as man against man, sinews bulging, lust brewing between their nearly interlocking loins. Angels were becoming sexy.

Yet it is among the Pre-Raphaelites and symbolists that we find most angels are no longer either/ors, but begin to metamorphose from male to androgynous, and then to pubescent females. Hugo Simberg (1873–1917), in his 'Wounded Angel', shows two young boys carrying off a blindfolded young female fallen angel on a stretcher – a wonderful analogy of the First World War. The ancient goddess messengers had returned, and the message, a long time coming, was 'she had never gone away'. The *Me* hidden by Inanna were about to be rediscovered. But behind the smokescreen of nineteenth-century materialism, the religious angel was absorbed under the loving wings of the Mormons and more esoteric movements, such as occultist Madame Blavatsky and the mystic scientist Rudolf Steiner, calling on anything from angels to ascended masters to get them out of trouble.

BLAVATSKY AND STEINER

Madame Blavatsky (1831–91) was a Russian medium who made a name for herself in New York in 1873, and went on to be one of the founders of the mystical philosophical school of Theosophy.

Her work, *Isis Unveiled*, published in 1877, promoted magic and occultism, while analysing the virtues and downfalls of science and theology. The Theosophists believe that selflessness and traditional virtues lead people ever closer to their divine nature. The solar system, cosmos and planets were regarded as conscious entities, fulfilling their own evolutionary paths. The spiritual units of consciousness in the universe were known as Monads, which could manifest as angels, human beings or in various other forms, including Ascended Masters.

Rudolf Steiner (1861–1925) was born in Austria and lived in Berlin and Weimar, where he became well-known and admired for his scholarly and scientific writings. Steiner became interested in philosophy, psychology and spirituality, and at the beginning of the twentieth century he began his spiritual teaching career through the Theosophical Society, and developed his own school of spiritual thought known as 'Anthroposophy'. From his own clairvoyant powers and experiences, Steiner confirmed the existence of spiritual beings, and in a series of lectures attempted to show how we must cooperate with the angels and their work, and how the modern mind can gain access to the angelic world and benefit from it.

According to Steiner, angels are our invisible guides and lifelong companions. They influence the life of the individual as well as the evolution of the cosmos and humanity. He described how guardian angels interact with other spiritual hierarchies, not just other angels, and believed we spend every night plotting the next day's events with our angel. In a lecture given during the First World War, he pointed out that, as adults, we must raise our consciousness to that of an angel. Children are naturally protected, but adults may not be. He called those who were not intrinsically evil 'luciferic' or 'ahrimanic' after Lucifer and Ahriman, our two favourite dark ones.

In *Angels – Selected Lectures by Rudolf Steiner, 1912–1914*, he states:

the Church, if it understands itself rightly, must consider its sole aim is to render itself superfluous on the physical plane as the whole of life becomes an expression of the realm that lies beyond the senses. Such at least, is the reason behind the work of Angels – to bestow complete religious freedom on humanity.

Someone who wanted complete control over humanity, however, came up with an improbable mythology, which at the time, and maybe even now, has proved Steiner slightly wrong in his prediction that the Church would simply fade away into the vapours. Individually, we may have raised our spiritual consciousness, but then came Joseph Smith and his angelic advisor, Moroni.

MORONI AND THE CHURCH OF LATTER DAYS SAINTS

The angel, Moroni, first appeared to American Joseph Smith, Jr (1805–44), the founder of the Church of the Latter Days Saints, in 1823. The Church and its various offshoots of religious denominations currently claims to have a membership of fourteen million worldwide. Are there enough angels to go round, the angel of Aquinas might ask.

Moroni was apparently the guardian of the 'golden plates', the sacred text of the Book of Mormon, said to be buried in a hill near Smith's home in New York State, USA. Sounding not unlike Inanna's Tablets of Destiny, and the later lost Books of Enoch, the golden plates revealed the answer to all questions ever posed. The angel was first identified by Smith as Nephi, and later, in 1835, identified as Moroni.

Described as an 'angel of light' (Satan in Corinthians II: 14–15), Moroni, according to Smith, told him where to find the golden plates. After they had been translated into English from some obscure made-up language, Smith returned the plates to the angel.

While preparing the first edition of *Doctrines and Covenants*, Smith made additional revelations that a host of angels would come to earth after the Second Coming, and drink wine with himself and Oliver Cowdery (1806–50), one of the first Latter Day Saints apostles. Among the angels would be, 'Moroni, who I have sent unto you to reveal the Book of Mormon containing the fulness of my everlasting gospel'. By 1838, most Latter Day Saints adherents preferred the Moroni 'angle' or angel, who must have embodied a spiritual ideal in a difficult period of American civil unrest, tension and political disorder.

The Book of Mormon, although now believed to be a fabrication of Smith's mind – church leaders would like to believe he was under some kind of divine guidance – was allegedly taken from engraved golden plates written over a thousand years earlier by an indigenous American prophet. The churches of the Latter Day Saints movements believe it was an historical account of God's interest in the affairs of the ancient indigenous peoples of the Americas, written by prophets as early as 2600 BCE.

Angel Moroni statues now flourish worldwide. By 1998, the well-known design for the Bern Switzerland Temple statue, sculpted by Carl Quilter, appeared in over one hundred temples around the world to boost the continuation of the Latter Day Saints movement.

PSYCHOLOGY AND ANGELS

'Man has awakened in a world that he does not understand, and this is why he tries to interpret it. For there is a cosmos in all chaos, secret order in all disorder.'

Carl Jung (1875–1961)

The archetype of the angel is ineffable. It pervades culture and religion at will, its own free will, its own energy. It waxes and wanes with the cycles of history or responds to the calling of the current collective needs. Yet the angel, or messenger, is always there, waiting in the wings. It always has purpose.

With the dramatic developments in psychology at the turn of the twentieth century, Jung for one, put his own stamp on the angel's changing face in the collective psyche. Saint Augustine had, like other Church fathers, believed the angel was basically there to do its job:

> Angels are spirits, but it is not because they are spirits that they are angels. They become angels when they are sent, for the name angel refers to their office, not their nature. You ask the name of this nature, it is spirit, you ask its office, it is that of an angel, which is a messenger.

Late nineteenth-century psychology was more science than art, and the behaviorist was king. But in the world of Jungian psychology, the mystic mind merged with the rational, and the development of existential, humanistic and transpersonal psychology soon followed. The angel and demon began to engage fully in our swamped consciousness again, while the daimon was to come later with the work of James Hillman.

Carl Jung pioneered the theory of the collective unconscious, and the archetypal realms of the cosmos. He suggested that, 'the angel personifies something new arising from the deep unconscious'. Jung was fascinated with good and evil, and in his work, *The Psychology of Transference* (1946), he writes:

> To live in perpetual flight from ourselves is a bitter thing, and to live with ourselves demands a number of Christian virtues . . . It is all very fine to make our neighbour happy by applying them to him, but the demon of self-reflection so easily claps us on the back and says, 'Well done!'

The demon of self-reflection meant that belief systems were changing. Christianity had built itself on Aristotle's deduction and reason, and managed to fit angels and demons into neat categories and hierarchies. The divine, meanwhile, usefully never explained, was considered separate, isolated, outside of man, a measure in itself. Yet for many people with other beliefs, which found meaning in symbol, coincidence, sychronicity and revelation, the turn of the twentieth century brought back to life the alchemist, the Neoplatonist, the Hermetic and the esoteric, hidden beneath the shroud of materialism and the darker aspects of politics and war.

The daimon, too, was unleashed into the psychological world, as the catalyst for change in the individual. The new psychology of Freud and Jung, and later Jung's unfurling of the individuation process, dressed the angel or demon, or both, in a suddenly responsible light. According to Jungian psychology, the quest to become oneself is helped along by the often radical, unexpected or frightening shifts that appear to come from outside of oneself. At the time, these appear to be unwanted by the ego, but later serve as a manifestation of our personal destiny. This was considered to be a 'daimonic force'. In *Symbols of Transformation* (1956), Jung writes:

> The daimon throws us down, makes us traitors to our ideals and cherished convictions – traitors to the selves we thought we were.

Others took it further. Rollo May (1909–94), the American existential psychologist, famous for his work *Love and Will*, attempted to fuse existential philosophy with Freud and Jungian psychology. He believed that the daimonic was a system of motivational forces, different within each individual, each energy personified by a specific daimon. These motivations include simple needs, such as sex, but also higher needs, such as love. The problem occurs when a daimon takes over the person, and the balance of all the daimons is disrupted. Then the daimon becomes evil. For example, the Greek god Eros (considered a daimon by May) is beneficial when still a participant in daimonic energy. But as soon as Eros takes over the persona, we become obsessed and therefore possessed by it. Then it is dangerous. His main doctrine was, 'many people suffer from the fear of finding oneself alone, and so they don't find themselves at all'. It is this existential gap that the angel now attempts to fill – or perhaps, collectively, we are calling for its help to find something to fill the gap that so far has never been filled.

Victor Frankl (1905–97)

Holocaust survivor Victor Frankl was a contemporary of May's, and a key figure in existential therapy. He described his life in a concentration camp in his autobiography, *Man's Search For Meaning*. From his own experiences of both transcendent awareness and extreme suffering, he developed 'logotherapy', a clinical approach to helping patients rediscover meaning in their lives. In his book, he comments:

> For the first time in my life I was able to understand the meaning of the words, 'The angels are lost in perpetual contemplation of an infinite glory.'

Interestingly, those lines don't appear in the Bible, as one would expect. But we can trace them to somewhere closer to home. Puritan clergyman Stephen Charnock (1628–80) writes in his book *Discourses upon the Existence and Attributes of God*, published posthumously in 1682:

> I am sure, under the laws, the figures of the cherubim were placed in the sanctuary with 'their faces looking towards the propitiatory', in a perpetual posture of contemplation and admiration.

Charnock refers here to the Exodus description of God's manufacture of the ark, when the cherubim spread out their wings to face the throne. These words, whether 'a perpetual posture' or 'perpetual contemplation', were the stuff of psychologists, mystics and philosophers. Frankl and May, both in their own small way, infused the collective psyche with a new way of viewing the angel. Contemplating one's fate wasn't too far from contemplating the infinite glory of the divine.

But it was the rise of the demon, perhaps a necessary evil as some might say, and the desperate need to project that evil on to something rather than accept it in oneself, that led to the growing belief that angels were mere fantasy and the demon was very real. And the demon had already been awesomely real in the minds of not only religious fathers, but the mass population, for some time.

12

DEVIL ON HORSEBACK

'The screech owl, the devil's messenger, an ancient familiar, came down that night and took the child. It was to the spirit a swift choice, but yet the she-demon strangled the boy softly, slowly. Each sinew in his neck, each vein that bubbled life, she took and held in her teeth too, and with his blood course left empty, drained of physical life, she hovered above him, taking his spirit, and his soul.'

'Lilith's Revenge'

Back in the early fifteenth century, the Inquisition's ongoing obsession with the extermination of heretics had reached fever pitch. The whole subject of demonology began to blossom as the quills and pens of both the devout religious theologian and the misogynist scholar scribbled and scratched their way across the pages *en route* for the printing press. Over the next few centuries, the Catholic Church expanded its anti-heresy campaign by imposing its papal authority in political and secular circles, too. The hunt was on for anything that reeked of *la diable*.

Across Europe, thousands of women and men were accused of being in league with the Devil for anything from mixing up a pot of herbal medicine and hugging a tree to fornicating with their dog. The link between witchcraft – Wicca still prospered in England among country communities and had nothing to do with the Devil – and Satan, although unproven, generated fear in the popular imagination and raised the testosterone levels of the sexually frustrated clergy.

While angels had proved themselves unreliable helpers against the bubonic plague, the demon and the Devil grew all powerful in the individual and popular imagination, while the fallen angels were still considered worthy of thwarting by occultists in their quests for spirit guides. Throughout Europe, the fashionable way to sway the believer of the opposite faith was through fairground displays of possession. Thousands of years before, in the ancient world, possession by 'demons' or rather 'daimons' or rather 'spirits', both good and bad, was globally accepted. Whether as the harbingers of sickness, or good health, to conquer love, or to requite it, the shaman, medium or witch doctor communed with the spirits, exorcising their evil influence or invoking their goodness.

Christians, both Catholic and Protestant, used the Devil as a deterrent for those who didn't quite get the hang of God, or who sided with anything remotely pagan. Fraudulent circus acts of demonic possession took Europe by storm in the seventeenth century, with sexually repressed nuns performing theatrical writhing acts, trick levitations and spouting obscene language. Often the 'possessed' received favours, possibly for sexual revenge, as in the case of Urbain Grandier (see page 211), or had other ulterior motives of provocation and reward.

An early fake possession, the Darling case occurred in 1596 in Burton on Trent, and was conjured up by a thirteeen-year-old boy, who claimed a witch cursed him for farting, as any mother would. Thomas Darling then began having fits and visions of green angels and green apples. 'How many green angels does it take for a boy to fart?' may have been one of Aquinas's questions that he asked himself. Jesse Bede, a 'man of trade', wrote up the case and sent it to the Puritan exorcist, Reverend John Darrell, who was convinced that Satan, disguised as an angel, was sending messages through the boy. He could only recommend no more green apples and lots more prayer. Shortly afterwards, friends and family of the boy apparently managed to exorcise the demon. Darling continued to have repeated visions of the odd green angel, followed by a multitude of helpful ones and a dove, which to all concerned meant he was cured. He later confessed to faking his demonic possession, then recanted and claimed that all messages were sent from God, not Satan.

Before we enter into the realms of the sexually frustrated nuns of Loudun, we need to see what had happened to the most sexually active she-demon of them all, Lilith.

LILITH

Lilith is described as child-killer, succubus, vampire, enchantress. Once the Sumerian–Babylonian goddess Belit-ili, she was also known to the Canaanites as Baalat, the 'divine lady', and by her earlier links with Inanna, as hand-maiden to the goddess, and as pure spirit, Lil. She has literally flown through Sumerian, Babylonian, Hebrew, Persian and Teutonic mythology, from around 3000 BCE, as destructive wind spirit, Lil, the dark aspect of the Great Mother, and on to her role as night demon or succubus, the cause of erotic dreams and nocturnal emissions feared by many a rabbi.

In the eighth century BCE, she was identified with the Syrian child-killing witch Lamashtu, and associated with stranglers, murderers, owls, hags and screeching nightjars. As the first wife of Adam, she demanded equality, which according to the

Hebrew scriptures, Adam refused. Lilith flew off in a temper to the Red Sea, so Adam sent three angels to bring her back. Finding more pleasure from her demon lovers than dull old Adam, who insisted on the missionary position as being the only way to have sex, she gave birth to a hundred demon children every day. She promised the angels that whenever she saw or heard their names, she would not harm mothers, men or children.

Also known as Leviathan's mistress, the wife of Samael, the Devil, and even God's consort when the Shekinah was in exile, Lilith has been suppressed and outcast since the sixth century BCE, and her only real appearance in the Bible is in her desolate location near the Red Sea (Isaiah 34: 14):

> Wild cats will meet hyenas there,
> The satyrs will call to each other,
> There Lilith shall repose
> And find her a place to rest.

Protective amulets against Lilith's apparently destructive powers were widespread in medieval times, perhaps as a result of the extreme, misogynistic accusations against her in the thirteenth-century's Jewish 'Book of Splendour', known as the 'Zohar':

> As soon as Lilith came forth, she went up and down till she reached the 'little faces' [cherubim] and desired to cleave unto them and be one of them, and was loathe to depart from them. But the Holy One, blessed be He removed her from them and made her go below.

The Zohar links Lilith and Eve in mutual sin, and warns men to be vigilant against the seductive wiles of women, most of whom are likely to be Lilith in disguise – 'Lilith is always present in the bed linen of man and wife when they copulate.' Lilith also hovers over men, and 'lays hold of them and cleaves to them, inspiring desire in them'. Origastic, enchanting Lilith is, according to the macho-packed Zohar, 'a despicable harlot'. However, by the twentieth century, Jung described her as a 'shamanistic anima', in other words, the feminine intermediary of the psycho-spiritual world. In terms of the psychological transformative process towards individuation, a conscious encounter with Lilith is necessary on the path to wisdom and enlightenment.

An amulet from the eleventh-century cabalistic work *Sepher Raziel*, published in 1701 in Amsterdam, shows the three angels sent by Adam to bring Lilith back to Eden, Sanvai, Sansanvai and Semangelof. Above the drawings of the angels, interestingly not in human form, but represented as birds, are the words: 'Adam, Eve away from Lilith'. Above is a list of seventy other angels plus further incantations. The bird motif can be seen in a parchment amulet held in the Sir Isaac and Lady Edith Wolfson Museum Collection in Jerusalem.

Jung also noted in *Symbols of Transformation*:

Angels are really birds . . . and that in the Jewish tradition angels are masculine. The symbolism of the three angels is important because it signifies the upper aerial, spiritual triad in conflict with the 'one' lower, feminine power [i.e. Lilith].

Babylonian incantation bowls were used to trap Lilith's power when the bowl was inverted. A sixth-century bowl depicts Lilith heavily bound in iron chains – common material for binding a demon – and an incantation reads: 'Bound is the bewitching Lilith with a peg of iron in her nose . . . bound is the bewitching Lilith with stocks of stone on her feet.'

Christianity found Lilith and her daughters, the Lilum, useful scapegoats for sexual guilt. As succubi, the Lilum visited celibate monks, who would sleep with hands over genitalia, clutching a crucifix rather than something else. It was believed that whenever a monk had a wet dream, Lilith laughed. Adam's denial of the dark goddess's message of equality, whether in bed or out of it, became a feminist metaphor of patriarchal civilization's cull of matriarchal power.

WITCH CRAZY

The Church's favourite pastime, witch-hunting, was getting out of hand. French lawyer Nicholas Remy (1530–1616) claimed to have sent over nine hundred witches to their deaths in Lorraine, and like his contemporary Jean Bodin, took up his own personal crusade against witches. Remy believed demons raised mountains and extinguished stars, and therefore advocated the torture and burning of all witches. After ten years of hunting out and prosecuting anyone who was remotely different, eccentric or suspiciously heretical, Remy sort to prove that demons and witches were in league in his book *Demonolatry*, published in 1595.

Earlier possessions were recorded by up-and-coming demon experts, such as German Jesuit priest Peter Binsfield (1540–1603), who was a prominent witch-hunter in campaigns against the Protestants. Famous for his association of the Seven Deadly Sins and seven specific demons, he was also responsible for the trial of more than three hundred people accused of witchcraft in Treves between 1587 and 1594.

The fraudulent French demoniac Marthe Brossier raised money from the naive and gullible at the end of the sixteenth century as part of a scam to undermine the Protestant Church by the Catholics. And possessions were recorded by the sixteenth-century Italian exorcist Girolamo Menghi (1529–1609), a leading exorcist of the Renaissance, who was famed for his own books on demonology and his writings on demonic pacts made by witches.

Father Louis Gaufridi

In Aix on Provence, in 1609, began the sensational mass possession case of the Ursuline nuns, their alleged pacts with the Devil and various perverted sexual acts. The case was unprecedented in France. This was the first conviction where a death sentence was based solely on the testimony of a demoniac (the person possessed by the demon). Before this, testimonies from demoniacs were deemed unreliable, because their words were believed to be uttered by the Devil himself.

Father Louis Gaufridi, a popular, good-looking priest from a fairly uneducated background, amused wealthy women with his charm and entertaining ways. He was called in to help fourteen-year-old Sister Madeleine de Demandolx de la Palud. Vain, highly strung and from an aristocratic Provençal family, she had recently been sent home from the new Ursuline convent in Aix en Provence, and was depressed. Gaufridi's visits became unusually frequent. It was no surprise that young Madeleine fell in love with the handsome priest.

Gossip reached the ears of Mother Catherine de Gaumer, head of the Ursuline convent in Marseilles. In 1607, Madeleine was sent there as a novice, and confessed lurid details of her intimacy with Gaufridi. Mother Catherine sent her back to the convent at Aix, well away from the charms of handsome priests.

Two years later, Madeleine's fits, convulsions and visions of demons began. Father Romillon, the spiritual director, tried to exorcise Madeleine, but the demonic possession, like a virus, spread to three other nuns. By 1610, during her manic fits, Madeleine accused Gaufridi of sexual perversity, of denying God, and of giving her a green demon as a familiar. Romillon attempted to exorcise Madeleine on many occasions, and five more nuns became possessed. One, Louise Capeau, performed on a par with Madeleine, and the frustrated Romillon hauled them off to see the grand Inquisitor of Avignon, Sebastian Michaelis, much feared for his recent trial and execution of eighteen witches at the stake.

Michaelis publicly attempted to exorcise the nuns, but failed, and the nuns were sent to another exorcist, François Domptius, a Dominican priest, where Louise became the veritable star of the show. Three demons, Gresil, Verin and Sonnillon, in 'Daf Veda' voices, spoke through Louise, taunting Madeleine with a total of 6,666 demons, who in response, screamed obscenities. Both were so convincing that the audience believed they were all genuinely possessed.

In December, the demon Verin, speaking again through Louise, accused Gaufridi of being in league with the Devil and causing Madeleine's possession. Accused of witchcraft, Gaufridi was jailed by Michaelis, but later released as there was no physical evidence. Madeleine's continued accusations of obscene sexual acts with Gaufridi, plus her horse-neighing impersonations, and wild stories of sabbats where sodomy was performed and babies eaten, brought pressure on Michaelis to do something.

In 1611, Gaufridi was finally brought before a civil court and Madeleine and Louise, the star witnesses, recounted every detail of their possessions, writhing on the floor in orgasmic fits. Madeleine, on some days, admitted she made everything up and was in love with Gaufridi. When examined, Devil's marks were discovered on the soles of her feet and under her left breast. Mysteriously the marks disappeared and reappeared. She twice attempted suicide.

Gaufridi was relentlessly prosecuted, and horrendously tortured until he confessed to being the 'prince of the synagogue' and to signing a pact with the Devil. Michaelis wrote a phoney confession for him, and on 18 April 1611, Gaufridi was found guilty of sorcery, idolatry and fornication, and sentenced to terrible torture, followed by an excruciatingly slow burn on a pile of bushes. He continued to be interrogated and tortured for names of accomplices, and at his final appearance before the court he said that the truth no longer mattered. After his particularly ghastly execution, Madeleine was instantly cured. Yet thanks to Louise continuing to promote her possession by witches, a few months later, a blind girl was convicted of witchcraft and burnt at the stake.

Other convents at Lille and Aix suffered from the possession epidemic and described sabbats similar to Madeleine's own detailed accounts. Were the nuns really witches themselves? Later, in 1642, at the age of forty-nine, Madeleine was accused of witchcraft, and again in 1652, when she was finally sentenced to life in prison.

Father Urbain Grandier

In 1617, not far from Poitiers, in the west of France, Jesuit Father Urbain Grandier had been appointed parish priest in Loudun, a town sharply divided into Huguenot Protestants and Catholics. Handsome, well-educated (unlike Louis Gaufridi) and worldly-wise, he had little trouble seducing women into his angelic arms. Successful and arrogant, Grandier's immoral goings-on were on the tip of most gossip-mongers tongues, as he openly courted Madeleine de Brou, daughter of the king's councillor, and was suspected of fathering a child by Philippa Trincant, the daughter of the king's solicitor. His enemy, the bishop of Poitiers, managed to gather enough evidence to find him guilty of immoral acts in 1630, but Grandier's political connections restored him to full clerical duties within a year.

Attracting local envy and resentment, his enemies approached Father Mignon, head confessor to the nuns at the Ursuline convent, in an attempt to persuade a few of the sisters to fake possession by demons, and to swear that Grandier had bewitched them, thus causing his downfall.

Jeanne des Anges, the mother superior, had recently been appointed, in 1627. An ambitious baron's daughter, Jeanne was rich, extravagant and mean. Hunchbacked and unattractive, she pretended to be pious and saintlike, climbing the ranks of high ambition to become mother superior, as a bitter compensation perhaps for her lack of feminine attributes or miserable deformity.

Jeanne and one other nun agreed to the fake possessions, putting on the usual husky voices and contortionist writhings.

Another version of the story tells that Grandier had turned down Jeanne's offer of the post of canon to the convent, admitting, quite innocently, that he was busy enough in his other priestly roles. This may well have been taken as a physical rejection by Jeanne, and in some accounts, it was Jeanne who enlisted Father Mignon's help to rid the world of Grandier, and to end her lurid sexual fantasies about him. In her reported sexually disturbed visions, he appeared as both angel and the Devil. But the priest had so many enemies, particularly among cuckolded husbands, resentful women and Catholic menfolk, that whether the plan was instigated by Jeanne or by Grandier's rivals, doesn't really matter. It was Mignon's and Jeanne's chance for revenge.

The Ursuline nuns were possessed and Grandier was responsible. The case, like any great play, was packed with theatrics, tricks and deception, as Grandier's enemies sought the back-up of Cardinal Richelieu, who was eager at the time to prove his power in the Church in France. Grandier was arrested as a witch, and although most experts doubted the possessions were genuine – the nuns couldn't speak in foreign tongues, levitate or show clairvoyant skills, which were all tests to prove demonic possession – the pressure against Grandier continued. He had become a political scapegoat in the war against the Protestant Huguenots, who, according to the nuns, were all disciples of Satan.

Former mistresses came forward with stories of sinful sex, and shocking tales of Grandier's diabolical nature escalated. By July 1634, Jeanne had faked a written statement of Grandier's pact with the Devil. All supporters, sceptics and defenders in a campaign to prove Grandier innocent were officially silenced.

In August, Grandier was sentenced to be burned alive at the stake. Protesting his innocence to the end, he told one of the exorcists that within thirty days he, too, would see God. The priest accordingly died, and many of the fraudsters, including witch prickers and torturers, met their end in obscure or unusual circumstances. The Loudun performances continued as a tourist attraction for a few years, but Richelieu, having proved himself all powerful, finally put a stop to the show-manship in 1637.

Louviers

Ten years after the end of the Loudun possessions, another public circus act of mass demonic possession was performed by sisters from various convents in Louviers, France, in 1647. Again, the conviction of the priest rested on the testimonies of the demoniacs. In one hit, eighteen nuns were possessed on the instigation of Sister Madeleine Bavent. The alleged bewitchment was from the dead spiritual director of the nunnery, Mathurin Picard, and the vicar of Louviers, Thomas Boulle. Accused of taking Bavent to a black mass, indulging in orgies and eating babies, the other nuns became possessed, too. Satan not only forced them to perform unspeakable sexual acts, but also attempted to lead them away from God. Exorcisms became public shows, Father Boulle was tortured and the parliament in Rouen finally passed sentence. There was mass hysteria in the streets of Loudun as the Inquisition swept through town, ready to burn anyone as a witch. Sister Madeleine was taken to the church dungeon and the innocent Father Boulle burned at the stake. Meanwhile, the body of the dead Picard was exhumed and burnt.

Salem

If the burnings, Inquisitors and 'tit for tat' Protestant and Catholic religious rivalry were not enough in Europe, the bewitchment craze had already spread across the seas to seven-teenth-century puritanical America. One particular mass possession in Salem, Massachusetts, created witchcraft hysteria and cost the lives of twenty innocent people.

When the Reverend Samuel Parris and his family arrived with their Barbados slaves, John and Tituba Indian, the exotic strangers appeared to have a startling effect on the prudish inhabitants of Salem Village. Tituba told stories of her native African witchcraft heritage to the young Betty Parris in her care, and some of the young village girls, no doubt excited by these accounts, began to dabble in the occult. In January 1692, Betty and some of the other girls (all around the age of twelve) began to have fits and contort their bodies. Whether they truly believed they were possessed or were playing a very dangerous game, no one ever found out, but the authorities believed the girls to be possessed.

The girls accused Tituba along with two other women, Sarah Good and Sarah Osborne, of bewitching them, and sending demons to attack them. Tituba confessed to being a witch, disclosed the whereabouts of a coven of witches in Massachusetts, along with names of those who had signed the Devil's Book, and thus shrewdly became one of the accusers rather than an accused. As the accusations mounted, tension-fuelled hysteria rose among the townspeople of Salem, complicated by the lack of the 'Massachusetts Bay's Charter', which meant they had no legal authority to try capital cases. But the witch-hunt was on. The first suspects were held in prison for nearly six months, and by May 1692, over one hundred people languished in chains due to the girls' accusations.

The new governor, Sir William Phips, established a court of 'Oyer and Terminer' (to hear and determine), and the witches were tried and most were found guilty. The first to be hung was Bridget Bishop in June. Many others followed. A wealthy land-owner, Giles Core, was pressed to death under a pile of stones for refusing to acknowledge the court's right to try him.

The girls' accusations turned towards prominent people, including the governor's wife. Wisely, Phips dissolved the court of 'Oyer and Terminer', and the whole affair was soon viewed as God's atonement for the sins of the colony. After the hysteria had long died down, in 1711, Massachusetts Bay became one of the first governments to pardon and voluntarily compensate victims and their families for its own mistake. In 1693, one of the Salem witch-hunters, Increase Mather, wrote a short treatise declaring that it was virtually impossible to determine if someone were a witch or not.

Which Witch?

Even if many people believed they could determine who was a witch, the number of outspoken critics of witch-hunts was growing, including Reginald Scot (1538–99). No demonologist or theologian, but a well-to-do English countryman and ordinary citizen, Scot was outraged at the tortures, trials and executions of innocent women. His refutation of witch-hunts and witchcraft, entitled *The Discoverie of Witchcraft*, was published in 1584 at the height of the frenzy. Scot was influenced by the German physician, Johann Weyer, who had a personal interest in the supernatural and occult literature, and was an expert in demonology.

Scot believed there were four categories of 'witches' – innocents who were falsely accused; evil people who had the intention to harm others but not by sorcery; people deluded enough to think they'd made a pact with the Devil; and charlatans, frauds and imposters, who persuaded others they could manipulate the spirit world. Although his work was well received by the clergy, James I ordered all copies to be burnt, and then published his own book, *Demonologie*, to prove the existence of witches and demons and refute Scot's work.

Throughout the sixteenth and seventeenth centuries, the topic of demonic possession was tackled by Lutherans, Protestants and Catholics alike. Symptoms of possession included knowledge of secret things; being able to predict the future; the ability to find lost people or items; being able to speak languages never learned, and other complex matters; having supernatural strength. However, insanity was not to be confused with possession, and possession could take place even when those symptoms were absent. It was a tricky subject.

A person suffering from demonic possession was known as a 'demoniac' and more recent ones include eighteenth-century Englishman George Lukins, known as the Yatton demoniac; South African Clara Cele in the early part of the twentieth century; American Roland Doe, who was also known as Robbie Mannheim, in the late 1940s – his story inspired William Blaty's book and the subsequent film *The Exorcist* ; and German Anneliese Michel in the 1970s.

In 1778, Sarah Barber, a visitor to the village of Mendip Yatton in Somerset, England, came across a man wandering the streets in a strange, deluded state. George Lukins, a tailor, aged forty-six, apparently 'sang and screamed in various sounds, some of which did not resemble a human voice; and declared doctors could do him no service'.

Sarah Barber contacted the Reverend Joseph Easterbrook, the local Anglican vicar, who subsequently exorcised Lukins. An account of the exorcism was published in the *Bristol Gazette*, which reported that George Lukins, during his alleged possession, claimed that he was the Devil, barked like a dog, sung an inverted Te Deum, and was extremely violent.

In 1906 , Clara Cele, a sixteen-year-old schoolgirl at St Michael's Mission in Natal, South Africa, was said to be able to speak languages she'd never heard before. Nuns reported that Clara revealed intimate secrets of people she didn't know, couldn't bear the presence of holy objects and had super-natural strength, often hurling nuns about the convent rooms or beating them. One nun also commented on her strange voices: 'no animal had ever made such sounds. Neither the lions of East Africa nor the angry bulls. At times, it sounded like a veritable herd of wild beasts orchestrated by Satan had formed a hellish choir.' According to other witnesses, Clara levitated five feet in the air, sometimes vertically and sometimes horizontally; and when sprinkled with holy water, she came out of the possession.

With the development of psychiatric and psychological approaches in the later twentieth century, possession became highly controversial, as in the case of Anneliese Michel, who was the inspiration for two films, *The Exorcism of Emily Rose* and *Requiem*. Born in Bavaria, Germany, in 1952, Anneliese was a devout Catholic, and slept on a bare floor in the middle of winter as an atonement for the sins of drug addicts or immoral priests. From her high-school days, she began to suffer epileptic fits, had hallucinations and heard voices telling her she would 'stew in hell'. By 1973, suicidal and depressed, she had developed a taste for coal, spiders and her own urine.

By 1976, Anneliese had physically deteriorated, doctors could do nothing and exorcisms proved futile. The demons had, according to her last experiences of exorcism, triumphed over good, and she died. The autopsy revealed the cause of death was starvation, but the case created a great deal of controversy. Pilgrimages were made to her grave by those who believed she'd sacrificed herself to God, and she became venerated to the level of sainthood. More controversy followed, when two exorcists and her parents were convicted of negligent homicide. Some believed she was possessed; others that she died from medical and psychiatric causes.

PSYCHIATRY AND DEMONIC POSSESSION
Psychiatric and psychological experts tend to stamp around the demonic world waving a large stick. Some, such as the pioneering American psychiatrists Scott Peck and Dr Ralph Allison, stir up journalistic fervour; others, more conventional psychiatrists, explain it all as abnormal functioning in the brain

and nervous system. Various disorders have symptoms that may, to some, seem similar to demonic possession. These include schizophrenia, periods of psychosis, dissociative identity disorder, and Tourette Syndrome.

Psychiatrists conclude that if all types of behaviour, including emotional states and cognitive states, are produced and mediated solely by the brain, that leaves no potential for such a phenomenon as demonic possession to exist, and such cases would clearly be instances of various illnesses. However, neuroscience has not yet been able to explain all characteristics common to purported cases of demonic possession, including levitation, wounds on the victim that have not been self-inflicted or are the result of some other physical source, knowledge of languages never before known, and psychic abilities, such as precognition. Science has yet to explain the changes in temperature of the room, which usually becomes icy cold, the appearance of words or writing, instances of odd sounds, and telekinesis. The controversy is ongoing, and probably will be until science discovers, dare one imagine it, a measurement for mystery – maybe something like three yards of mystery equals four to the power of God.

Scott Peck (1936-2005)

Prominent American pyschiatrist Scott Peck is best known for his 1978 bestselling book *The Road Less Travelled*, which teaches 'that our growth as human beings is being assisted by a force other than our conscious will'.

In *People of the Lie: The Hope For Healing Human Evil*, Peck claimed that two of his patients suffered not only from multiple personality disorders but some kind of possession. After several possible cases of possession had been referred to him, and being involved in two exorcisms, he was convinced of the existence of Satan.

Peck theorized that people who are possessed are victims of evil, but not inherently evil themselves. Influenced, and based on specific accounts, by Malachi Martin, his diagnostic approach to possession has since been questioned. It has been argued that it is not possible to find formal records to establish the veracity of Martin's cases, since all exorcism files are sealed by the Archdiocese of New York. Peck later admitted that Martin was a charlatan, manipulator and liar.

Malachi Martin (1921–99)

Malachi Brendan Martin, Catholic priest, theologian and professor at the Vatican, had a major success with his 1970s book on Exorcism, *Hostage to the Devil*. A controversial bestseller, and at the time raved about as 'a chilling account of modern American culture, evil and possession', it recounted five cases of possession and exorcism, now seemingly fabricated. In his last introduction, to the 1992 edition, Martin attacked Satanism, Ouija boards, the Enneagram and Transcendental Meditation, which were all popular at the time. He writes:

> the effective cause of Possession is the voluntary collaboration of an individual, through his faculties of mind and will, with one or more of those bodiless, genderless creatures, called demons.

He goes on to claim that possession isn't a static state, but an ongoing process whereby an individual receives and internalizes knowledge, then chooses to act upon that knowledge. The disposing factors that are likely to induce the individual to collaborate with a possessing demon include 'instruments', such as tarot cards, and attitudes, such as Transcendental Meditation, astrology and other psychic phenomena. It is interesting that Harry Potter books have recently been added to the Vatican's list of don'ts 'if you want to avoid possession'.

Father Gabriele Amorth (b 1925–)

Another controversial figure, Father Gabriele Amorth is head exorcist of the Catholic Church, and has published many mass market books detailing instances of exorcisms. From an article in *The Times*, (13 March 2010), it appears that Father Amorth has experienced over 70,000 exorcisms.

Father Amorth. Memoirs of an Exorcist. My life fighting against Satan, compiled by Marco Tosatti and published in November 2010, received a great deal of attention when Amorth, in various interviews, claimed that not only were the Nazis, Hilter and Stalin possessed by Satan, but that the current sex scandals within the Catholic Church are the result of demonic possession. His intention was to help rid the Church of its demonic persecutor.

Father Jose Antonio Fortea Cucurull, a Spanish priest and theologian who specializes in demonology and is currently studying for his doctorate of theology in Rome, has recently refuted Amorth's claims that 'legions of demons have lodged' in the Vatican, and Amorth's other sweeping statements, such as 'all evil is due to the intervention of the Devil, including paedophilia'.

Back in 2000, in an interview with the *Sunday Telegraph*, Amorth stressed, 'People need to know what we do.' His was another of the voices that warned parents about the Harry Potter novels, noting the books' attempt to make a false distinction between black and white magic, when the distinction 'does not exist, because magic is always a turn to the Devil'.

He also observed that the new Catholic rite of exorcism is 'a farce, an incredible obstacle that is likely to prevent us from acting against the demon'. He noted that the rite forbids exorcisms on people who have been reportedly subjected to evil spells. Father Amorth exclaimed:

Absurd! Evil spells are by far the most frequent causes of possessions and evil procured through the demon: at least 90% of cases. It is as good as telling exorcists they can no longer perform exorcisms. [The new rite] Solemnly declares that one should not carry out exorcisms if one is not certain of the presence of the devil. [He considered it]

A blunt weapon . . . Efficacious prayers, prayers that had been in existence for twelve centuries, were suppressed and replaced by new ineffective prayers.

In *The Times* interview, he commented:

Angels exist, and how, but they are not as depicted in art – they are pure spirit. We all have guardian angels. Demons are, of course, fallen angels who rebelled against God; that is why they are so intelligent, and so arrogant.

Of course.

But it was angels in their new-age packaging who became the new threat to orthodox religion. The angel has freed itself from the very thing that tried to pin it down, for the angel, whether fallen or not, seems to have more free will than was believed. If demons possessed us for a while, it is Hesiod's 'mist-apparelled' daimones of the Golden Age who have recently made their secret comeback.

13

TOUCHED BY AN ANGEL

Antony: Say to me,
Who's fortunes shall rise higher, Caesar's or mine?
Soothsayer: Caesar's.
    Therefore O Antony, stay not by his side;
Thy daemon – that's thy spirit which keeps thee,
– is Noble, courageous, high, unmatchable,
Where Caesar's is not; but near him thy angel
Becomes afeard, as being o'erpower'd; therefore
Make space enough between you.
                    William Shakespeare, *Antony and Cleopatra*,
                                        Act II, Scene III

The word, 'ecstasy' derives from a Greek root, meaning 'a standing outside oneself'. It is this mystical 'standing outside of oneself' that has led many to believe they have seen or encountered angels. If the Church had mostly frowned upon the worship of angels, and if the summoning of them by occult means induced hysteria under the Protestant and Catholic frocks of the Renaissance, then their recorded apparitions have, ironically, been welcomed by those of Christian faith as evidence that at least something exists 'up there'. But who are the people who have seen, tasted, touched an angel? Not all recorded mystical encounters are religious ones, and many are now considered to have been induced by altered states of consciousness or out-of-body experiences.

The accounts related here are mostly drawn from examples of experiences by Christian female mystics. It is hardly surprising, in the flurry of witch-hunting and misogyny, that women married to the Church expressed their 'ecstasies', both spiritual and covertly sexual, through communion with God or Jesus. On the other hand, the ordinary 'Mary Pilcher' of East Gibbings was accused of having sex with the Devil if she even dared to smile at a priest. Interestingly, most of the people who have seen angels have also recorded sightings or experience of demons, and conveniently managed to overcome all devilish temptations. But mystics, whether Christian, pagan or of another faith, have something in common – they are all inspired, by either a divine intervention or their own psychological one, to transcend this earthly lot and 'stand outside themselves'.

Inevitably, there are many 'ordinary' people who have visions of angels, although according to theology scholar Emma Heathcote-Jones, they are often reluctant to talk about these experiences, either from embarrassment at being laughed at, or because, to them, it's an intimacy not to be disclosed. Her insightful and uplifting book, *Seeing Angels*, presents accounts of contemporary angel sightings and experiences as a feature of our current subcultural obsession with all things spiritual .

The following visions and encounters with angels are examples that have influenced the collective and individual imagination. Whether we believe in them or not hinges on whether we have ourselves experienced an angelic encounter, or merely 'entertained angels unawares'.

Cecilia

Beginning at the latter end of the third century, a legend grew around a young Roman virgin, Cecilia, who was to become the well-loved Christian saint of music. Cecilia was born to a Roman senatorial family. As was the custom, an arranged marriage was agreed; Valerianus was her dashing young pagan suitor. On their wedding night, Cecilia told Valerianus that she was secretly betrothed to an angel, who jealously guarded her virginity, and therefore Valerianus on no account was allowed to consummate the marriage.

Another version suggests that Cecilia's angel was simply her conscience telling her not to consort with a pagan, and unless Valerianus converted to Christianity she was certainly not going to have sex with him. Valieranus, desperate to see this angel, and rather desperate to get in the sack with Cecilia, agreed to meet her mentor Bishop Urbanus, to be baptized. His conversion to Christianity would ensure him a sighting of both the angel and the boudoir. On his return, the angel presented the couple with crowns of roses and lilies, before flapping its wings and returning to heaven. Tibertius, Valerianus's brother, wanted to see the angel, too, and so agreed to be baptized.

After more angelic meetings, the brothers devoted them-selves to burying the daily pile-up of slain Christian martyrs, sent for execution by an obscure Roman Prefect. Their sticky ending is uncertain, but their conversion to Christianity meant they were duly executed.

Cecilia had by now, according to various accounts, converted over four hundred people, and was eventually arrested and sentenced to death by suffocation in her own bath. However, for whatever legendary reason, she survived, and an executioner was sent to chop off her head. The man struck three times, but

couldn't sever the head from the body, and left her dying. She
bled for three days, and as she passed away sang praises to God,
the basis for her patronage of music.

Paintings of Cecilia's legend show how the fashion for
depicting angels changed from the medieval era to the Renaissance.
In the early fifteenth-century version by Botticini, a winged,
characterless creature hovers over the couple, while Lelio Orsi, in
the sixteenth century, shows a sensuous, feminine angel, involved
in all the passionate goings-on of the earthly martyrs.

Seventeenth-century artist Domenichino portrays a putti-
like child in attendance while Cecilia plays her cello, heralding
the way for John Waterhouse in the late nineteenth century.
His photographic-like St Cecilia, dressed in Plantagenet
gowns, sleeps on a stylish throne in an Italianate rose garden
beside the sea. The two accompanying angels are beautiful
winged young girls, as graceful, feminine and sensuous as
Cecilia herself. These romanticized angels, along with the
putti of the high Baroque and rococo eras, are what survives
most in the collective imagination today. But then there were
the 'real' mystics, too.

Hildegarde of Bingen (1098–1179)

> 'And thus I [God] remain hidden in every kind of reality
> as a fiery power. Everything burns because of me in the
> way our breath constantly moves us, like the wind-tossed
> flame in a fire.'
>
> Vision 1: 2, *The Book of Divine Works*

A new wave of music, writing and art was evident across
medieval Europe, and the otherworldliness of Christianity was
at its height. Against this background, women tithed into
marriage with God (the purpose of nunneries) were gaining a
voice, among them Hildegarde of Bingen, Elisabeth of Schonau
and Julian of Norwich.

Hildegarde was born into a family of German nobility. As the tenth child, she was dedicated to the Church, and sent to an 'anchoress', Jutta, to be educated. When Jutta died in 1136, Hildegarde was elected head of the small convent at Disibodenberg. She moved to Bingen on the banks of the Rhine in 1136, where she ran the convent and monastry.

From a young child, Hildegarde had visions, but it was not until she experienced a serious illness in her early forties that she began to put pen to paper. After consulting with the pope and St Bernard of Clairvaux, she published her journal, but more as a precedent for other women to tithe themselves to the Church, rather than to champion her experience. *Scivias* was her first account of her visions, and she followed it with two more. Not only did she communicate openly with archbishops, popes and kings, but spoke out against corruption in the Church, wrote music and songs, and painted symbolic paintings of her visions. She often depicted herself as a tiny seated figure with an open book, gazing upwards at a mandala of the cosmos, dotted with angels, demons, winds and stars.

Hildegarde claimed that all her senses were evoked in her 'visions', but most importantly, she saw a brilliant light, and inside the light she saw an even brighter light, which she called 'the living light'. A vision of falling stars turning black as they plunged into the ocean she interpreted as the rebel angels falling from heaven. For all her mystical legacy, her extraordinary influence on holistic healing and the revival of her work by feminists today, she was very much a woman in an insular patriarchal religious world.

She venerated marriage and believed that a man without a woman wasn't much of a man, but condemned adultery and other forms of sexuality as being Satan's doings:

> God united man and woman, thus joining the strong to the
> weak, that each might sustain the other. But these perverted

adulterers change their virile strength into perverse weakness, rejecting the proper male and female roles, and in their wickedness they shamefully follow Satan, who in his pride sought to split and divide Him Who is indivisible. They create in themselves by their wicked deeds a strange and perverse adultery, and so appear polluted and shameful in my sight . . . a woman who takes up devilish ways and plays a male role in coupling with another woman is most vile in My [God's] sight, and so is she who subjects herself to such a one in this evil deed . . . And men who touch their own genital organ and emit their semen seriously imperil their souls, for they excite themselves to distraction; they appear to Me [God] as impure animals devouring their own whelps . . .

Hildegarde of Bingen's bright lights, Satanic perversions, fallen angels and sexual confusions enabled her to leave a memorable legacy. Likewise, Catherine of Siena (1347–80), whose visions of guardian angels began when she was six, left a lasting impression, becoming known as 'Doctor of the Church' for her peace-making activities. A wool dyer's daughter from northern Italy, Catherine became a Dominican tertiary when she was sixteen, and continued to have visions of Jesus, Mary and the saints until her death at the age of thirty-three, mostly due to her ascetic, anorexic lifestyle.

JEANNE D'ARC (1412–31)

'And came this voice, about the hour of noon, in the summertime, in my father's garden . . . and rarely do I hear it without a brightness . . . and after I had thrice heard this voice I knew it was the voice of an angel.'

Joan of Arc by Herself and Her Witnesses,
Regine Pernoud

Jeanne d' Arc's political and religious crusade at the end of the Hundred Years War has remained a symbol of feminine courage, and she has been honoured as a political heroine in France since the time of Napoleon.

Her visions of angels, including the archangels Michael and Gabriel as well as angelic hosts, have, on the whole, been accepted by not only religious but also secular commentators and writers. Recently, Italian neurologists G. D'Orsi and P. Tinuper have sought to prove she was suffering from some delusional state or brain malfunction. Yet it was her own utter belief in the messages that God had sent her through the angels that generated the collective notion that angels maybe do come down to those who can change the course of history. Joan of Arc is perhaps one of the few examples to demonstrate such a spiritual influence on the political and royal goings-on of the era.

TERESA D'AVILA (1513–82)

> '*I know by frequent experience that there is nothing which puts the devils to flight like holy water.*'

One mystical woman may not have changed the course of political history, but she did revive the whole cult of mystical spirituality in the Catholic Church in her role as Carmelite reformer and founder.

Born in Avila, not far from Madrid, in 1515, Teresa ran away from home as a child in an attempt to throw herself on to the daggers and swords of the blood-thirsty Moors as a martyr. However, her uncle managed to bring her back to the family, and later entered her into a nunnery. Increasingly suffering from nutritional illnesses (like many other mystics), she began to have visions and mystical experiences. Studying medieval manuscripts, such as the works of our friendly Cabalist, Ramon Lull, Teresa kept a record of her ecstasies. One experience became the inspiration for the Catholic Counter Reformation's favourite Baroque artist, Bernini.

This classic, sensuous, erotic, provocative sculpture in soft white marble, entitled the 'Ecstasy of St Teresa', dominates the Cornaro Chapel in Rome. The idealized angel, personified as a Cupid-like messenger, has just withdrawn his spear from Teresa's heart, contrary to popular belief that he is just about to thrust it into her. When Teresa describes this vision, we are invited to wonder whether her experience is a representation of physical orgasmic fulfilment or spiritual fusion, or maybe both?

> I saw an angel close by me, on my left side, in bodily form . . . He was not tall, but short. Marvellously beautiful . . . In his hands was a long golden spear and at the point of the iron there seemed to be a little fire . . . He appeared to me to be thrusting it at times into my heart, and to pierce my very entrails; when he drew it out, he seemed to draw them out also, and to leave me all on fire with a great love of God. The pain was so great, that it made me moan; and yet so surpassing was the sweetness of this excessive pain, that I could not wish to be rid of it . . .

She describes her mystical states as ecstasies, and ecstasy as a 'detachable death', as if her soul awakened to God while all bodily senses were dead. Teresa's angelic visions were at the time a bonus for the Catholic Church. The Reformation, led by Luther and Calvin, focused on intellectual asceticism, self-discipline and purging of the soul. The merging of soul with the divine in mystical meditation was considered acceptable. With the appointment of the Father General of the Jesuit Order to clean up the Catholic Church and rid it of its pagan elements, which were thought to be the underlying cause for its moral degeneration, spiritual prayer and devotional meditation were welcomed as a form of ritual, rather than personal experience.

By the end of the sixteenth century, Teresa d'Avila and John of the Cross, and their books on mystical prayer, became key works in the Catholic Church.

Later, Spanish priest Miguel Molinos (1628–97) and Frenchwoman Jeanne Guyon (1648–1717) attempted to revive mystical spirituality. Molinos was the main exponent of a cultish religion known as Quietism, and his book *The Spiritual Guide* became a bestseller across Europe. They were both accused of heresy under the auspices of the Jesuits, and subsequently, the mystical element in the Roman Catholic Church was also stamped out. Those who practised mystical prayer scurried underground, while the precious works of Teresa and John of the Cross were hidden away from view.

STIGMATA

'Never desire nor seek any face or image during prayer. Do not wish for sensory vision or angels, or powers, or Christ, lest you lose your mind by mistaking the wolf for the shepherd and worship the enemies – the demons.'

St Francis of Assisi

Contrary to his own words, Francis of Assisi (1181–1226) had a vivid vision – an encounter with an angel who then, luckily, transformed not into a wolf, but into the crucified Jesus.

Most stigmatics are usually Catholic, imitating Francis's first recorded thirteenth-century visionary experience. Firstly, they believe their guardian angels, or some form of tutelary spirit, is responsible for the wounding. Secondly, they 'become', or believe themselves to be, Jesus Christ. The psychology behind the passion of the mystic to suffer or martyr oneself for Jesus is peculiarly fascinating, and too complex to be fully developed in the context of this book. But the stigmatic's state has been associated with a religious fervour for Jesus, invoking a need for the subject or 'victim' to produce 'symptoms' of their suffering.

Stigmata researcher Ian Wilson, author of *The Bleeding Mind: An Investigation into the Mysterious Phenomenon of Stigmata*, proposes that stigmata are self-induced by people suffering from stress who then turn to prayer, causing multiple personality-type symptoms. Just what causes the actual stigmata remains unclear, but the ability to cause bodily scarring or self-mutilation by mind power alone may be more common than is believed.

In 1224, two years before his death, St Francis embarked on a journey to Mt La Verna for a forty-day fast. One morning, around the feast day of the Exaltation of the Cross, the seraph allegedly appeared to Francis while he prayed. Humbled by the sight of the angel, who transformed into the crucified Jesus, Francis was both ecstatic and filled with pain and suffering. When the angel departed, Francis found wounds in his side as if caused by the same spear that pierced Christ's side. The image of iron nails immediately appeared in his hands and feet, and the wound in his side seeped blood. Brother Leo, who had been with Francis at the time, left the first definite account of the phenomenon of stigmata:

> Suddenly he saw a vision of a seraph, a six-winged angel on a cross. This angel gave him the gift of the five wounds of Christ.

Others, such as Anne-Catherine Emmerick (1774–1824), St Gemma Galgani (1878–1903) and St Pio (1870–1968), were put under round-the-clock observation to see if they were fakes. Current scientific research suggests that stigmata sufferers are most likely linked to dissociative identity disorders, starvation, anorexia and obsessive compulsive disorders. In his paper, 'Hospitality and Pain', Christian theologian Ivan Illich states: 'Compassion with Christ . . . is faith so strong and so deeply incarnate that it leads to the individual embodiment of the contemplated pain.' His thesis is that stigmata result from profound and unbearable religious faith, plus the desire to associate oneself with the suffering Messiah. Interestingly, no recorded stigmatics occurred before St Francis's visions in the twelfth century.

Anne-Catherine Emmerick

Mystic, stigmatic and ecstatic, Anne-Catherine Emmerick is still considered by Catholics to be one of their greatest visionaries. Born at Flamske, Germany, on 8 September 1774, Anne-Catherine became a nun of the Augustinian Order at Dulmen. She believed she was being led on some spiritual journey by her guardian angel. The angel also told her that the wounds, which usually appeared immediately after a vision, signified she had been ravished in body and spirit.

Anne-Catherine wanted someone to write down the revelations, and from 1819, the date of an examination to determine the validity of her stigmata, until her death in 1824, Clemens Brentano, a well-known poet, believing her to be a chosen 'bride of Christ', recorded forty volumes of her visions. These were detailed, graphic accounts of her direct experience of New Testament events and communications with the Virgin Mary. Reading more like an epic work of fiction than the Bible itself, Brentano apparently read back all of Anne-Catherine's dictations, and only made changes once she had given her approval.

Her best-known visions were published in 1833 in *The Dolorous Passion of Our Lord Jesus Christ according to the Meditations of Anne Catherine Emmerich*. This is a sourcebook of imagination and utter obsession with suffering as Christ's bride. To Anne-Catherine, it seems, the angels, the Devil and the presence of Christ in the Eucharist – that is the transformation of bread and wine into the body and blood of Christ – were as real to her as so-called reality. Yet, in the religious storms that continued to blow across Europe, Anne-Catherine, like many a mystic, was a useful PR figure. While scientific knowledge increased, and the industrial revolution got going, she had visions to support the wonderful beliefs of the Catholic Church.

All over the world I saw numberless infusions of the Spirit; sometimes, like a lightning-stroke, falling on a congregation in church, and I could tell who among them had received the grace; or again, I beheld individuals praying in their homes, suddenly endowed with light and strength. The sight awoke in me great joy and confidence that the Church, amid her ever-increasing tribulations, will not succumb.

Gemma Galgani

An Italian mystic, known as the 'Daughter of Passion' by the Roman Catholic Church, Gemma Galgani first experienced stigmata, and simultaneous visions of angels and Jesus, at the age of twenty-one. According to her testimonies, she spoke with her guardian angel as well as the Virgin Mary and Jesus. In *Mysteries, Marvels, Miracles in the Lives of Saints* by Joan Carroll Cruz, she is reported as recounting her first ecstasy:

Jesus appeared with his wounds all open; blood was not flowing from them, but flames of fire which in one moment came and touched my hands, feet and heart. I felt I was dying, and should have fallen down but for my Mother (Blessed Virgin Mary) who supported me and kept me under her mantle. Thus I remained for several hours. Then my Mother kissed my forehead, the vision disappeared and I found myself on my knees; but I still had a keen pain in my hands, feet and heart. I got up to get into bed and saw that blood was coming from the places where I had the pain. I covered them as well as I could and then, helped by my Guardian angel, got into bed.

One eyewitness testimony came from the esteemed head, or Provincial, of the Passionists – a Catholic order founded by St Paul of the Cross – Father Peter Paul of the Immaculate, who later became Monsignor Moreschini, Archbishop of Camerino. He went into lengthy detail about his visit to Lucca on 20 August 1899:

> I saw that drops of blood were oozing from the skin around her head, especially from her temples. After the lapse of twenty minutes, when she had come out of the ecstasy and washed, I saw that there no longer existed the death-like pallor and indication of pain which made her resemble Our Saviour on the Cross. She had returned to her natural color; nay, after the sweat of blood had ceased, her countenance assumed an angelic beauty.

One wonders if he were more interested in promoting Gemma's imminent transformation into an angel, than the one she had apparently sighted.

Padre Pio

A Capuchin priest, miracle worker and charismatic mystic, Padre Pio lived more like a New Testament apostle than a twentieth-century man. He was convincing. Angels visited him and translated his foreign language fan-mail; he conversed with the guardian angels of the sick, ready to heal them before they even knew it; he cast out the Devil here, there and everywhere; and was beaten by furious demons in his cell. Of course, a contingent of sceptics tried to prove him either mad, a fraud, skilled at hypnosis or in league with the Devil. Perhaps he was one of the greatest illusionists ever, or just the product of people who desperately needed some of his magical holy water. As his cult built, so did his delusions, while others simply dismissed him as psychotic. In 1918, he received visible stigmata, which stayed with him, apparently, for the next fifty years of his life.

OTHER VISIONARIES

Catherine Labouré (1806–76) from France was no stigmatic, but she was famous for her vision of the Virgin Mary and the Miraculous Medal, worn by millions of Catholics today. She was a sister of the 'Daughters of Charity', and while sleeping in her curtained bed in the dormitory with the other novices, she was awakened by her guardian angel, who whispered to her several times. She saw the angel as a dazzlingly bright, beautiful child. The angel whispered, 'Come to chapel; the Blessed Virgin is waiting for you.'

The remarkable Marto children, Jacinta (1910–20) and Francisco (1908–19) and their cousin Lucia dos Santos (1907–2005), living near Fatima, Portugal, reported three separate apparitions of an angel. The angel bade them fall on their knees, rest their foreheads on the ground and be ready for the coming of the Virgin Mary, from whom they subsequently reported several controversial prophecies, resulting in a massively popular pilgrimage to the site every year.

In San Sebastian de Garabandal in northern Spain, between 1961 and 1965, controversy developed over the so-called 'Garabandal' apparitions. Four teenaged girls reportedly saw the Virgin Mary, baby Jesus, the archangel Michael and other holy angels. The apparitions, although never refuted by the Catholic Church, have never been truly approved either, and were considered as 'preternatural' events, rather than supernatural.

Scenes of the girls in their 'ecstasies' – bending their heads back to stare at something in the sky above them – were at the time recorded on rather dodgy video. Stiff necks and profiting osteopaths come to mind. And, not totally without a hint of scepticism here, why would any angel worth its salt give a girl such a hard time and stay suspended in the air above her? Secondly, the clip where Conchita receives a

Holy Communion wafer on her tongue is one of the most obvious pieces of camera trickery ever. Indeed, angels could easily be endowed with preternatural perks.

Padre Pio and Mother Teresa both endorsed the apparitions, which, along with a series of prophecies and seemingly false predictions, created a renewal of interest in April 2007, when Joey Lomangino, founder of a large organization for 'Garabandal devotees' in the US, dedicated to spreading the word of the 'Garabandal prophecies', received from Conchita a copy of a letter from the Archbishop of Sierra, Spain, expressing keen enthusiasm for a new investigation into the apparitions. But then, angels had become big business again.

Born to Greek parents in Helipolis, Egypt, in 1942, Vassula Ryden is best known for her writings *True Life of God*. A modern mystic if ever there was one, in the Christian Church's eyes at least, Vassula's compilation of thousands of messages from God came to her in 1985 when she was living in Bangladesh with her family. She maintains that while writing a grocery list, she experienced a tingling sensation in her fingers, and an invisible presence guided her hand to write, in a totally different style from her own: 'I am your Guardian Angel and my name is Daniel.' Believing she had been called by God to promote Christian Unity and spread the word, she still organizes ecumenical pilgrimages, attracting attention from Orthodox, Catholic and Protestant denominations.

The following day my angel returned to me as before. I spent endless joyful hours communicating with him. Again, the next day he returned, but this time, to my great surprise, he brought with him a multitude of angels of different choirs. I felt that the gates of heaven were suddenly wide open because I could easily sense this great movement of angels from above.

BILLY GRAHAM (b. 1918)

If Vassula Ryden was one of previous little faith turned Christian mystic, then American Billy Graham, the evangelical spiritual advisor to many of the US presidents since Harry S. Truman, has been one of the twentieth-century's media stars of religion, whose fanatical beliefs have converted many of no faith to accept Jesus Christ as their saviour.

His book, *Angels, God's Secret Agents*, first published in the mid-seventies and reprinted as many times as there are, apparently, angels, was an extraordinary publicity drive for the re-emergence of angel power. The book is based on the premise that the cultural fascination for the occult and assorted dark delights of spirituality, relies on a whole army of angels, who will save us from our own terrors and, of course, the wrath of the demon. The publishers' preface reads:

> At a time when many people have lost touch with their Christian heritage, there is a great risk of falling for ideas that sound exotic and appealing but are actually misleading and extremely dangerous.

The book makes rather naive suggestions about how to tell a demon from an angel – mostly with references to the Bible. As we know, even St Paul had his doubts and was probably speaking about his own psychological metamorphosis from persecutor to saviour. The preface goes on to maintain that, 'yes, there are angels in our very midst – but not all supernatural forces are good and not all angels are from heaven.' Didn't we know that anyway?

Graham's book arrived, handily, just when the collective obsession for all things occult was at a peak. The film of *The Exorcist* suggested that evil forces marched unseen among us, and we could be possessed at any moment. The Devil, maybe, really did exist. People fled from central London cinemas to take solace in the nearest pub and the great demon drink. Tame by comparison with more recent films, it was still a cultural reminder that there was something to fear after all – fear itself. Billy Graham also worked on the age-old religious fear factor. Sharing his evangelical crusades with over two hundred million people worldwide, Graham said, 'If we had open spiritual eyes, we would see not only a world filled with evil spirits and powers – but also powerful angels with drawn swords, set for our defence.'

His Christian angels became a source of reassurance and protection in times of dread. If we hadn't already noticed, the angels are, and always have been, here to save and guard us. The revival of this ancient idea of guardian angels, whether Christianized ones or the daimon from the ancient world, came leaping back into the collective psyche like a veritable bat out of hell.

ELISABETH KUBLER-ROSS (1926–2004)

From a different perspective, research is currently being carried out on exceptional human experiences, particularly near-death experiences, by Doctor Sam Parnia at Southampton University and across selected hospitals in the UK. A programme started in 2008 is due to end in 2011, and the study will report on the common 'symptoms' of near-death experiences, such as deep feelings of peace, hearing music, entering a tunnel of light and sightings of angels.

Research into near-death experience was pioneered by Swiss-born psychiatrist Elisabeth Kubler-Ross. In her book *On Death and Dying* (1969), she described five stages of grief when faced with one's own impending death, and similar stages for those left to grieve for their loved ones. This became known as the Kubler-Ross model.

Her close association with a self-professed medium and psychic, Jay Barham, in the late 1970s, jarred with the softly softly finality of death that she had championed. Barham had founded the rather obscure 'Church of the Facet of Divinity' near San Diego, where Elisabeth bought a ranch, 'Shanti Nilaya', turning it into a centre for her workshops. Referring to herself as 'an immortal visionary and modern-day cartographer of the River Styx', Elisabeth was impressed by Barham's séances in which the participants, usually widowed wealthy women, had sex with spirit entities. She believed, 'this man [Barham] has more gifts than you have ever seen'. Barham claimed that the spirits of the dead materialized by cloning themselves from his body cells, and then proceeded to have sex with the grieving widow. And he recruited women to act as 'sex channellers' for male initiates.

Barham's cultish tricks were exposed by a friend of Kubler-Ross's in the early eighties, when she turned on the light during a session with an 'afterlife entity' and discovered the opportunistic Barham, naked except for a turban – one dares to wonder where he was wearing it.

Yet Kubler-Ross's faith in Barham remained unshaken, and she declared 'there are those who might say this has damaged my credibility', later conceding that his behaviour 'did not meet the standards' of her retreat.

By the 1990s, her interest in the after-life and out-of-body experiences seemingly challenged her own earlier beliefs that death was, simply, death. Her interest turned to angels, who might help us to move beyond life. She wrote in *Death is of Vital Importance*:

Dying patients become aware of the presence of beings surrounding them who guide and help them. This is the first reason you cannot die alone. Young children often refer to them as 'their playmates'. The churches have called them guardian angels . . . From the moment of birth, beginning with the taking of the first breath, until the moment when we make the transition and end this physical existence, we are in the presence of these guides or guardian angels. They will wait for us and help us in the transition from life to life after death.

THE NEW AGE AND BELIEF

Angels have became big business. Bookshops have dedicated sections for New Age and Mind, Body, Spirit titles, and angel iconography embellishes many a food, fashion and furniture shop. Angel cards, amulets and jewellery are also rife, and there are now as many experts on angels as there are angels in history. Doreen Virtue, for example, has merged the spiritual and psychological aspects of angelology to create her own angel therapy. White feathers appearing on the doorstep are a sign that an angel has visited, yet how many times has your feather pillow leaked little white signs of angels, too?

But what has caused their return to popular culture? According to Jungian psychology, there has always been an 'angel' archetype within the human psyche, deep down inside each of us. Based on Plato's Theory of Forms, Jung's archetypal psychology proposed that there is an underlying essence to everything, and these essences, or archetypes, are expressed through symbols, metaphors, images and ideas in the 'real' world. Yet they themselves are always numinous, invisible and autonomous, hidden deep within our psychic inheritance.

The angel archetype, that is the symbol of goodness, connection to the divine, guardianship and protection, manifests when a culture is in need of spiritual meaning, or some kind of supernatural fix. The angel embodies good and bad human qualities, so we can see the angel as a 'reflection' of our spiritual longings and human failings. We can identify with fallen angels as readily as we can with the goody-goodies in films such as *City of Angels*, *It's a Wonderful Life* and the TV series *Touched by an Angel*. We want to contact the angel, because deep within the collective unconscious, the message is inevitably more important than the conveyor of the message. We therefore cheat. We want to contact Michael, or Gabriel, or Another-el, not because we want to know them, but because we want to know about ourselves, and our future. Yet the only messages that the daimon and angel brings us are that we're not alone and we should trust in the universe, God, or the eternal now. This, of course, never truly relieves the human angst of aloneness, and the idea that life is a pig and then you die.

Yet we still seek proof of the numinous, but the more we look for proof, or concrete evidence, the more we become disillusioned. Why do angels favour some and not others? Why is it wars still happen and angels are not powerful enough to combat the black death or bird flu? We relentlessly want to believe in something and find meaning in our lives. But the more we dig around in our spiritual vanities and attempt to reach out to the angels, the more we contact other people with egos and similarly unfulfilled hopes and dreams. This doesn't make for an easy belief in angels.

This basic human need for salvation is at the root of the glitz of angel books and angel cards. We are now more open to the existence of extraterrestrials, conspiracy theories and harnessing our own psychic power. Angels are non-threatening, and importantly, they symbolize the ancient shamanic experience of the divine.

The angel archetype is no longer just a messenger sent from God, not just the mounted courier on his way across the desert, but a distributor of individual destiny, too. The angel is like Hermes, a guide who takes you on a journey to find yourself.

In 2008, a survey conducted by Baylor University's Institute for Studies in Religion in the USA, revealed that more than half of all adults, including a poll of one in five people who were not particularly religious, believe they have been protected by a guardian angel at some time in their lives. The US, a predominantly religious nation, according to another poll from the Pew Forum on Religion and Public Life in 2007, found that 68 per cent of Americans believe that angels and demons are active in the world.

Whether we believe in angels or not, as Italian writer Luciano de Crescenzo recounts, 'we are each of us angels with one wing, and we can only fly by embracing one another.' Angels are no longer necessary when we realize we can be enlightened through the angel of ourselves. It is the daimon within who gives us hope, courage, self-belief and love as we travel along the road of our unfolding destiny.

The guardian angel is there for us all. Yet take care, as Patrick Harpur in his book, *A Complete Guide to the Soul*, writes:

Anyone who invokes their guardian angel, therefore, should beware. It may not be as friendly and sweet as the many little New Age books on angels will have you believe. It will protect you, yes – but only the 'you' who serves its plan for yourself. It will guide you, certainly – but who knows what sojourn in the wilderness this might entail? . . . You will inevitably be led way, way out of your depth.

Secret truths, whether taught by Hermes Trismegistus, Ficino, Pythagoras or Blake, are about the invisibility of everything, once known as the *deus absconditus* – the concealed god. And it is the gods, angels and demons, whether imagined or real, who give us the chance to experience these hidden secrets. Yet at the same time, our need to personify, isolate and separate angels from demons, and both of them from us, has occluded the divine in nature. As the Hermetic magician, the yogic and the cabalist would remind us, this can be found and experienced in oneself, if one only dares to look.

We have been cloaked in Judaeo-Christianity's ambivalence towards the messenger. Either angels do only God's will and therefore have no free will, or angels do have free will, but become fallen and demonic. What this means is that angels are stupid instruments of God, while demons, daimons and other miscellaneous deities are handy scapegoats for religious persecutors, simply because they *are* human in nature. To have free will then, is to be daimonic and human; to be fated is to be an angel. Our heavenly choirs of angels *have no choice* but to comtemplate not so much our fate, but their own never-ending one.

In the 1998 romantic drama film *City of Angels*, actor Nicolas Cage plays Seth, an angel who falls in love with the a human being, Maggie. After giving up his angelic existence to be with her, Maggie is then dramatically killed in a road accident. Grief-stricken and doomed to the fate of a mortal, he reflects on how human love is more like being in heaven than his existence as an angel. The sentiment, that one touch of Maggie's skin is enough to relinquish eternity, is beautifully echoed in the lyrics of the hit song 'Iris' by the Goo Goo Dolls from the same film. If an angel would give up the City of God for human love, maybe that says a lot more about finding our heaven or hell right here on earth? Both are states of being, as Eckhart so astutely pointed out nearly one thousand years earlier.

Inevitably then, the common or garden angel's 'fate' is no longer all it's cracked up to be. Yet the more attractive fait accompli of the cosmos has always been our equivocal dance with life, led on by our own personal, daimonic chaperone.

Et vous danseriez en la terrible danse

LAST WORDS

Back in the church in Bar-sur-Loup, the painting it still the same but the perceiver has changed. The demons, the angels, the benign Michael, the tricky Devil, the repentent Count, foolish dancers, naive revellers and debauched chroniclers are now a reflection of whoever gazes at the painting. Look again. Look twice. Look carefully in the words of this book, for as seventeenth-century French astrologer Jean Baptiste Morin de Villefranche noted, not from the stars, but from some occult opus:

> The secret hidden here is easy to discover if you know what you are seeking. And if you, the reader, should find it in these pages, then you will find it within yourself.

Filled with our own angels and demons, we might assume that we don't need to look for them outside of ourselves. The daimon of our psychic life is always here, within. But if our 'mist-apparelled' guardian spirits are looking after us, maybe they are also looking at us, right now?

EPILOGUE

A woman sat in mourning clothes in a long pew in a Cambridge College chapel. The bright daylight outside shot blue, amber, red and golden slivers of light through the stained-glass windows, filled with Christian angels and someone she thought was probably Jesus. A pagan by choice, the woman was filled with awe, for as any fool knows, a place built for worship, whether for religion or for dreaming, is still infused with the divine, as is every tree.

It was the occasion of her father's funeral. The dons in the opposite pews sat in stony silence. Family and colleagues soliloquized on the life and works of the popular and influential academic, and then they all rose to sing her father's favourite song, 'Jersualem'. Blake's words, the stirring music, memories and sadness brought tears to her eyes. As they sat down to listen to some loving prayer or other, a hand rested gently, perhaps for ten seconds, no more, on the top of her head. A warm, loving hand filled her with comfort, a sense of being at one with the universe, and a feeling of release as some kind of divine revelation spread through her. She turned round to smile at whoever had kindly touched her, perhaps someone who was sitting in the pew behind. But there was no one there. She knew then, just for the immeasurable moment, that she had been touched by an angel.

That woman was me.

BIBLIOGRAPHY

Baring, Anne and Cashford, Jules, *The Myth of the Goddess*, Arkana, London, 1993

Black, Jeremy and Green, Anthony, *Gods, Demons and Symbols in Ancient Mesopotamia*, British Museum Press, London, 1992

Brakke, David (trans.), *Evarius of Pontus: Talking Back. A Monastic Handbook for Combating Demons*, Cisterian Studies Series, Minnesota, 2009

Brenk, Frederick E., *Relighting the Souls: Studies in Plutarch, in Greek Literature, Religion and Philosophy, and in the New Testament Background*, Franz Steiner Verlag, Germany, 1998

Burkert, Walter, *Greek Religion*, Blackwell Publishing, London, 1987

Campbell, Joseph, *The Hero with a Thousand Faces*, Fontana Press, London (Reissue), 1993

Certeau, Michel de, (trans.) Smith, Michael B., *The Possession at Loudun*, University of Chicago Press, 2000

Charlesworth, James H., (ed), *The Old Testament Pseudepigraphia*, Doubleday, New York, 1985

Davidson, Gustav, *A Dictionary of Angels*, Free Press, New York, 1971

Darmesteter, James, (trans.) Muller, Frederick Max, *The Zend Avesta*, Clarendon Press, Oxford, 1880 d'Este, Sorita (Ed), *Both Sides of Heaven*, Avalonia, London, 2009

Flint, Valerie I. J., *The Rise of Magic in Early Medieval Europe*, Princeton University Press, New Jersey, 1991

Fowden, Garth, *The Egyptian Hermes*, Princeton University Press, New Jersey, 1993

Givry, Grillot de, *Witchcraft, Alchemy and Magic*, George Harrap and Co, London, 1931

Godwin, Malcolm, *Angels: An Endangered Species*, Simon and Schuster, New York, 1990

Graham, Billy, *Angels: God's Secret Agents*, W. Publishing Group, Tenessee, 1995

Guiley, Rosemary Ellen, *Encyclopedia of Demons and Demonology*, Visionary Living Inc, New York, 2009

Harpur, Patrick, *The Philosopher's Secret Fire*, Penguin, London, 2002

Harpur, Patrick, *The Complete Guide to the Soul*, Rider, Random House, London, 2010

Harrison, Jane Ellen, *Prolegomena to the Study of Greek Religion*, (first published 1903, Cambridge University Press.) Princeton University Press, New Jersey, 1991

Hastings, James (Ed), *Encyclopedia of Religion and Ethics Vol 8, 1912*, Kessinger Publishing's Rare Reprints, New York, 2003

Hillman, James, *The Soul's Code: In Search of Character and Calling*, Warner Books, New York, 1996

Hughes, Pennethorne, *Witchcraft*, Longmans, Green and Co. Ltd, England, 1952

Jacobsen, Thorkild, *The Treasures of Darkness: A History of Mesopotamian Religion*, Yale University Press, 1976

Johnson, Buffy, *Lady of the Beasts*, Harper and Row, San Francisco, 1988

Jovanovic, Pierre, *Enquête sur l'Existence des Anges Gardiens*, Le Jardin des Livres, Paris, 2008

Jung, C. J., *The Archetypes of the Collective Unconscious*, Routledge, 2nd edition, London, 1991

Jung C. J., *Symbols of Transformation. The Collected Works by C. J. Jung Vol 5*, Routledge & Kegan Paul, London, 1967

Koltuv, Barbara Black, *The Book of Lilith*, Samuel Weiser, Maine, 1986

Kramer, Samuel N., *Sumerian Mythology: A Study of Spiritual and Literary Achievement in the 3rd Millenium BC*, University of Pennsylvania Press, 1972

Kramer, Heinrich & Sprenger, James, *The Malleus Maleficarium*, Dover, New York, 1971

Martin, Malachi, *Hostage to the Devil*, Harper Collins, 1992

McGinn, Bernard, *Meister Eckhart: Teacher and Preacher (Classics of Western Spirituality)*, Paulist Press International, New Jersey, 1986

McKenna, Stephen (trans.), *Plotinus: The Enneads*, Faber & Faber, London, 1956

Meyer, Marvin W. (Ed), *The Ancient Mysteries, A Sourcebook of Sacred Texts*, University of Pennsylvania Press, 1999

Ogden, Daniel, *Magic, Witchcraft and Ghosts in the Greek and Roman World: A Sourcebook*, Oxford University Press, Oxford, 2009

Pagels, Elaine, *The Gnostic Gospels*, Orion Books, London, 2006

Prophet, Elizabeth Clare, *Fallen Angels and the Origins of Evil*, Summit University Press, Montana, 2000

Robinson, James M., (Ed), *The Nag Hammadi Library in English*, Harper Collins, 1988

Schur, Edouard, *Pythagoras and the Delphic Mysteries 1906*, Forgotten Books

Steiner, Rudolph, (trans.) Wehrle, Pauline, *Guardian Angels: Connecting with our Spiritual Guides and Helpers*, Rudolph Steiner Press, UK, 2000

St John Chrysostom, (trans.) Harkins, Paul W., (trans.) *Fathers of the Church. On the Incomprehensible Nature of God*, Catholic University of America Press, 1984

Swedenborg, Emanuel, (trans.) Dole, George F., *Heaven and Hell*, Swedenborg Foundation, New York, 1976

Tarnas, Richard, *The Passion of the Western Mind*, Random House, London, 1996

Walker, Barbara G., *The Woman's Encyclopedia of Myths and Secrets*, Harper Collins, USA, 1983

Wender, Dorothea (trans.), *Hesiod and Theognis*, Penguin, London, 1973

Yates, Frances A., *Giordano Bruno and the Hermetic Tradition*, University of Chicago Press, 1964

Yates, Frances A., *The Occult Philosophy in the Elizabethan Age*, Routledge Classics, London, 2001

Vermes, Geza, *The Complete Dead Sea Scrolls in English*, Penguin, London, 2004

Zuffi, Stefano (Ed), *Angels and Demons in Art*, Getty Publications, Los Angeles, 2005

Internet Sacred Text Archive at www.sacred-texts.com

INDEX

Abgal 45
Agathos Daimon 28, 38
Agrippa, Henry Cornelius 159, 163,
        166–9, 170, 172
Ahriman 57, 58, 80, 149, 196
Ahura Mazda 49, 50, 54–5,
        56, 57, 58, 66, 67, 80, 149
ahuras/asuras 48–9
Akkadians 11, 45, 65, 68–9, 139
alchemy 41, 50, 127, 157, 167, 173, 175,
        177, 186, 187, 188, 200
    see also mysticism and esotericism
Ambrose, Saint 119, 123, 127
Amesha Spentas 54–5, 57, 66, 74
Ami-Hemf 79
Amorites 11, 45, 47
Amorth, Father Gabriele 219–21
ancient Greece see Greece
angels 6, 13–14, 15, 74–5, 94–6, 97,
        123–4, 133, 173, 178–9, 182,
        205–6, 207, 238, 241–4
    archangels 83, 112, 119, 121–2,
        124–7, 128, 133, 137, 157, 166,
        170, 175, 181, 193–4, 229, 236
    cherubim 68–71, 121–2, 139, 201–2
    early angel cults 117–19

encounters with 125, 145, 197–8,
        224–37, 247–8
and the Essenes 131–2
fallen angels 69–71, 79–85, 86, 87,
        109–10, 114, 129, 149, 181, 194,
        204, 221, 227, 241, 243
as guardians 17, 21, 69–70, 93, 98,
        122–3, 129, 179, 187–8, 196,
        197, 221, 231, 233, 234, 236,
        237, 239, 240, 242–3
in Islam 128–9
mal' ak 67–8, 88
in medieval Christianity 138–9, 143,
        145, 146–51
as messengers 67–8, 72–3, 75, 76, 110,
        111, 112, 113, 114, 121, 129,
        137, 164, 181, 186, 199, 243
and Origen 108–11
and Philo of Alexandria 87–9
and Pseudo-Dionysius 120–2, 124,
        148, 159, 169, 179
and psychology 199–202, 241–2
seraphim 71–2, 112, 121–2, 139,
        232
Zoroastrian archetypes 54–6, 57, 66,
        84

see also Apkallu; art and
iconography; bibles; Cabala;
Catholicism; Christianity;
daimons; demons; goddesses;
gods; guardians and guides
(non-Judaeo-Christian);
humanists; messengers
(non-Judaeo-Christian); mystics
and esotericism; Protestantism;
saints by name
Angra Mainyu 50, 54, 57
anthroposophy 196–7
Apam Napat 49
Apkallu 45, 64, 66, 68–9
Apocryphal texts 32, 44, 81–4, 85–6,
118, 122, 127, 130–2
apologists 96–8
Apuleius 19, 102–3, 114
Aquinas, Thomas 120–1, 143, 144,
147–51, 153
archangels 83, 112, 119, 121–2, 124–7,
128, 133, 137, 157, 166, 170,
175, 181, 193–4, 229, 236
archons 94
Aristotle 39, 58, 106, 144, 147, 148, 199
Ark of the Covenant 69, 201–2
art and iconography 14, 15, 16, 18, 20,
28, 33, 44, 45, 69, 113,
118–20, 123, 124, 126, 144, 145,
158, 162, 180–1, 193, 194–5,
198, 207, 226, 230, 245, xiii–xiv
Artemis 29, 111
Aryan beliefs 9, 10–11, 16, 47,
48–50, 67
see also Zoroastrianism
Asherah 17, 45, 67, 79–80
Asmodeus 93–4, 126, 144, 181
Assyrian culture 44, 48, 52, 63–4, 69,
73, 79
astrology and astronomy 12, 50, 51, 58,
63–4, 114, 131, 154, 159, 164,
166, 168, 174, 180
see also cosmic realm
Attis 4, 114
Augustine of Hippo, Saint 70, 80, 84,
85, 102, 111, 113–15, 119, 123,
143, 199
Avesta 52–3, 54, 55, 56, 57
Azazel 83

Ba see Ka and Ba
Baal 46, 67, 78, 80
Babylon 11, 12, 47, 48, 51, 63–7, 69, 76,
79, 80, 207
Bede 143, 145
Beelzebub 86–7, 144
see also Devil/Satan; demons; fallen
angels; Lucifer; possessions and
exorcisms; witch hunts and
trials
bibles 140, 178
Greek and Latin translations 6, 67,
70, 74–6, 79, 81, 88, 93–4, 97,
111
Hebrew bibles and Christian Old
Testament 11, 46, 48, 64–6,
67–75, 76, 78, 79, 80, 81, 82, 85,
88, 110, 112, 122, 124–5, 126,
133, 141, 146, 155, 206
New Testament 11, 75, 79, 80–1,
84–5, 86, 91–2, 93–4, 115, 120,
122, 126
see also apocryphal texts
bird associations 14–15, 18, 24, 30–1,
33, 56, 207
Blake, William 192–3
Blavatsky, Madame 195–6
Bronze Age 8
Browne, Thomas 186–9
Bruno, Giordano 173
Bundahishn 58
Byzantine Empire 109–10, 119, 127–8,
143

Cabala 127, 131, 139, 154, 155–9, 163,
167, 175, 190, 207, 229
Calvin, John 178–9, 230
Canaanites 11, 46, 66, 67, 78, 79–80, 86,
205
Cassian, John 139, 140
Catal Huyuk, Turkey 14, 15
Catholicism 121, 133, 138, 139, 155,
158, 164, 166, 170–1, 177–8,
180, 181–2, 203–4, 208, 211,
213, 215, 220–1, 223–4, 229–31,
233–7
see also Byzantine Empire;
Constantinople; monks; papal
authority; possessions and

exorcisms; visions; witch hunts and trials; individual saints by name
Cecilia, Saint 225–6
Celsus 103–4
Celts 11, 28
Cernunnos 11, 144–5
Chaldean culture 52, 58, 73, 98, 154, 157–8, 167
Charnock, Stephen 201–2
cherubim 68–71, 121–2, 139, 201–2
China 13–14
Christianity 3–4, 8, 16, 72, 76, 81, 87, 91–8, 108–15, 117–24, 137–53, 177–81, 197
    see also angels; apocryphal texts; bibles; Cabala; Catholicism; Devil/Satan; individual saints by name; possessions and exorcism; Protestants; witch hunts and trials
codes and cryptography 164–6, 175, 176
Constantinople 110, 119, 125, 127, 140, 156
cosmic realm 7, 12, 15–16, 17, 18, 20–1, 29, 39, 79, 98, 154, 159, 166, 168, 169, 170, 173, 196, 227
    see also astrology/astronomy
Cybele 4, 9, 114–15
Cyrus, King of Persia 12, 52, 63–5, 66–7, 81

d'Abano, Pietro 170
daevas 48–9, 57, 66
daimons/daemons 7–8, 35–7, 88–9, 107–8, 142, 154, 162, 168, 173, 181, 188, 194, 199–201, 243
    ambiguous nature of 7, 28, 31, 32, 39–40, 41, 99–101
    as guardian and guides 7, 27–8, 31, 32–3, 35, 38–9, 98, 99, 101, 102, 103, 104–5, 106
    influence of translations 59, 75, 76, 97, 169
    as messengers 6, 7, 102–3, 104, 114
    as soul/ inner self 37, 42, 100, 102, 103–5

see also demons
Dante 79, 85, 124, 148, 193
D'Avila, Teresa 229–31
Dead Sea Scrolls 81, 130–2
Dee, John 159, 162, 163, 165, 166, 173–7
demons 6, 93–4, 95, 97, 109, 110, 114, 115, 123, 126, 127, 140–2, 144, 145–7, 149–50, 153, 154, 157, 162, 165, 170–1, 176–7, 179–80, 181, 182, 187, 199–200, 202, 203–10, 211–20, 238–9, 242
    see also daimons/daemons; Devil/Satan; fallen angels; Lilith; possessions and exorcisms; witch hunts and trials
Devil/Satan 77–8, 80–1, 84–6, 91–2, 97, 142, 144, 145, 149, 157, 166–7, 170–2, 179–80, 182, 183, 186, 194, 203–4, 205, 206, 209, 210, 212, 213, 214, 216, 218–20, 224, 227–8, 233, 235
    see also Beelzebub; demons; fallen angels; Lucifer; possessions and exorcisms; witch hunts and trials
dews 58, 142
Dionysius the Areopagite, Saint see Pseudo-Dionysius

Eckhart, Meister 151–3, 190
Egyptian culture and beliefs 8, 9, 10, 12, 16–21, 33, 34, 69, 77, 154, 167, 168
    Greek influenced 17, 18, 19, 24, 74–5
El 45–6, 176
Emerald Tablet 15–16
Emmerick, Anne-Catherine 233–4
Empedocles 35–7
Enki 7, 44, 45
Enoch, Books of 32, 81, 82–4, 86, 127, 131, 175, 176, 197
Enuma Elish 47, 48
Epictetus 35, 101–2
Er 105–6
Erinyes 29, 30
esotericism see mysticism and esotericism
Essenes 130–2

Eudaemons 32
Evagrius the Solitary 139–43
exorcism *see* possessions and exorcisms
Ezekiel 68, 69–71, 110

fallen angels 69–71, 79–85, 86, 87,
        109–10, 114, 129, 149, 181, 194,
        204, 221, 227, 241, 243
    see also demons; Devil/Satan
Ficino, Marsilio 154, 157, 162, 173, 243
Francis of Assisi, Saint 231, 232–3
Frankl, Victor 201
Fravashis 54, 56, 108

Gabriel 83, 112, 124, 126, 128, 133, 166,
        170, 181, 229
Galgani, Gemma 234–5
Garabandal apparitions 236–7
Gathas hymns 49, 52–3, 55, 56, 57
Gaufridi, Father Louis 208–9, 210
Genesis 68–9, 81, 82, 88
Genius 40–1
Giorgi, Francisco 159
Gnostics 72, 81, 94–6, 112, 118–19
God 3, 38, 68, 70, 71, 73, 75, 76, 78, 79,
        81–2, 83, 84, 85, 87, 88, 92, 94,
        96, 97, 102, 104, 108, 109, 110,
        111, 112–13, 118, 119, 121, 123,
        124–5, 127–8, 133, 141, 145,
        148, 152–3, 154, 155, 158, 170,
        171, 172, 173, 174, 175, 178,
        179–80, 188, 204, 206, 226, 229,
        230
goddesses 5, 7, 8–9, 10–11, 14–15, 36,
        66, 118, 125, 195, 205–8
    Egyptian 17–19, 33, 77
    Greek 4, 21–3, 29, 31, 100, 107, 111,
        114–15, 154
    Semitic 9, 17, 44, 45, 47–8, 67, 79–80
gods 5, 9, 10, 11, 15, 20, 48–9, 54, 66, 79,
        104, 105, 118 144–5
    Greek 5, 21–2, 23–5, 31, 32, 35, 36,
        51, 101–2, 139, 154, 180, 200–1
    Semitic 7, 9, 44, 45–6, 63–4, 66, 67,
        79–80
    see also bibles; Catholicism;
        Christianity; Jesus Christ;
        Protestants; Zoroastrianism
Graham, Billy 238–9

Grandier, Father Urbain 211–12
Greece 4, 11, 12, 15, 50, 51–2, 87, 100,
        156
    Empedocles and Heraclitis 35–7
    influence in Egypt 17, 18, 19, 24,
        74–5
    Keres, Harpies and Erinyes 21, 23,
        25, 28–31
    origins of messenger archetype 21–5,
        41
    Sirens 33–4
    see also daimons/daemons;
        goddesses; gods
Grimoire, The 169–70
guardians and guides (non-Judaeo-
        Christian) 17, 21, 31, 32, 35,
        38–9, 41, 45, 56, 67, 98, 99, 101,
        102, 104–5, 106

Hammurabi, King 11, 47
Harpies 21, 23, 30–1
Hathor 17
Hebrew culture and language 6, 11–12,
        17, 38, 44, 45–6, 48, 59, 67, 72,
        88, 125, 133, 138–9, 155–6, 158,
        168–9
    see also bibles; Essenes; Jews and
        Judaism
Hecate 29
Heraclitis 37
Hermas 122–3
Hermes (Greek god) 7, 15, 21, 23–5, 29,
        139
Hermeticism 41, 95–6, 154, 157, 159,
        167, 168, 173, 186–7
Hesiod 23, 28, 30–1, 32, 38, 87, 99, 100
Hildegarde of Bingen 145, 162, 226–7
Hinduism 13, 49
Hittites 48, 52
Homer 22, 24, 28, 30, 31, 32, 33–4, 87,
        99
Humanists 154, 157, 158, 167, 180
Hunmanit 21

Iamblichus 105–7, 120, 154
Inanna 9, 19, 44, 45, 46, 79, 82, 205
Indra 9
Inquisitions 151, 159, 171, 203,
        209, 213

see also possessions and exorcism; witch hunts and trials
Iranian culture and beliefs (Persian) 11, 12, 48, 49–50, 74, 75, 80
see also Cyrus, King; Zoroastrianism
Iris 21–3, 25
Isaiah 64–6, 68, 71–2, 80, 85, 112, 122
Ishtar 44
Isis 9, 17–19, 40, 69, 99, 102, 105
Islam 128–30, 155–6
Israel 66, 67, 68, 69, 72, 131

Jamshid/Yima 50
Jerome, Saint 79, 85, 93, 109, 123
Jesus Christ 19, 80, 84, 86, 87, 92, 103–4, 110, 114, 120, 121, 126, 128, 145, 174, 178, 189, 224, 228, 231–5, 236, 238
see also bibles; Catholicism; Christianity; Protestantism; stigmata
Jews and Judaism 16, 45, 75, 87, 95, 126, 132, 133, 155, 156, 178, 206–7
pre-release from Babylon 51, 52, 58, 59, 63–5, 67
see also bibles; Cabala; Hebrew culture and language
Jinn 129–30
Joan of Arc 228–9
Job, Book of 78, 81
John of Chryosostom, Saint 111–12, 121
John the Baptist 110, 126, 127
Judaeo-Christian religion *see* bibles; Christianity; Jews and Judaism
Jung, Carl 5, 48, 199–200, 207, 241

Ka and Ba 19–20, 34
Kakodaimons 31, 32
Karibu 68–9
Kelly, Edward 173, 175–7
Keres 25, 28–31
Kramer, Heinrich 171–2
Kubler-Ross, Elisabeth 239–40
Kurdistan 15

Lascaux caves, France 14, 15
Lilith 44, 205–8
Louviers convents 213

Lucifer 29, 70, 71, 85, 144, 179–80, 196
origins of 'light bearer' mythology 79–81
see also Beelzebub; demons; Devil/ Satan; fallen angels; possessions and exorcisms; witch hunts and trials
Lull, Ramon 155–6, 229
Luther, Martin 178, 179–80, 230

Madimi 176–7
Magi 50–1, 59, 80, 168
Magus, Simon 118–19
mal'ak 67–8, 88, 111
Malleus Maleficarum 170–2
see also possessions and exorcism; witch hunts and trials
Marduk 7, 46–7, 64, 66
Martin, Malachi 219
Martyr, Justin 96–7
May, Rollo 200–1, 202
Me 9, 44, 46–7, 79, 82
medieval period 139–53
Mesopotamia 9, 14, 19, 47, 74
see also Semitic cultures; Sumerian cosmology
messengers (non-Judaeo-Christian spirits) 6–8, 10, 12, 16–25, 33, 38, 41, 45, 54, 65, 67, 76, 95
see also daimons
Michael 119, 124–5, 126, 129, 133, 137, 175–6, 229, 236
Milton, John 85, 182–3
Minoan beliefs 4, 14, 28
Mithrasism 49, 96
monks 139–43, 145, 146–8, 158, 159, 163, 171, 207
monotheism 10, 16, 42, 45, 47, 51, 54, 65, 78, 94, 108, 132, 133
see also bibles; Catholicism; Christianity; Jews and Judaism; Protestantism; Zoroastrianism
Mormons 197–8
morning star 18, 29, 71, 79, 80, 81
Moroni and the Church of the Latter Days Saints 197–8

Moses 44, 66, 68, 72, 87, 88, 121, 154, 155
mystery cults 96, 154
mysticism and esotericism
    Eckhart and Porete 151–3, 190
    post-Renaissance 186–94, 195–7
    Renaissance 159, 162, 163–70, 172, 173–7
    see also Cabala; humanists; Neo-Platonism; visionaries (Christian)

Nabonidus, King of Assyria 63–4, 71, 80
Nag Hammadi Library 95–6
Naqdas 16
near-death experiences 239, 240
Neith 8, 9, 17
Neo-Platonism 41, 104–7, 121, 148, 154, 162, 179, 186, 188, 192
    see also mysticism and esotericism
Neolithic period 14, 33
Nephythys 18, 69
New Testament
    see under bibles
Nike 23, 25
Nikita the Recluse, Saint 146–7
Nippur, Iraq 7
Noah 82, 83, 127

Old Testament see under bibles
Origen 108–11, 123, 142, 143

papal authority 125, 127, 143, 145, 158, 170, 171, 177–8, 203–4, 227
    see also Catholicism; Christianity; Protestantism; Reformation
Paul, Saint 84–5, 87, 92–3, 95, 118, 121, 132, 238
Peck, Scott 218–19
Persia see Iran
phallic symbolism 77–8
pharaohs 18, 20, 69
Philo of Alexandria 87–9, 131
Phosphorus see Lucifer
Pico Della Mirandola, Giovanni 157–8, 172
Pio, Padre 235, 237

Plato 18, 20–1, 24, 27–8, 32–3, 34, 38–40, 87, 89, 95, 96, 98, 99, 101, 104, 105, 106, 107, 113, 144, 154, 188, 241
    Middle-Platonism 98–104
    see also Neo-Platonism
Plotinus 104–5, 154
Plutarch 18, 34, 39–40, 58–9, 87, 97, 98–101
Porete, Marguerite 151–2
Porphyry 41, 107, 154, 188
possessions and exorcisms 87, 204–5, 208–21, 238–9
Proclus 107
Protestants 170–1, 178–80, 181–2, 204, 208, 230
Pseudo-Dionysius 120–2, 124, 148, 169, 179
psychology 199–202, 207, 241–2
Pythagoras 35, 36, 51, 188

Raphael 83, 93, 124, 126–7, 129, 133, 162, 166, 170, 181, 182–3
Reformation 170, 177–81, 183, 230
Remy, Nicholas 208
Renaissance 99, 120, 139, 153–9, 162, 163–77
Reuchlin, Johannes 158, 166
Revelations 73–4, 124, 125
Rig Veda 49
Romans 4, 16, 18, 23, 25, 28, 29, 40–1, 117–19, 127
Ryden, Vassula 237

Salem witch trials 213–15
Sanskrit 78
Satan see Devil/ Satan
Saul of Tarsus see St Paul
Savonarola 158
Scot, Reginald 215
séances 175–7, 240
Semitic beliefs and culture 7, 9, 10–12, 16, 17, 38, 44, 45–8, 52, 63–4, 66, 67, 68–9, 76, 79–80
Sephiroth 155–6, 157, 158, 159
Septuagint see bibles
seraphim 21, 71–2, 112, 121–2, 139, 232
serpents 72, 77–8, 80, 85, 125
seven deadly sins 139–44, 208

sex 171–2, 189, 190–2, 205–8, 209–10, 211–12, 213, 225, 227–8, 240
Shaher 79–80
shamans 14–15, 24
Sirens 20–1, 29, 33–4
sky-gods 10, 11, 67, 79
Smith, Joseph 197–8
Socrates 38, 97
souls 12, 14–15, 19, 25, 48, 67, 86, 87–8, 131, 173, 189
    in Christianity 95, 96, 109, 142, 145, 152–3, 157, 230
    and daimons 28, 31, 34, 35, 36, 39–40, 41–2, 98, 99, 100, 101, 102–3, 104, 106–7
    Zoroastrianism 51, 52, 54, 55, 56
spirits 28–9, 46, 48, 59, 74, 75, 112, 129–30, 175, 196, 199, 204, 240
    Egyptian 9, 17, 19–20
    guardians and guides 12, 17, 31, 32, 35, 38–9, 41, 45, 56, 67
    messengers 6–8, 10, 12, 16–25, 33, 38, 41, 45, 67
    Semitic 7, 11, 12, 16, 44–5, 52, 64, 67, 73
    Zoroastrian influence 49, 53–6, 58, 66–7, 84
    see also angels; daimons/daemons; demons; souls
Steiner, Rudolf 196–7
stigmata 231–6
succubi 205–7
Sumerian culture and beliefs 4, 7, 8, 9, 16, 38, 43–5, 65, 67, 68, 76
    see also Semitic cultures and beliefs
sun-gods 47–8, 77–80
Swedenborg, Emanuel 189–92, 193

Tablets of Destiny/Heaven 9, 44, 46–7, 79, 82, 175, 197
Talmud 133
Teresa of Avila, Saint 229–31
Theosophy 196
Thoth 24, 25

Tiamat 9, 46–7
Tobit, Book of 93–4, 126–7
Trismegistus, Hermes 95–6, 168
Trithemius, Johannes 163–6, 175
Tyre, King of 69–71, 110

Ugarit 46
Uriel 124, 127, 175–6, 181
Ursuline nuns 208–13
Utukku 7

Varuna 9, 49
Vedic culture 9, 11, 48–9, 50, 57
Vendidad 57
Virgil 28, 30, 31
Virgin Mary 57, 145, 233, 234, 236
visions and visionaries (Christian) 125, 145, 189, 224–37
    see also mysticism and esotericism
Vulgate see bibles

Watchers see fallen angels
witch hunts and trials 170–2, 204, 208–16
Xenocrates 39–40

Yahweh 45–6, 64–5, 67–8, 69, 72, 75
Yakut mythology 14–15
Yam 46, 78
Yama 50
Yazatas 54, 55
Yezidis cult 15
Yima/Jamshid 50

Zawi Chami people 15
Zeus 5, 22, 23, 31, 32, 35, 36, 101–2
Zohar 206–7
Zoroastrianism 11, 16, 45, 49, 50–9, 65, 66–7, 74, 76, 95, 108, 128, 149, 154
Zorzi 159
Zostrianos 96
Zu 79
Zurvan Akarana 50
Zurvanism 57–8, 80